LLEWELLYN'S 2023

Witches'
Spell-A-Day
Almanac

Holidays & Lore
Spells, Rituals & Meditations

© 2022 Llewellyn Worldwide Ltd.
Cover design by the Llewellyn Art Department
Interior art © 2018 Laura Tempest Zakroff: pages 9, 31,
49, 69, 89, 111, 131, 151, 173, 193, 215, 237
Spell icons throughout © 2011 Sherrie Thai

You can order Llewellyn books and annuals from *New Worlds*,
Llewellyn's catalog. To request a free copy of the catalog, call toll-free
1-877-NEW WRLD or visit our website at www.llewellyn.com.

ISBN: 978-0-7387-6405-4

Llewellyn is a registered trademark of Llewellyn Worldwide Ltd.
2143 Wooddale Drive
Woodbury, MN 55125

Printed in the United States of America

Contents

A Note on Magic and Spells

The spells in the *Witches' Spell-A-Day Almanac* evoke everyday magic designed to improve our lives and homes. You needn't be an expert on magic to follow these simple rites and spells; as you will see if you use these spells throughout the year, magic, once mastered, is easy to perform. The only advanced technique required of you is the art of visualization.

Visualization is an act of controlled imagination. If you can call up in your mind a picture of your best friend's face or a flag flapping in the breeze, you can visualize. In magic, visualizations are used to direct and control magical energies. Basically the spellcaster creates a visual image of the spell's desired goal, whether it be perfect health, a safe house, or a protected pet.

Visualization is the basis of all good spells, and as such it is a tool that should be properly used. Visualization must be real in the mind of the spellcaster so it allows him or her to raise, concentrate, and send forth energy to accomplish the spell.

Perhaps when visualizing you'll find that you're doing everything right, but you don't feel anything. This is common, for we haven't been trained to acknowledge—let alone utilize—our magical abilities. Keep practicing, however, for your spells can "take" even if you're not the most experienced natural magician.

You will notice also that many spells in this collection have a somewhat light tone. They are seemingly fun and frivolous, filled with rhyme and colloquial speech. This is not to diminish the seriousness of the purpose, but rather to create a relaxed atmosphere for the practitioner. Lightness of spirit helps focus energy; rhyme and common language help the spellcaster remember the words and train the mind where it is needed. The intent of this magic is indeed very serious at times, and magic is never to be trifled with.

Even when your spells are effective, magic won't usually sparkle before your very eyes. The test of magic's success is time, not immediate eye-popping results. But you can feel magic's energy for yourself by rubbing your palms together briskly for ten seconds, then holding them a few inches apart. Sense the energy passing through them, the warm tingle in your palms. This is the power raised and used in magic. It comes from within and is perfectly natural.

Among the features of the *Witches' Spell-A-Day Almanac* are an easy-to-use "book of days" format; new spells specifically tailored for each day of the year (and its particular magical, astrological, and historical energies); and additional tips and lore for various days throughout the year—including color correspondences based on planetary influences, obscure and forgotten holidays and festivals, and an incense of the day to help you waft magical energies from the ether into your space. Moon signs, phases, and voids are also included to help you find the perfect time for your rituals and spells. (All times in this book are Eastern Standard Time or Eastern Daylight Time.)

Enjoy your days and have a magical year!

Spell-A-Day Icons

 New Moon

 Meditation, Divination

 Abundance

 Money, Prosperity

 Altar

 Protection

 Balance

 Relationship

 Clearing, Cleaning

 Success

 Garden

 Travel, Communication

 Grab Bag

 Air Element

 Health, Healing

 Earth Element

 Home

 Fire Element

 Heart, Love

 Spirit Element

 Water Element

2023 Spells at a Glance by Date and Category*

	Health, Healing	Protection	Success	Heart, Love	Clearing, Cleaning	Balance	Meditation, Divination
Jan.	28	9, 27	1, 4, 17, 25, 31		3, 15	26	2, 8, 10, 20, 23
Feb.	2	3, 7, 12, 23	22	14	6, 8, 18, 21, 25	11, 19, 27	13
March	19	5	8, 12, 20, 27	4, 15, 31	6, 10		14, 16, 22, 26
April	16, 23	14, 29	7, 17		8, 12, 19, 25		13
May	23, 28	26	1, 3, 12, 17	2, 9, 16	4, 13	6, 24	31
June	13, 28	22	2	1, 5, 7, 19	8, 12	26	10
July		13, 14, 22, 26, 27	7		2, 15, 18	5	1, 11, 12, 23
Aug.		15, 29	5, 19, 20, 22	3, 17	21, 24, 31	7, 11, 13, 26, 28	10
Sept.	6, 9, 12	11, 16, 20	21, 26	22, 24	1, 17, 25	7, 8	3, 4, 5, 18, 27, 30
Oct.	2, 7	16, 24, 27	4		10, 21	8, 9	6, 13, 25, 30
Nov.	5, 22	3	7, 18	9	4, 14, 21	16, 23, 25	10, 11, 24
Dec.		1, 14, 22		4, 17	2, 5, 28, 31	20	3, 6, 9, 15, 18, 21

*List is not comprehensive.

2023

Year of Spells

January

Happy New Year! The calendar year has begun and even though we may be in the depths of winter (in the Northern Hemisphere) or the height of summer (in the Southern Hemisphere), we stand at the threshold of fifty-two weeks filled with promise. Legend has it that this month is named to honor the Roman god Janus, a god of new beginnings and doorways, but it is also associated with Juno, the primary goddess of the Roman pantheon. Juno was said to be the protectress of the Roman Empire, and Janus (whose twin faces look to both the past and the future simultaneously) encourages new endeavors, transitions, and change in all forms. Since this month marks the beginning of the whole year, we can plant the seeds for long-term goals at this time, carefully plotting the course of our future success.

In the United States, there are three important holidays occurring in January: New Year's Day, Martin Luther King Jr. Day, and Inauguration Day. Each of these days exemplifies powerful change and transition. The dawn of a new year heralds a fresh start, and whether snow-covered or bathed in summer heat, January offers renewed possibilities for all.

Michael Furie

January 1
Sunday

2nd ♉

Color of the day: Orange
Incense of the day: Almond

New Year's Day – Kwanzaa ends

Goal-Setting Candle Spell

Happy new year! This spell sets your goals for the coming year and helps manifest them over the seasons.

Materials:

- 1 white seven-day jar candle
- Paint
- Brushes
- A pen and paper

On the morning of January 1, place your candle outdoors or on a windowsill where it can absorb the fresh, hopeful energy of New Year's Day. Retrieve it in the evening.

Write down all the things you wish to manifest this year, then create a simple symbol or drawing to match each goal. These symbols only need to have meaning for you and no one else, so don't worry if you're not an artist. They can be as simple or complex as you wish.

Paint these symbols onto the glass of the candle, visualizing each one manifesting exactly as you wish it to be. When you're done, flip the candle upside down and paint a star on the bottom of the glass. This star is you, beaming energy into all the goals and dreams you have illustrated.

Throughout the coming year, light the candle once a month and allow it to burn for a couple of hours. Snuff it out in between, and repeat. Each time you light it, the flame helps bring your desires to fruition.

Kate Freuler

Notes:

January 2
Monday

2nd ♉

☽ v/c 5:16 pm

☽ → ♊ 9:44 pm

Color of the day: White
Incense of the day: Lily

A New Path

So now we begin a new year and a new path. This meditation will help you set out on your new path with a clear vision. You'll need one small twig or branch. Select one that has some twists and bumps. Sit with it before your altar. Hold it; feel its curves and bumps. Project your feelings and concerns about the coming year into it. When you're ready, say:

The new year may hold twists and turns,

But from my challenges I shall learn.

And when my road is smooth and straight,

Then my victories I shall celebrate.

Keep the twig on your altar throughout the coming year. Now and then, hold it and think about what has happened in your life this year.

James Kambos

January 3
Tuesday

2nd ♊

Color of the day: Gray
Incense of the day: Ginger

Toss the Fruitcake Spell

We love the holidays, but by early January we are ready to move on and embrace all the new year has to offer. Just as strange energies accumulate in late December/early January, our refrigerators also acquire a lot of leftovers that need to be gotten rid of. Clear out both unwanted food and unwanted energy with this spell.

Peek into your refrigerator and find any items that are past their expiration date. For many of us in early January, that might include a fruitcake. Once you've gathered your unwanted/spoiled leftovers, take them out to the compost pile or trash can and say:

The holiday season has passed, and I throw away all that doesn't serve me from that season. I shall be rid of any negativity and bad feelings. All will be renewed. So mote it be!

Put any lingering concerns about Yuletide out of your mind.

Amanda Lynn & Jason Mankey

January 4
Wednesday

2nd ♊

☽ v/c 7:08 pm

Color of the day: Topaz
Incense of the day: Lilac

Double Capricorn "Boss Vibes" Oil

Today both the Sun and Mercury are expressing peak Capricorn energy as they travel through the depths of this sign, giving us major boss vibes. By "boss vibes," I mean that ability to manage, prioritize, and delegate the things that need to get done to achieve personal and shared goals. This is a good time to take practical steps and see things through. You can bottle this energy by creating the following ritual oil.

Into a half-ounce bottle, blend the following oils and allow to charge on your altar for forty-eight hours:

22 drops cypress essential oil

11 drops cedar essential oil

Once the oils are charged, fill the rest of the bottle with the carrier oil of your choice. (Fractionated coconut, olive, and grapeseed work well.)

Add Saturnian herbs such as comfrey, elm, and thyme to enhance this energy. Label the bottle and use the oil whenever your energy is dragging or when tackling big projects.

Devin Hunter

January 5
Thursday

2nd ♊

☽ → ♋ 9:15 am

Color of the day: Crimson
Incense of the day: Nutmeg

Abundance Talisman

Prepare yourself for a prosperous new year by creating a talisman to carry with you in your purse, your backpack, or even your pocket. First, wrap a dollar bill around a small cinnamon stick. As you wrap it, chant three times:

Let my assets multiply—
all my needs be met.

Burn clove incense. Pass the bundle through the smoke several times and chant three times:

Bring abundance to my life,
as much as I can get.

As the incense burns, visualize the abundance you desire and deserve. Keep the talisman with you as often as possible. When you have more than enough, remember to share with others by giving something back.

Ember Grant

January 6
Friday

2nd ♋

☽ull ☾oon 6:08 pm

Color of the day: Pink
Incense of the day: Violet

Full Moon Family Blessing

The Full Moon in the watery, intuitive, emotional, and nurturing sign of Cancer tonight is an ideal time to heal and strengthen family bonds, with both those who are family by birth and those who are chosen family. For this spell you will need a bowl of water and slips of paper to write down the names of those in your family you wish to bless using a pen. Then, under the Full Moon, place the name papers into the water and say:

Cancer Moon, as you do shine,

Bless those who are family of mine.

Heart to heart, our bonds are strong,

A seat of blessing to all who belong.

Be they through blood or
be they through feeling,

I bless us all through the
Moon's power of healing.

Leave the bowl of water under the Moon until morning. The words of ink should have dissolved. Remove and dispose of the papers, and pour the water at the roots of a nearby tree.

Mat Auryn

January 7
Saturday

3rd ♋

☽ v/c 5:23 pm

☽ → ♌ 9:40 pm

Color of the day: Indigo
Incense of the day: Ivy

Flower Power

January is a cold and snowy month for many people in the Northern Hemisphere. While it is dark and cold outside, bring flowers into your home to add vibrant new life to your space. You can choose flowers based on their color meanings. Red flowers bring power, passion, and love to your space. Yellow flowers add an uplifting joy. White flowers have the energy of purity and innocence. Orange flowers represent enthusiasm.

Once you have flowers and colors in your space, this chant will evoke the energies to magnify and show gratitude for nature's gifts:

I am grateful for the flowers
that are now in my space.

May their energies enhance my home
with their magick and grace.

This spell can be done to liven up the energy of your home and add more magick to your days at any time of the year.

Sapphire Moonbeam

 January 8
Sunday

3rd ♌

Color of the day: Yellow

Incense of the day: Juniper

Right Path Tarot Reading

New years are exciting, but the terrain can seem unfamiliar at times. This reading gives you signposts to indicate you're on the right path. Hold a deck of tarot cards in your hands and take a deep breath. In a clear, strong voice, say:

Signs to know and signs to see.

Six months of signs, please send to me.

Draw six cards from the middle of the deck. Place them before you in a rainbow arc, starting on the left and continuing to the right. These cards represent signs for each of the six months:

1. Sign in January

2. Sign in February

3. Sign in March

4. Sign in April

5. Sign in May

6. Sign in June

Write down the information in your book of shadows, along with the symbols on the cards. Over the next six months, watch for these signs to know you're on the right path.

Astrea Taylor

January 9
Monday

3rd ♌

☽ v/c 8:52 pm

Color of the day: Gray

Incense of the day: Neroli

Embodied Consent Spell Protection

This spell requires your body and voice, and repetition. Stand with your feet hip-distance apart, arms at your sides.

Step forward with your dominant foot (if you are right-handed, then you are right-footed) while pushing away with your palms facing out in front. Say, "No." Step back to your neutral starting position.

Step forward, raising your arms forward, with palms facing down toward the ground, and say, "Maybe." Step back to neutral.

Stand firmly with your feet hip-distance apart. Roll your shoulders back, with arms loosely at your sides, palms up, and say, "Yes."

Envision a situation that requires your consent. Practice using your voice and body to respond. Practice "stepping into it" and saying what is needed: *no, maybe,* or *yes.* Feel the power of embodied consent.

When you repeat this practice 300 times, you develop muscle memory. And when you repeat it 3,000 times, you create new neurological pathways that will make future access to these skills almost automatic. Then, without having to think about it, you can practice embodied consent even when confronted with a sudden stressful event. And that embodied consent is the magic we most need to use in a crisis.

Dallas Jennifer Cobb

NOTES:

January 10
Tuesday

3rd ♌

☽ → ♍ 10:15 am

Color of the day: Maroon
Incense of the day: Cinnamon

Seeking New Knowledge

If you have ever searched for just the right book or new area of study but weren't quite sure exactly what you wanted, then this spell may help. You will need a small blank notebook, a white candle, and a candleholder.

Hold the notebook in your hands and visualize that it is filled with exactly the new information you wish to learn. Set the book down and pick up the candle. Envision a bright orange light (a color of Mercury and learning) streaming down your arms and into the wax. Place the candle on the notebook, light the candle, and say:

> Words of power, a brand-new course,
>
> Seeking knowledge from a new source.
>
> Candle's flame, now light my way,
> to ideal form and topic for me.
>
> As I do will, so mote it be.

Allow the candle to burn for as long as it is safe, then extinguish it.

Michael Furie

January 11
Wednesday

3rd ♏

Color of the day: Brown
Incense of the day: Marjoram

Eleven for Justice

Eleven is a most magical number! In just about any spiritual or occult system, the number eleven is celebrated as having wonderful energetic associations. Today is the eleventh day of the Gregorian new year, so let's harness some of that energy to make magic fitting for our times.

Currently we are seeing valiant fights for justice by people from marginalized populations. The scales have been tipped against many people for far too long, and balance is being sought. The eleventh card of the major arcana in the tarot is the Justice card. Tarot's Justice is cosmic justice, justice with a capital J. It's not an individual's opinion of what is right, but the Truth of Justice.

For this spell, gather eleven tea light candles in safe holders, and place them in a reasonably large circle on a table or other safe space where they can be supervised. Place an image of Justice from your favorite tarot deck in the center of this circle. And as you slowly light the candles, recite:

*Justice! Justice! We call
upon your power,*

On this eleventh day, full of power.

*We ask that you arrive
at a timely hour.*

*May the Truth of Justice win
out at the appointed hour!*

Extinguish the candles.

Blake Octavian Blair

Notes:

January 12
Thursday

3rd ♍

☽ v/c 6:06 pm

☽ → ♎ 9:56 pm

Color of the day: Turquoise
Incense of the day: Apricot

Magical Year Resolution Spell

With the holiday celebrations well and truly over for another year, now is the time to make your New Year's resolutions into solid plans.

At the post-holiday sales, buy yourself a journal. Using numerology, add the digits of the new year together:

$$2023 = 2 + 0 + 2 + 3 = 7$$

Thus, the magical year number for 2023 is seven. Using this powerful number, make seven resolutions for the year. Think about your ultimate dreams and what your heart truly desires, and write them down in your journal. Then look at them and say three times:

2023 is my year.

Magical manifestations of seven,

Empower my resolutions to make my year heaven.

Work toward your plans throughout the year and check on them halfway at Midsummer. Tick the ones that you have accomplished and repeat the spell for the remaining resolutions.

Use the power of seven throughout the year to manifest the life you want.

Each year, add the digits of the year the same way, and use that magical number to power your resolutions.

Tudorbeth

NOTES:

January 13
Friday

3rd ♎

Color of the day: Purple
Incense of the day: Alder

Find Your Voice Spell

January 13, 1910, was the first public radio broadcast in New York City, and it featured Enrico Caruso and other Metropolitan Opera stars. I love radio, so in homage to this day, I created this "Find Your Voice" spell.

You will need a pen and paper. Take three deep breaths, and think about where you feel you aren't being listened to/heard in your life. Write a list. Example:

When my friends and I talk about where to go out, my suggestions aren't used.

When you finish the list, take three more breaths. Now rewrite each item, turning them into positive statements. Example:

My suggestions delight my friends, and we have a wonderful time.

Go outside with the rewritten list. Face south, for action and identity. Speak the list.

The next time you are in one of the negative situations, remember your positive rewrite, and speak up to make it happen.

Cerridwen Iris Shea

January 14
Saturday

3rd ♎
4th Quarter 9:10 pm

Color of the day: Blue
Incense of the day: Patchouli

The Sweet Smell of Sustainability

Balancing our books is an eternal journey of karma and self-sustainability. We can be profoundly impacted by the energy of the quarter moon today as Libra and Capricorn begin to calculate our course in life. The following anointing oil is formulated to draw wealth and fulfill our need for balance. Our finances and our karma can have a lot in common. Use this oil on your bookkeeping journal or wallet and wear or carry it to business meetings that favor a healthy bottom line.

Place the following ingredients in a 2-ounce amber glass vial with a roller:

- 8 drops vanilla extract
- 8 drops pure essential wheatgrass oil
- 8 drops pure essential bergamot oil
- 8 drops pure essential orange flower oil
- 8 drops pure essential sage oil
- 8 drops pure essential sandalwood oil

- 8 drops pure essential lavender oil

- 8 drops pure essential mulberry oil

- 8 drops of sweat from your own brow

Estha McNevin

NOTES:

January 15
Sunday

4th ♎

☽ v/c 3:40 am

☽ → ♏ 7:08 am

Color of the day: Amber
Incense of the day: Eucalyptus

hat Day

If you are one of those people who puts off taking down all the holiday decorations, perhaps this is the day to do just that and make what may be seen as a chore into fun.

As you remove decorations, set aside the care-worn tree trimmings and baubles. Do not discard them. Next seek out a hat that has seen better days. With magickal intent, combine the two. Using your imagination, a needle and thread, and some glue, create a headpiece fit for a goddess or god, or the Lady and Lord. Save the hat in a hat box or other sturdy container. You now have a wonderful conversation piece. Wear it to a holiday event or use it as a wall or table decoration next year. Don't forget to cleanse the hat with burnable purifying herbs before storing it. As you do so, chant:

*These items have served me
well over the years.*

New life they find as creative memories.

Emyme

January 16
Monday

4th ♏

Color of the day: Silver
Incense of the day: Clary sage

Martin Luther King Jr. Day

Understanding and Peace Ritual

Today we honor Dr. Martin Luther King Jr. This ritual reminds us of Dr. King's commitment to understanding and peace. You'll need a crystal with one point. Hold the crystal while sitting at your altar. The point of the crystal should be pointing away from you. Think about understanding and peace filling our world. In your mind, see a brilliant blue-white light streaming from the crystal. Then speak these Words of Power:

> *Understanding and peace*
> *begin with me,*
>
> *Understanding and peace*
> *begin at home.*
>
> *It's not just a dream; it's our destiny.*
>
> *But we must work together, not alone.*

End by meditating on the words you've just said. Begin to think of ways you can bring help to those in need. Visualize yourself acting upon your Words of Power. Together we can bring understanding and peace to all.

James Kambos

January 17
Tuesday

4th ♏

☽ v/c 9:27 am
☽ → ♐ 12:33 pm

Color of the day: Black
Incense of the day: Bayberry

Aiming for Career Advancement

The Sun in Capricorn is ideal for endeavors related to work and career. With the Moon in the hunter sign of Sagittarius, ruled by the kingly Jupiter, for most of the day, this is an opportune time to perform workings related to seeking out a new job or position or expanding or advancing the career you already have.

Get into a meditative state and imagine that you are wearing a crown and holding a bow and arrow. Visualize your career goal ahead of you. Physically pull back your imaginary arrow, and before shooting it at your target, say with confidence:

> *By hooves and crown, I draw my bow.*
>
> *I'm aiming past the status quo.*
>
> *My arrow speeds to the goal,*
>
> *Unlocking doors as I stroll*
>
> *Along the career path that's best for me,*
>
> *That enhances my life like royalty.*

Visualize your arrow hitting your target.

Mat Auryn

January 18
Wednesday

4ᵗ⃗ ♐

Color of the day: White
Incense of the day: Lavender

Find Your Magickal Tools

Finding just the right tools for Witchcraft can be a challenge. Make your search just a little bit easier with this spell.

You'll need a few pieces of paper, a pair of scissors, and a pen/pencil. Start by thinking about what's missing from your altar, and draw each item on a piece of paper. Add as much detail as you can, but don't worry too much if your picture doesn't exactly match what's in your head. Most of us aren't artists! Cut out the items you have drawn and place them where you envision them going on your altar.

As you place the cutouts on your altar, say something like this:

These tools will come to me.

The energy of the cutouts and your desire will draw the tools you're looking for in the coming months.

Amanda Lynn & Jason Mankey

NOTES:

January 19
Thursday

4th ♐

☽ v/c 5:09 am

☽ → ♑ 2:11 pm

Color of the day: Purple
Incense of the day: Mulberry

Magical Mouthwash

Words are powerful. What we say out loud has a tendency to manifest. This magical mouthwash will help your words flow in a positive direction. As an added bonus, the herbs in this recipe contain antibacterial properties that are actually good for your oral hygiene!

Ingredients:

- 5 fresh sage leaves
- 5 fresh peppermint leaves
- 1 organic rose petal or 3 drops rose water
- Glass jar with a tight lid
- ½ teaspoon sea salt
- 5 ounces boiling water

Put the leaves and rose petal/rose water in a glass jar with a tight-fitting lid. Dissolve the salt in boiling water. Pour the water over the leaves, allow it to cool, then strain. Stir the mixture with your finger and say:

I speak with wisdom,
gentleness, and confidence.

When you wish to use the mouthwash, shake it in the jar and repeat the affirmation. Take a mouthful, swish it around in your mouth for twenty seconds, then spit it out.

Keep the mouthwash in a tightly lidded jar in the fridge for up to one week.

Kate Freuler

NOTES:

January 20
Friday

4th ♑

☉ → ♒ 3:30 am

Color of the day: Coral
Incense of the day: Mint

Reflection Meditation

Use this meditation to reflect on self-improvement or self-care. Look deeply and honestly at yourself and discover things you'd like to change or new goals you'd like to set.

You'll need some incense and a mirror. Any size is fine as long as you can see your face in it. Position the mirror so you can gaze into it and then light the incense. You may wish to dim the lights and use candles. Allow the incense smoke to rise up in front of the mirror, creating a screen. Close your eyes and imagine you're walking through dense fog; revelations are waiting for you beyond it. Whisper these words:

Like an open book,

I need an honest look.

With open eyes I see

Who I truly want to be.

When you're ready, open your eyes and blow the incense smoke away, revealing your reflection in the mirror. Look into your own eyes. Ask yourself what you truly want and need. Promise yourself to pursue it.

Ember Grant

 **January 21**
Saturday

4th ♑

☽ v/c 10:52 am

☽ → ♒ 1:29 pm

New Moon 3:53 pm

Color of the day: Brown
Incense of the day: Sage

Spirit Guide Communication Amulet

Both the Sun and the New Moon are in the sign of Aquarius today, ushering in a flood of positive energy that is sure to inspire, move, and even tantalize us. Ride the wave by directing this energy into projects that make you feel connected to your life's purpose and by reaching out to spirit guides that help you see the big picture. This is also a good time to create magical tools, such as this amulet, that can help you connect with your spirit guides. All you need is a small piece of clear quartz.

Cleanse your stone in whatever way you prefer, then draw the energy of Aquarius into it by holding it with both hands and visualizing a light blue light sparkling within. Chant this incantation three times, allowing the light to grow brighter each time:

Water bearer, pouring light;
stars and spirits, guide my sight!

Carry your amulet with you to enhance spirit guide communication.

Devin Hunter

January 22
Sunday

1st ♒

Color of the day: Gold
Incense of the day: Heliotrope

Lunar New Year (Rabbit)

Sweeping Success

Today marks the new moon in Aquarius and the Lunar New Year of the Rabbit. (The new moon occurred yesterday in Eastern Standard Time, but it falls early this morning in the UTC +8:00 time zone, or China Standard Time.) It's an auspicious day to cleanse your home to make way for the influx of fresh energy. This spell uses the magical action of sweeping a broom to accomplish this. It also uses mood music, which can be anything from a song to ambient sounds or tonal frequencies—whatever gets you into the right mindset.

Turn on the music and decorate your broom with ribbons and bells. When your broom is all decorated, start sweeping in the middle of your home and sweep toward the exits. Use a dustpan to gather the debris, and place the sweepings in the trash. Light some incense and continue playing the music. If you wish, you can dance with your broom to raise the energy even more. Let the incense burn out completely if possible.

Astrea Taylor

January 23
Monday

1st ♒

☽ v/c 5:19 am
☽ → ♓ 12:36 pm

Color of the day: Lavender
Incense of the day: Rosemary

Tea Leaf Spell

Divination is a way to discover and see magical signs. You can drink a cup of tea in the winter and do a bit of scrying to get a glimpse of the future in the tea leaves. Tea leaf divination requires practice but can be done with minimal supplies. Use a loose leaf tea. Boil the water and allow it to steep and infuse the water for three to five minutes before pouring it into your cup.

As you drink the tea, think of the question you have about your future. After you have finished, place the teacup upside down on a saucer and say these words:

May the tea leaves show the story unfold and reveal signs and symbols of what the future may hold.

Turn the cup right side up and study the tea leaves. Turn the saucer clockwise to find symbols from a different perspective to discover the answer to your question.

Sapphire Moonbeam

January 24
Tuesday

1st ♓

Color of the day: Scarlet
Incense of the day: Geranium

Manifest Abundance with Ekeko

On this date in La Paz, Bolivia, begins the monthlong celebration of Alasitas. The main figure honored during this event is Ekeko, a god of abundance. Ekeko is depicted as a man carrying money and household items related to abundance. If presented with wheat, he provides a good harvest. If he is presented with money, the household will prosper.

Miniature items are sold at the festival. These items are exchanged as gifts to bring specific types of abundance. It is believed that if you are gifted a miniature version of something, you will get the real object sometime the following year. Create a simple statue of Ekeko decked out in symbols of the wealth you already have or the wealth you wish to manifest. Miniatures are found in almost every hobby store. When Ekeko occupies a place of honor in your home and with appropriate intention, riches will come your way.

Emyme

January 25
Wednesday

1st ♓
☽ v/c 11:12 am
☽ → ♈ 1:48 pm

Color of the day: Yellow
Incense of the day: Bay laurel

Mystical Renovations

My village is gentrifying, and I often feel unsafe. On a bad day, I feel "less than," unworthy, and worthless. I see how much time and money are being spent on the upgrade, rebuilding, and renovation of houses, and I am deeply aware that my financial resources are very different from "theirs." Why do they deserve more than I? From there, it's a quick spiral down into worthlessness. *Ugh.*

In order to change consciousness around this dynamic, choose to undertake mystical renovations. Renovate your spirit. Repeat after me:

I don't need new windows;
I choose to see more clearly.

I don't need to replace the doors;
I replace my fearful thinking.

I won't add a sunroom or pool; I will go out and commune with nature.

While I "live" in this home,
I dwell in spirit.

I don't have to rebuild this place; I rebuild my life.

Dallas Jennifer Cobb

January 26
Thursday

1st ♈

Color of the day: Green
Incense of the day: Myrrh

Spousal Symbiosis

Today is National Spouses Day. The day is meant for people to celebrate the bond they share with their spouse and to show each other appreciation and gratitude. If you have a spouse, hopefully you do this regularly anyway; however, it's always nice to have a celebration! If you don't have a spouse, today is a great day to do a meditation on self-care and being your best self, as this will help you be the best possible partner to a future spouse and also identify what qualities in a person would make the best spouse for you, if that is your desire. If you do have a spouse, meditate on how you balance each other and complement each other.

Culminate the meditation by visualizing a healthy balance of two fully realized individuals who support each other in healthy ways. Outwardly express to your spouse the positive ways in which they support your life together.

Blake Octavian Blair

January 27
Friday

1st ♈

☽ v/c 4:01 pm
☽ → ♉ 6:42 pm

Color of the day: White
Incense of the day: Vanilla

The Prismatic Crystal Shield

A fast yet surprisingly powerful means of magical protection is to form an energetic crystal shield. This is very similar to other methods of creating a shield, such as the mirrored shield, but the effects are quite different.

To form the crystal shield, close your eyes and envision being surrounded by a brilliant white light. Concentrate on it condensing around you to form a crystalline egg of power that will act as a magical prismatic filter. In other words, any harmful energy that is sent your way will be drawn through the crystal prism (as opposed to being repelled) and its power will be transformed from a single (and harmful) intention into a rainbow of constructive energy that you can utilize to your own benefit. In this way, you are not only preventing harm, but also transforming the energy to serve the greater good—a powerful piece of magical recycling.

Michael Furie

January 28
Saturday

1st ♉

2nd Quarter 10:19 am

Color of the day: Black
Incense of the day: Rue

Treasures of the Earth

Sweet bean soup is a bit like liquid trail mix. Often served for Lunar New Year in many countries in Asia, it is a restorative food that has its roots in ancient curative cuisines. Nuts, spices, and dried fruits are slow-stewed for days, along with sweet adzuki and lotus beans. The result is a thick, richly spiced broth with many sweet treasures suspended beneath the surface.

Here's a Crock-Pot version that is easy and rewarding. Cook the following on low heat for three to five days. Serve over rice to promote longevity.

- 1 pound adzuki beans, soaked overnight
- ½ pound lotus beans, soaked overnight
- 1 cup walnuts
- 1 cup dried cherries
- 1 cup dried plums
- 1 cup dried apples
- 1 cup diced oranges or marmalade
- 1 cup dates, sliced
- 8 cups apple juice
- ¼ cup diced candied ginger
- 1 cup sliced candied winter melon
- 1 cup honey
- 1 vanilla bean, split lengthwise
- 3 star anise pods
- 2 cinnamon sticks
- 8 clove buds
- 3 teaspoons cinnamon powder
- 2 teaspoons ginger powder
- 1 teaspoon cardamom powder
- 1 teaspoon allspice
- 1 pinch mace

Estha McNevin

January 29
Sunday

2nd ☿

Color of the day: Orange
Incense of the day: Frankincense

A house Protection Spell

Use this spell to bring stability, peace, and security to your home. You'll need the Ten of Pentacles card from your favorite tarot deck, a light blue candle, some rose water, and a cotton ball.

Place the candle on your altar, and lay the tarot card in front of the candle, facing you. Set the rose water and cotton ball off to the side. First, safely light the candle. Meditate on the card.

Think about what you want your home to be like. Calm? Peaceful? Stable? Now gaze at the candle flame and say:

From this home I banish all negativity.

Only positive forces dwell here.

Peace surrounds me

And those who carry my key.

Safely snuff out the candle. You may use it for other positive magic. Put the card back in the deck. End the ritual by moistening the cotton ball with the rose water. Use it to wipe off all exterior doorknobs of your home as you focus on peace.

James Kambos

January 30
Monday

2nd ☿

☽ v/c 12:52 am

☽ → ♊ 3:35 am

Color of the day: Ivory
Incense of the day: Narcissus

Spell to Wipe Away Debt

The bills are in and repayment on those Christmas and New Year festivities may have taken a toll on your bank account. It's time to put some action into your finances. If you have debts, especially credit card bills and loans, then do a manifestation spell to consciously wipe them away using this snowball practice. This spell involves paying off the smallest debt first, then snowballing that money and carrying it on to the next bill until you are completely debt-free.

Write down your debts on a piece of white paper, and look at them and acknowledge them. Don't be frightened; instead, accept them. Then safely light a green candle and imagine a snowball wiping away those debts, starting with the smallest one, until it wipes them all clean whilst gathering momentum and growing larger.

To manifest a debt-free life, think of how you will feel when you've paid everything off and then, while holding the paper in your left hand, say:

Snowball, snowball, rolling bright,

Debts disappear with all my might.

Blow out the candle, and keep the paper in a special place where you can see it every day to acknowledge it but not where everyone can see it.

Make a conscious effort to pay the debts off. Contact the credit card, loan, or debt company to arrange a repayment plan and ask for them to lower your interest rate. Actively pursue clearing those debts. Show the universe how capable you are, and keep imagining that snowball wiping away all those debts.

Tudorbeth

January 31
Tuesday

2nd ♊

Color of the day: Red
Incense of the day: Cedar

Feast for hecate

By January 31, some of the ambitions we had on the 1st have lost momentum, and we feel disjointed. It's a good time to ask Hecate for guidance and blessings.

Clean your house, and cleanse it with the smoke of lavender and rosemary incense.

Hecate is connected to the crossroads. Take two yards of black fabric and two yards of white fabric. Create a crossroads on your floor by putting the pieces of fabric at right angles to each other, and place a table in the middle of the crossroads.

Now make a simple meal. Decorate the table with candles, keys, and offerings of honey, arranged in groups of three, on a black and white cloth.

Ask for Hecate's guidance in anything where you feel you are at a crossroads. Eat the feast and let the candles safely burn out.

Cerridwen Iris Shea

February

The word *February* is based on the Latin *februa* and refers to the Roman festival of purification of the same name. This festival later became integrated with February's infamous Lupercalia. Since ancient times, February has been observed as a month of cleansing, cleaning, purification, and preparation for the warm months ahead. We see the Celtic Imbolg (Candlemas) celebrated in February to perpetuate the summoning of solar light. In many parts of the world at this time, the promise of sunlight seems bleak, even imaginary. The world around us is slowly awakening from its wintery slumber, and some semblance of excitement begins to grow in the hearts of those attuned to the seasonal tides.

Daylight hours are short in February, so this time of year can sometimes feel depressive. We must actively cultivate our inner light through regular exercise, solid sleep, meditation, yoga, ritual, studying, artwork, and planning ahead for the year. When performing magickal work this month, remember that your energy levels may be lower than usual and you must summon your own inner light to strengthen and illuminate your efforts. Do whatever it takes to stay on top of your game, keep energized, cultivate happiness, and embrace February's cleansing rebirth!

Raven Digitalis

February 1
Wednesday

2nd ♊

☽ v/c 6:58 am

☽ → ♋ 3:11 pm

Color of the day: Topaz
Incense of the day: Honeysuckle

Creativity Imbolc Spell

At sundown we begin to celebrate Imbolc, the Celtic festival in honor of Brigid. She is known as a goddess of wisdom, poetry, and inspiration, among other things. Imbolc is also a fire festival, a celebration of the return of the light. The light and fires of Imbolc represent a luminous, radiant hope after experiencing harsh, cold winter days. Fire is the element of transformation and passion. It is a perfect time to renew and transform your creativity.

A simple way to celebrate Imbolc is to light a white candle to "spark" your creativity and celebrate the return of the light. Once your candle is lit, cup your hands around the candle at a safe distance and say:

> On this Imbolc night, as my
> candle burns bright, help my
> passion and creativity reignite.

Safely extinguish the candle once you are done.

Sapphire Moonbeam

 February 2
Thursday

2nd ♋

Color of the day: White
Incense of the day: Carnation

Imbolc – Groundhog Day

Sadness, Be Gone Spell

February 2 is an auspicious day for many: it is Candlemas, Imbolc, and Groundhog Day. Moreover, February can be one of the coldest months in the Northern Hemisphere, with snow heavy on the ground. Fragile snowdrop plants begin to push their way up through the frozen land to greet us, a sign that the earth is once again emerging from her winter sleep. In Hedgewitchery, we often call Imbolc the Snowdrop Festival.

The festivals around this time are regarded as celebrations of light, as the light is dawning after a dark winter's night. Further, even though magic is within everything, there are a number of traditional symbols of magic. One in particular is the bell, which is said to drive away evil spirits, including the winter blues. In the Craft, bells are used to invoke the Goddess or to call the elementals and to drive away winter and sadness.

If you have been suffering or feeling low, cast this spell today to renew your spirit and embrace the coming of spring. You will need a bell of any size,

a white candle, and a snowdrop plant or a picture of one. If you don't have a bell, there are lots of videos online of a bell ringing, or you might have a bell sound effect on your phone.

Safely light the candle and look upon the snowdrop. Hold the bell in your left hand (if you're using one) and say:

Festival of light,

Release the pain that I feel

When thrice the bell peals.

Then slowly ring the bell three times and blow out the candle. Watch the smoke rise, taking your pain with it.

Tudorbeth

February 3
Friday

2nd ♋

Color of the day: Rose
Incense of the day: Orchid

Push It Protection Spell

Salt and pepper are not just good for seasoning food—they're also used for magickal protection. This is because salt neutralizes negative energy, and pepper acts as a potent guardian against harm. You can prepare this protection spell nearly anywhere and anytime. You will need a plate, some salt and ground pepper, a spoon, and a small pouch.

On a plate, make two equal-size mounds, one of salt and one of pepper. Hover your right hand over the mounds, then start mixing them together with your fingers in a clockwise motion. Push your intention for protection into them as you repeat this phrase:

Salt and pepper, protect me from harm.

Do this for at least three minutes. When you feel they have absorbed your will, use a spoon to gather the powder into the pouch. To use it, take a pinch of the powder with your left fingers and throw it while pushing the protective energy out with your hand. Take a deep breath and walk away.

Astrea Taylor

February 4
Saturday

2nd ♋

☽ v/c 1:19 am

☽ → ♌ 3:48 am

Color of the day: Gray
Incense of the day: Magnolia

Kitchen Witch Intentions

There is no need to buy special ingredients to work magic, cast spells, or change consciousness at will. Just reach for these magical kitchen basics.

Whether you're cooking, baking, or stewing, adding common ingredients with strong scents can increase magical energy. Today, as you prepare food for yourself or another, set an intention of what you want to convey, instill, or magnify, then use an herb, fruit, or spice to fix the intention in the food, inviting the energy into yourself, your food, and your kitchen.

To invite love, protection, and feelings of belonging, use cinnamon. Need comfort, quieting, and soothing? Try chamomile. For energy, memory, and attention, choose coffee. Want a calm, mindful focus? Choose lavender. To promote clearing, cleaning, and uplifting, use lemon. You can add clarity and inspiration with mint, promote abundance, success, and enlightenment with orange, and nurture a sense of wellbeing with vanilla.

Dallas Jennifer Cobb

 February 5
Sunday

2nd ♌

Full Moon 1:29 pm

Color of the day: Gold
Incense of the day: Hyacinth

Balancing Lunar and Solar Energies

Today is the full moon! We all know about today's powerful lunar energies for working magic; however, we can work a special bit of balancing magic by bringing in some solar energy. Why don't we have a meditation and a toast to balance?

This evening, after the moon is visible in the sky, pour or brew yourself a drink with solar energy. Try a nice glass of local mead, which is made from honey, or perhaps choose a hot cup or thermos of a decaffeinated tea of your choice with some honey stirred in. Honey has fiery, masculine, solar energies that balance out the moon's watery, feminine, lunar energies.

Raise your drinking vessel in a toast to the full moon. Take a sip of your libation and bask in the moonlight, meditating on the fact we all contain a mix of these solar and lunar energies within us. As you take another sip, visualize yourself balancing these energies as your solar-inspired drink moves down through your body and you bask in the gentle lunar light.

Blake Octavian Blair

 # February 6
Monday

3rd ♌

☽ v/c 9:15 am

☽ → ♍ 4:14 pm

Color of the day: White
Incense of the day: Hyssop

Break a Bad Habit Spell

There are several ways to carry out this spell to break a bad habit. The point is to write the habit you wish to break on an object that you can literally shatter. One easy way to do this is by using craft clay, which is easily found in craft stores or online. There are many types that air-dry and don't need to be baked. Just form a portion of clay into a thin piece that's large enough for you to write your bad habit on using a toothpick. Let it dry completely, then break it and throw away the pieces.

You can also perform this spell by writing on a rock and breaking it with a hammer. However, if you do this, be sure to work outdoors and wear eye protection. Another option is to use an old plate. Again, be careful and watch for flying shards. You may wish to put the object in a plastic bag before breaking it. The act of literally breaking something can be very satisfying and empowering.

Ember Grant

February 7
Tuesday

3rd ♍

Color of the day: Black
Incense of the day: Basil

Cosmic Influence Shield

The Moon is in Virgo today and our insecurities may be getting the best of us. While usually I am a fan of working with the energies afforded to us by the movement of heavenly bodies, sometimes these energies can stir up unwanted thoughts and emotions. If you are feeling insecure, overwhelmed, or even incapable right now, it could very well be related to the current placement of the Moon. Cast this spell to temporarily shield yourself from these effects.

Visualize yourself standing on top of a six-foot-wide pentacle of white light. Say:

> I call upon the Earth, my
> home, to shield and protect
> me from the Virgo Moon!

Take a few deep breaths and visualize the light that shines from beneath you morph into a chrysalis of crystallized light, then say:

> Let the will of the Earth be
> victorious over all others!

Devin Hunter

February 8
Wednesday

3rd ♏

Color of the day: Yellow
Incense of the day: Lilac

Clean Out Your Social Media

Let's get in the spirit of spring cleaning and bring it to our electronic devices and social media accounts. Throughout the year we collect and store lots of things on our phones, computers, tablets, etc. Whether it's unopened files on your laptop or just a slew of random friends you don't know or haven't connected with in a while, now is the perfect time to clear out all the digital clutter that has no room in your life anymore.

Spend a couple of hours today sifting through your old files, knowing that you are getting rid of things that have no relevance to your life anymore. Thank them for the memories or purposes they once served and then delete them. As you clear out the unwanted clutter, say, "Be gone!" or "Thank you for you for your service," or whatever is appropriate. When you are done, burn some clearing incense and welcome in a fresh start!

Amanda Lynn & Jason Mankey

February 9
Thursday

3rd ♏

☽ v/c 1:40 am
☽ → ♎ 3:47 am

Color of the day: Green
Incense of the day: Balsam

Finding Strength in a Tree

In the winter when the trees are leafless, their beauty and strength are more visible. That's when you can see their power and majesty. To increase your own strength, form a pact with a tree. Follow the instructions in the following verse:

Walk into the winter wood,

Where bare trees sleep and brood.

Select a tree majestic and great.

Now you each have a shared fate.

With this tree your strength is bound.

Leave a gift—a crumb, a seed,
or a rock you've found.

As the seasons turn and pass,

Your strength will grow and last.

Return to your tree from time to time. Touch it. Thank it. Be grateful for its presence in your life. If for some reason the tree is destroyed, create a bond with another tree.

James Kambos

February 10
Friday

3rd ♎

Color of the day: Pink
Incense of the day: Rose

Spell for a New True Friend

With the Sun in Aquarius and the Moon in Libra today, this is the perfect time to cast a spell for friendship. When I was a child, we would wear friendship bracelets as a sign of our bond. In this spell you will be braiding three different colored pieces of yarn of your choice to make a bracelet. One yarn represents you, another represents your future friend you are summoning, and the third represents the friendship. Braid the pieces together while reciting and focusing on the intent of these words:

I draw a friendship near to me,

One that's built on sincerity.

A friend who cares, a friend who shares,

A friend who always treats me fair.

A friendship that isn't superficial,

One that is mutually beneficial.

A friend with motives that are pure,

A solid friendship that will endure.

Tie the braided friendship bracelet comfortably on your left ankle until it comes off on its own. Be open to meeting new people.

Mat Auryn

February 11
Saturday

3rd ♎

☽ v/c 11:41 am
☽ → ♏ 1:34 pm

Color of the day: Brown
Incense of the day: Sandalwood

Spell for Balance

Eleven is considered a master number, connected to enlightenment and balance. Today is perfect for a balance spell. Gather these items:

- A candle of any color in a glass jar/votive holder (I like yellow.)
- Calm music
- A yoga mat (optional)

Light the candle. Listen to the music for a few minutes, following your breath.

Pinpoint where your life is out of balance. Imagine what is out of balance on one side of a scale. Put yourself on the other side of the scale. Visualize the two sides evening out, so they are in balance. Hold this image for at least five breaths.

Embody the balance by doing your favorite yoga balancing pose, such as Tree, Dancer, or Crow. Hold the pose as long as it feels good.

Release the pose and extinguish the candle. Repeat the ritual any time you feel out of balance, visualizing the balance of eleven.

Cerridwen Iris Shea

February 12
Sunday

3rd ♏

Color of the day: Orange
Incense of the day: Marigold

Calling the Light to Aid You

From the moment we exist, good spirits watch over us. Over time, the good intentions of all those who love us evolve along with us into an intelligent guardian spirit. This lights-witch spell draws electricity to recharge this connection every time you use a light switch.

Use a gold glass marker to draw a pentacle on each light switch in your home. Then anoint each switch with sesame essential oil and repeat the following blessing for each room:

From womb to grave; life, with me weave, bound as we are to each other.

Be kindness and mercy reflected through me, drawn upon the light; let's work together.

I seek to understand. I am ready to listen. I can see your perspective from within any light that glistens.

So mote it be.

Estha McNevin

 # February 13
Monday

3rd ♏
4th Quarter 11:01 am
☽ v/c 6:52 pm
☽ → ♐ 8:31 pm

Color of the day: Ivory
Incense of the day: Lily

Magical Third Eye

This is a simple spell designed to enhance your ability to be influential in all situations. To begin, find a comfortable place to sit where you will not be disturbed. Relax and close your eyes. Let your mental focus fix upon your third eye (the area essentially in the middle of your forehead), and envision that a large glowing eye opens there, radiating power and light. This light is the light of your third eye chakra. Set the intention that this light will continually shine forth, granting you greater authority and influence, and that it will continually draw in light from the universe to maintain its strength. When you feel ready, say:

The third eye opens, and with its gaze, shall influence, fascinate, enchant, and amaze.

Universal light empowers for me This flowering gift; so mote it be.

Open your eyes and it is done.

Michael Furie

February 14
Tuesday

4℠ ♐

Color of the day: Maroon
Incense of the day: Ylang-ylang

Valentine's Day

Meditation on Self-Love

Today is Valentine's Day. In addition to the romantic love that is so commonly celebrated and emphasized today, it is also important to love yourself. We need not be in a state of perfection to have love for ourselves. Today let's show our love for ourselves and practice a bit of meditation on the topic. All you need for this simple meditation is a piece of rose quartz of any size, a pen and paper, and ten minutes of quiet time to yourself.

Have a seat where you'll be undisturbed and make yourself comfortable. Write on the piece a paper a list of three to five personal affirmations of qualities you like about yourself, such as "I am a generous person," "I am a dedicated musician," or "I am a loving sibling." Hold the rose quartz in the palms of your hands and, with eyes open, enter a light meditative state. Repeat the affirmations for five or six minutes, slowly and calmly. Then proclaim, "So mote it be."

Blake Octavian Blair

NOTES:

February 15
Wednesday

4th ♐

☽ v/c 8:06 pm

Color of the day: White
Incense of the day: Bay laurel

Watering Can Spell for Emotional Growth

The element of water is often associated with the emotions, always swelling then receding, coming in storms or a gentle nourishing rain, much like our feelings. Water is also essential to the growth of all living things. This spell combines water and plants to steadily encourage emotional expression and healing.

Materials:

- A watering can
- Water to fill the can
- 1 seed of any kind to symbolize growth
- 1 small stone to create stability
- Potted plant(s) or an outdoor space where plants grow

Put the stone and the seed in the watering can. As you fill the can with water, recite:

Water helps emotions flow, seeds make healthy feelings grow.

A stone to bring stability, while nurturing my heart and soul.

Water your plants with the watering can and repeat as needed. As your plants grow steadily and flourish, your ability to express emotion will mature and gain stability.

Kate Freuler

NOTES:

February 16
Thursday

4th ♑

☽ → ♑ 12:00 am

Color of the day: Crimson
Incense of the day: Jasmine

Aurora Borealis Enchantment

The *aurora borealis* is named after Aurora, the Roman goddess of the dawn, and Boreas, the Greek god of the north wind. Also known as the northern lights, the *aurora borealis* is the result of particles colliding with atoms high in the atmosphere.

There are many wondrous names for the northern lights, from the Dance of Spirits to the Charge of the Equinoxes, and strangely enough, they do seem to appear around the time of the equinoxes, especially in the spring. They are also connected to geomagnetic storms set off by the sun.

To see the *aurora borealis* is a rare opportunity and is said to bring luck. Channel the Dance of Spirits into your magic by creating an enchantment on something you love. It could be anything you wear every day, such as shoes. Gather a picture of the *aurora borealis*, a green or blue candle, and a favourite pair of shoes. Put the shoes on and safely light the candle. As you hold the picture of the *aurora borealis*, imagine the magic and luck from the swirling colours going into your shoes. Recite this spell over the shoes you're wearing:

> *Blessed shoes upon my feet,*
>
> *Bring me luck with those I meet.*
>
> *Chances are rare and hard to find,*
>
> *Opportunities now become mine.*

Then blow out the candle and imagine the rising smoke as colours from the *aurora borealis* bringing luck and opportunities to you every time you meet someone whilst wearing the shoes.

Tudorbeth

NOTES:

 # February 17
Friday

Self-Love Bathing Spell

February is the month of love. Whether you are in a relationship or not, self-love and positive body consciousness are important. Your inner dialogue with yourself and your body helps your self-love blossom from the inside out. When you wash your body, the water cleanses your emotions and spirit. Rose, vanilla, and lavender are scents associated with love. Find a scent that you love for this bathing ritual.

As you wash different areas of your body, tell yourself why you appreciate that part of yourself. For instance, you could say:

I love my feet. They help me walk on my magical path.

I love my legs. They give me strength for new adventures.

I love my stomach. It accepts nourishment that benefits my entire body.

You get the idea. You can repeat this spell whenever you need to reset your inner dialogue about body consciousness and self-love.

Sapphire Moonbeam

 # February 18
Saturday

4th ♑

☽ → ♒ 12:35 am

☉ → ♓ 5:34 pm

Color of the day: Blue
Incense of the day: Pine

Burn and Banish

Banishing is a powerful way to rid yourself of something that's troubling you. It could be a bad habit, an unhealthy relationship, or any other situation that is causing you pain. You'll need a photo of the person, or simply write on a piece of paper the problem you wish to be rid of.

Burn the paper in a heatproof dish. As it burns, chant these words three times:

Out of my life, out of my way,

You will no longer trouble me starting today.

Visualize yourself being free of the troublesome situation. Feel how light you are. See yourself being at peace. Soak the ashes in water and then bury them or let the wind blow them away.

Ember Grant

February 19
Sunday

4th ♒

☽ v/c 9:00 pm

☽ → ♓ 11:56 pm

Color of the day: Yellow
Incense of the day: Juniper

Serenity Jar

The serenity jar spell is helpful for all of the problems that you don't have the power to change. It encases them in a peaceful setting and lets you breathe a little easier. You will need a small jar with a lid, six drops of lavender oil, a cleansed amethyst, a marker, and some scraps of paper.

Drop the lavender oil and the amethyst into the jar. Inhale the peaceful aroma, and for one minute meditate on the feeling of serenity. Slowly and mindfully write "Serenity" on the jar with the marker.

Write down a problem on a scrap of paper. Uncap the jar, take a whiff of the aroma, and place the paper inside. Recap the jar and say:

> Serenity, take this worry
> from me. I release it.

Repeat, writing more items on the papers. When you're done, seal the jar tightly. Place it in a safe and secret place. Repeat the spell whenever you need more serenity.

Astrea Taylor

February 20
Monday

4th ♓

New Moon 2:06 am

Color of the day: Lavender
Incense of the day: Rosemary

Presidents' Day

Charging Items with the Power of the Moon

Witches love working with lunar energy. While we often are obsessed with full moons, we can sometimes overlook the subtle but powerful energy of the new moon. It's a time of new beginnings, to refresh and to look inward. This is also a great time to charge our magical items.

Within the darkness of the night sky, the new moon is invisible to us, but it emits such a powerful aura for magical work! For this spell, all you need to do is take whatever items you feel need a good energetic cleanse and charge. It could be a piece of jewelry or even your wand or athame. Just after sunset, place your items in a safe space where they will be under a clear sky. Feel free to sit with your items and set the intention out loud that you are cleansing and charging them with new moon energy. Bring the items in the next morning and use them as you normally would.

Amanda Lynn & Jason Mankey

February 21
Tuesday

1st ♓

☽ v/c 11:06 pm

Color of the day: Red
Incense of the day: Ginger

Mardi Gras (Fat Tuesday)

Fat Tuesday Purge and Splurge

This holiday is celebrated around the world the day before Lent begins. It's a day of feasting before fasting. Approximately two to three months after Yule, it is a good time to begin a spring clean-out. Bake hot cross buns or a king cake, or prepare a nourishing soup and let it simmer. While working in the kitchen, purge any outdated items and unused or broken tools. Whether there is snow on the ground or you are in the middle of a heat wave, invite friends and loved ones over for the evening meal. Dress in green, gold, and purple. Send everyone home with a portion of the meal and a slice of cake or a bun.

Emyme

February 22
Wednesday

1st ♓

☽ → ♈ 12:14 am

Color of the day: Brown
Incense of the day: Marjoram

Ash Wednesday

Manifestation Spell

The number 22 is palindromic, which means it reads the same way backward and forward. It's associated with making your deepest desires come true.

For this spell you will need:

• 2 pieces of paper, to make a list

• 2 small green candles in holders, rubbed with patchouli or rosemary oil

• 2 moss agate stones

• A firesafe dish

• Matches

Write two identical lists of what you want to manifest over the next six months. Limit the list to three items, so it stays focused.

Light both candles, placing the stones in front of them.

Burn one list in the firesafe dish, visualizing the manifestation of your goals. Extinguish one candle when the list finishes burning. Let the other candle burn down safely.

Put the extinguished candle, the remaining list, and one stone in a safe place until the spell manifests. If you have more than one goal on your list, tear off each goal as it manifests, light the candle, and light that part of the list to burn in a firesafe dish, burning the candle all the way down when the final goal has manifested.

Carry the other stone with you until the spell manifests.

Cerridwen Iris Shea

NOTES:

 # February 23
Thursday

1st ♈

Color of the day: Turquoise
Incense of the day: Clove

Stop Gossip Spell

The energy today is heavy in the air and fire elements, despite the Sun being in the early degrees of Pisces, a water sign. One of the things that can arise from this energy is a tendency to gossip, which can spread even faster than usual at this time. Cast this easy spell to freeze gossip in its tracks. All you need is a box of matches, a black pen, some water, and a container to put the spell in to freeze.

Hold the box of matches in your hands and think about the people spreading gossip, the rumors themselves, and how it makes you feel. Draw a big *X* on the inside of the box and say:

Not today, there is no way. I freeze this from happening and all that you say!

Put the box of matches in the container, fill it with water, and freeze! Thaw it out once the threat has passed and throw away what remains of the matches.

Devin Hunter

February 24
Friday

1st ♈

☽ v/c 2:22 am

☽ → ♉ 3:29 am

Color of the day: Coral
Incense of the day: Yarrow

Seasons of Rebirth Spell

In this ritual two elements, earth and water, are combined to honor the return of spring, the season of rebirth. Snow and ice may still dominate the landscape in many regions, but spring isn't far away. You'll need a garden hoe or shovel and a watering can. If you live in an apartment, you may use a dish of potting soil and an old spoon, or any suitable substitute.

Begin by going out to your garden or yard. Turn a small spot of earth with your hoe or shovel, just enough to loosen the soil. Then sprinkle the turned soil with some water. As you do so, say:

Water, combine with the earth.

Earth, combine with water.

May your union bring about the season of rebirth.

Visualize yards and parks turning green and lush again. Put away your tools and wait for spring. It'll be here before you know it!

James Kambos

February 25
Saturday

1st ♉

Color of the day: Black
Incense of the day: Sage

Good Riddance Spell Banishing

After years of abuse, belittlement, and intimidation, I left my husband one February 25th. After years of compromising, trying harder, making peace, and doing more, better and faster, I came to the end of the enchantment. I was aware of what I hated in him. I said, "I'm not doing this anymore. I'm done."

While many of us are in safe, secure relationships with people who love and cherish us, we all have situations with people, places, practices, or things where we need to break the spell of enchantment and be free.

To cast your own good riddance spell, you need pen and paper, a pinch of courage, a dash of self-worth, and a good measure of fortitude. Write down everything you hate about the person, place, practice, or thing. Feel the depth of despair. Crumple the paper, throw it in the garbage, and say:

Good riddance. I'm done. Be free.

Repeat daily if needed.

Dallas Jennifer Cobb

February 26
Sunday

1st ♉

☽ v/c 9:42 am

☽ → ♊ 10:48 am

Color of the day: Amber
Incense of the day: Almond

Spirit Guide Communication

With the Sun in visionary Pisces and the Moon in Gemini (ruled by Mercury) for most of the day, this is an ideal time to connect with your spirit guides and open up those channels of clear communication. This is a simple prayer to your help on the other side using the traditional offering of a white candle and a clear glass of water. Simply set out the glass of water and safely light your white candle, and with an earnest heart recite the following:

I call to those on the other side.

I call forth my highest spirit guides.

By this candlelight and a water libation,

Open the channels of clear communication.

Spirit allies of integrity that I can trust,

May there always be a peaceful bond between us.

Pay attention to any visions, synchronicities, and dreams for signs of guidance from your spirit allies. Extinguish the candle.

Mat Auryn

 February 27
Monday

1st ♊

2nd Quarter 3:06 am

Color of the day: Gray
Incense of the day: Neroli

The Blessing Word

Ordinary words can be empowered with magical ability for power and blessings. Many people have sayings or phrases they say from time to time, but if focused upon, giving them specific intention, these words can become words of power. For this spell you'll need a piece of paper, a pen, a white candle, and a heatproof cauldron or bowl.

To begin, choose a word or small phrase you already use and would like to empower. It could be something said in mild frustration (like dang, darn, crap, etc.) or even a nonsense word (like gerflooffen). Write your choice on the paper and light the candle. Hold the paper and fix in your mind that whenever you speak the word, it shall carry a blessing energy. Then say:

(Word), from this point you shall be filled with blessing energy; whenever spoken aloud by me, a shift of power then set free.

Burn the paper in the cauldron to seal the spell.

Michael Furie

February 28
Tuesday

2nd ♊

☽ v/c 8:07 pm

☽ → ♋ 9:40 pm

Color of the day: White
Incense of the day: Cedar

Honoring the Spirit of Place

Everywhere you go, whether a building, field, or forest, there is a spirit of place. Honoring this spirit is important, especially if you intend to do magic there. This ritual is a way to connect to the spirit of a place by showing respect, which in turn will create a better atmosphere for your workings.

To honor the spirit of place, you can offer a gift. It must be something of personal value to show that you're authentic in your wish to connect. Only you know what this might be: a special crystal, a meaningful herb, a pretty feather, or something completely personal.

Sit in the space you wish to connect to and close your eyes. Listen to the sounds, feel the air on your skin, breathe in the smells. You might sense a presence. When you reach this state, say:

With this gift I offer respect to the spirit of this place. May we exist together in harmony.

If you're outdoors, place the gift on the ground. Inside, find a corner or shelf space that feels right. Now when you do your magical workings, you'll have the spirit of place on your side.

Kate Freuler

NOTES:

March

March is upon us! March is a month of unpredictable weather. Will the weather spirits decide to bring us a last hurrah of winter in the form of a blustery snowstorm or instead bring us signs of spring's beginning in the form of budding trees and perhaps rain showers sprinkled with mild, sunny days? There really is no telling! However, for those of us who follow the Wheel of the Year, the spring equinox is a time of new beginnings, regardless of the weather.

Rituals of spring and new beginnings will take place around the globe this month. Druids still gather at Stonehenge to welcome the rising sun on the morning of the equinox. March also is the time to celebrate the festival of Holi, popular in India and Nepal. People engage in paint fights, covering each other in festive splatters of vibrant color, welcoming the arrival of spring and all its vibrancy.

In March, however you choose to celebrate, work the magick of new beginnings!

Blake Octavian Blair

March 1
Wednesday

2nd ♋

Color of the day: Yellow
Incense of the day: Honeysuckle

The Magick of Compliments

When we think of magick, we often think of the full moon, candles, and burning incense, but magick can also be incredibly simple. There is a great deal of power and energy that comes from our voices and what we say to one another. This is not a spell you actively cast for yourself. Instead, it's a series of gifts for those you interact with.

Spend your day actively and sincerely complimenting others. Tell people they have made good decisions or are great at their job. Praise a lover or partner in a way that maybe you have not before. Let a customer know they are brilliant for buying a certain item. As you compliment and say nice things to others, you'll notice a shift in them as they receive your positive energy. In most instances, that energy will be returned to you too!

Amanda Lynn & Jason Mankey

March 2
Thursday

2nd ♋

Color of the day: Green
Incense of the day: Nutmeg

A Green Man Garden Blessing

For this garden blessing, you'll need to fashion a Green Man from grasses or other plant materials. You can do something simple, like fold a few stems of grass over to form a humanlike shape and tie in the middle with jute twine to form a waist. Or you could get fancier and make a corn doll. It's up to you. When finished, the Green Man form should be about the size of a child's doll. When it's done, place the Green Man on your altar and say:

Green Man, protect my garden during spring rain,

Protect my garden during summer's heat,

Protect my garden during autumn's frost,

Protect my garden during winter's ice and snow.

Now take your Green Man out to your garden. Place it where it won't be disturbed, such as a far corner. Leave it alone. Let it return naturally to the earth.

James Kambos

March 3
Friday

2nd ♋

☽ v/c 9:22 am

☽ → ♌ 10:16 am

Color of the day: Rose
Incense of the day: Thyme

Birdseed Blessing

Today is World Wildlife Day. It is important to remember to contribute to efforts to save exotic animals in far-off lands, as we are all connected; however, don't forget the importance of your local wildlife, whether you live in an urban area or someplace more rural.

At this time of year in late winter, it is still appropriate for many of us in the Northern Hemisphere to keep our bird feeders well stocked. Today, top off your bird feeder or hang one if you do not yet have one, and enter into a symbiotic relationship with your wild siblings in the animal kingdom. After you fill your feeder but before you hang it, hold your hands with palms over the birdseed and say a blessing. Here is an example for inspiration:

Hand to wing we join together,

Even in chilly winter weather.

In this season I offer seed to you,

So we may sustain a relationship all year through.

Health and happiness to both you and me.

We are but fellow animals on this earth, blessed be.

Blake Octavian Blair

NOTES:

March 4
Saturday

2nd ♌

Color of the day: Indigo
Incense of the day: Sandalwood

Love Spell Mist

When we're searching for love, we often have a fixed notion of what that should look like, an expectation that can end up standing in our way. This spell is designed to welcome all forms of love into your life, including the unexpected!

Materials:

- A misting bottle
- ½ cup rose water
- 3 fresh rose petals
- 1 cleansed rose quartz
- 1 tablespoon sugar

Combine the rose water, rose petals, and rose quartz in the misting bottle. Place it in direct sunlight and sprinkle the sugar around it in the shape of a heart. Leave the bottle for three days to absorb the loving rays of the sun. On the third day, hold the bottle in your hands and visualize a vaporous pink glow surrounding it. This glow is filled with many kinds of love, without judgment or labels.

Each day, open your door or windows and spray the mist into the openings, imagining them glowing bright pink.

Recite:

Open door, open mind,

The love I seek will soon be mine.

Wait and see who walks through your door.

Kate Freuler

NOTES:

March 5
Sunday

2nd ♌

☽ v/c 10:18 pm

☽ → ♍ 10:38 pm

Color of the day: Yellow
Incense of the day: Marigold

Energetic Vehicle Protection

To magically protect your vehicle in a completely inconspicuous way, a bit of energy magic is very useful. Using the index and middle fingers of your dominant hand, trace a pentagram over the middle of the steering wheel while visualizing an electric-purple energy forming the symbol. Beginning at the top, move down to the lower left, then up to the right, then across to the left, then down to the lower right, and finally back to the top to complete the pentagram. As you form the symbol, say:

> Witch's star of magical power,
> protect this vehicle from all harm.
>
> Draw force from the universe
> hour by hour, to keep the
> spell and seal the charm.
>
> Shielded from accidents, from danger
> you're free. As I will, so mote it be.

> Michael Furie

March 6
Monday

2nd ♍

Color of the day: Silver
Incense of the day: Narcissus

Purim begins at sundown

Cleansing Spell

Since the full moon is tomorrow, it's a great day to get your altar and sacred space cleansed and prepared. Gather up any supplies that you plan to use during your full moon practice. Place the items (candles, crystals, athame, etc.) in a bowl of salt. White salt is known for its purification and protection energies. Submerge your tools/crystals in the salt in a glass or wooden bowl. Do whatever feels right to you, but do some research and make sure your crystals and supplies won't be damaged by the salt. Use these words to assist the energetic cleanse:

> On this day and in this hour,
>
> As the moon is nearly in full power,
>
> I purify and cleanse these
> magickal things
>
> To increase the effect that
> each item brings.

Leave the items in the salt overnight. Rinse them with water, then allow them to dry so they are ready for your magickal workings.

> Sapphire Moonbeam

March 7
Tuesday

2nd ♍

Full Moon 7:40 am

Color of the day: Scarlet
Incense of the day: Cinnamon

A Time to Charge Tools

Take this opportunity at the full moon to charge your tools, candles, crystals, and other magical items. Find a spot in your home where the moon will shine in for at least one hour. If no window ledge is wide enough, set up a table. If an item is flat, like your athame, let it bathe in the moonlight for a while and then flip it over. You may also want to charge some organic matter for use in spells, such as spices, herbs, or a jar of water.

Ground and center, then call upon the elements and the directions. As you charge your items, chant:

*Lady of the moon, look down
upon these items. Cleanse them
of past spells and infuse them
with clean energy for use in future
incantations. In your honor.*

Emyme

March 8
Wednesday

3rd ♍

☽ v/c 9:07 am

☽ → ♎ 9:44 am

Color of the day: Topaz
Incense of the day: Lavender

Eggzactly Unstoppable

Ancient Europeans worshiped the first eggs of spring, to honor with gratitude the return of the regenerative fertility and life-sustaining cycles of Earth. This Ukrainian parlor game is a lively way to learn to maintain your compassion and tenderness under pressure. It teaches us that every egg is a treasure and our own endurance and patience are redeeming survival skills, because with time and practice we can all steadily develop any ability.

Nestle an egg between two teaspoons, holding one spoon in each hand. Cross your arms to make it more of a challenge. The trick is to apply enough pressure to grip the egg but not so much that the spoons will crack the shell. How long can you hold it? Can you dance with it, climb with it? Can you sit, stand, or roll around on the ground while still gripping the egg safely? Challenge your abilities today. Chant:

*May joy and laughter abound,
should no egg befall the ground.*

Estha McNevin

March 9
Thursday

3rd ♎

Color of the day: White
Incense of the day: Clove

Incantation for Peace

An incantation is a series of words used as a magical spell, to "change consciousness at will," as defined by Dion Fortune. Whether spoken, chanted, or sung, words have power. The power of their meaning and the effect of their sound vibration can uplift, inspire, and manifest.

The Sanskrit words *Om shanti shanti shanti* have been popularized by yoga and yogis. *Shanti* translates to *peace*. Chanting it three times is said to bring peace from the three disturbances: the disturbance of the world around us, the disturbance from within, and the disturbance from the sacred. Literally, this chant evokes peace of body, mind, and spirit, and when repeated three times, it can represent the past, present, and future.

Today, chant *Om shanti shanti shanti* and hold the intention of purifying your body, mind, and spirit to relieve you of all suffering. You can alternately chant *Oh peace peace peace* for a similar effect.

Dallas Jennifer Cobb

March 10
Friday

3rd ♎

☽ v/c 6:37 pm
☽ → ♏ 7:06 pm

Color of the day: Purple
Incense of the day: Cypress

Wash Away the Day

Use this cleansing bath to relax and unwind, especially if you've had a challenging day. Prepare as you normally would for a relaxing bath or shower. For example, light some candles and play some music. If you're using a tub, add some Epsom salts, bubble bath, essential oils, or a bath bomb. Create the most relaxing atmosphere you can imagine. If you don't have a bathtub, prepare the room with the candles and use an infuser for essential oils.

Visualize the water literally washing away stress and tension. As you bathe or shower, chant these words over and over until you're completely relaxed.

Water, wash the day away,

Help me keep the stress at bay.

If you need a quick fix, splash water over your face while you chant.

Ember Grant

 ## March 11
Saturday

3rd ♏

Color of the day: Blue
Incense of the day: Patchouli

Ancestor Tray

Today is National Genealogy Day, a time to commit to a regular pattern of honor and communication with a specific ancestor until Samhain.

Choose a deceased grandparent or older relative with whom you either feel or would like to build a strong connection. Put a photograph of them in a beautiful frame. (If you don't have a photograph, create a sketch or write and decorate the individual's name, and frame it.)

Prepare a tray with the photograph (or framed sketch or name), a candle in a firesafe dish, a crystal, a feather, a small mirror, and a token that is specific to that person (such as a horseshoe charm if they rode horses, a pen if they liked to write, etc.).

Light the candle and meditate on what you know about this ancestor and the relationship you would like to form with them. Once a week until Samhain, make time to have a conversation with this ancestor in different spaces or outside. Extinguish the candle when done. Keep your ancestor tray visible for daily communication.

Cerridwen Iris Shea

 ## March 12
Sunday

3rd ♏

Color of the day: Gold
Incense of the day: Hyacinth

**Daylight Saving Time
begins at 2:00 a.m.**

Spring Forward Spell

Today, many people will "spring forward," as we adjust our clocks and our schedules for one hour in the future. While we aren't physically moving ahead, we can use this change to reframe our mindsets and help us roll with the changes. For this spell you'll need a pinch of dried mint and a bit of soil, either in a potted plant or outside.

Hold the mint in your hand and get close to the soil by sitting or crouching near it. Take a few deep breaths. Focus on your future self—envision yourself springing forward with more power, mindfulness, fun, wisdom, clarity, or whatever you wish to bring about. Hold that vision of yourself as you crush the mint between your fingers and release it to the soil. Say:

*I offer this mint to my
future empowered self.*

*As I spring forward, may I find
the paths that lead to you.*

Astrea Taylor

March 13
Monday

3rd ♏︎

☽ v/c 2:58 am

☽ → ♐︎ 3:21 am

Color of the day: Lavender
Incense of the day: Clary sage

Four Seasons of Magic

Today, begin a new magical tradition for celebrating the seasons. Pick a spot in nature that you find especially sacred, striking, and spiritually significant. Choose a place that you can access easily within an hour radius of home. Visit it today in the current season. Soak in its energy and the feelings you perceive as well as what you can visually see, smell, touch, and hear. Make note of all the sensory experiences of this place in this season. Remember to make an eco-friendly offering to the land.

Then make a commitment to revisit this exact same location in all four seasons. Each time, take note of the changes at this place as you progress through the Wheel of the Year. You might like to journal about each visit. You will build a relationship to the spirits of place and with the land in which you live as you become familiar with your sacred place throughout the year, through all seasons and weather.

Blake Octavian Blair

 ## March 14
Tuesday

3rd ♐︎

4th Quarter 10:08 pm

Color of the day: Gray
Incense of the day: Basil

Saturnian Cycle Oracle Working

Something major is happening right now. Saturn has just crossed the threshold into Pisces, ushering in a new era of collective soul-searching and reflection that will last roughly thirty years. During this period we are going to break down spiritual walls and redefine what spirituality means to us as a collective. Find out what this cycle means for you specifically by performing this easy reading, which can be done with tarot, runes, or any draw system of divination. Draw five lots and place them in a pentagram pattern, starting at the top:

Position 1: What you are bringing with you from the last Saturnian cycle

Position 2: What your personal challenge will be during this cycle

Position 3: Unseen influences to be aware of

Position 4: Overall personal theme for this cycle

Position 5: Message from Spirit to you about this cycle

Devin Hunter

March 15
Wednesday

4th ♐

☽ v/c 4:50 am

☽ → ♑ 8:06 am

Color of the day: Brown

Incense of the day: Lilac

A Daffodil Love Spell

Ruled by Venus, daffodils are spring's flowers of love. During the days of the old-time herbalists, daffodils were sometimes used in love spells. They were frequently placed on the altar during the casting of a love spell.

For this spell you'll need two daffodils with their stems intact. You'll also need one pink and one light blue ribbon. As you think of your spell's intent, but without thinking of anyone specific, tie the daffodil stems together using both ribbons. As you tie them, say:

With a ribbon of pink
and a ribbon of blue,

I bind these flowers of love together,

To bring me a love special and true.

Place the daffodils in a small vase of water and set it on your altar. Wait for love to come to you. After the daffodils fade, respectfully place them in a compost pile or lay them on the ground in a wooded area.

James Kambos

 ## March 16
Thursday

4th ♑

Color of the day: Crimson

Incense of the day: Myrrh

Tea for Prophetic Dreams

For this spell you will need the following ingredients:

- 1 teaspoon mugwort
- ½ teaspoon rose petals
- 1 teaspoon peppermint
- ½ teaspoon lavender
- ½ teaspoon chamomile
- Honey to taste

Mix the ingredients well and steep them in boiled water for ten to fifteen minutes. As they steep, stand over the teacup and recite the following chant:

Tea of dreams, tea of wonder,

Bring me visions while I slumber.

Aid me in my sacred rest.

Guide me on my psychic quest.

Provide the answers I must know.

As above, so below.

Drink the tea at least thirty minutes before you go to bed or take a nap. When you wake up, write down any interesting or pertinent visions from your dreams in your journal.

Amanda Lynn & Jason Mankey

March 17
Friday

4th ♑

☽ v/c 10:14 am

☽ → ♒ 10:25 am

Color of the day: Coral
Incense of the day: Alder

Saint Patrick's Day

Sweeping in the Luck

Saint Patrick's Day is often associated with the concept of luck (the luck of the Irish). Jupiter, the planet that governs luck, is in fiery Mars-ruled Aries now, so we're going to tap into those aspects.

For this spell we will be using two common household spices that have associations with luck: nutmeg (ruled by Jupiter and associated with the element of fire) and allspice (ruled by Mars and corresponding with fire). You will also need either your besom or your household broom.

Sweep all the dust and dirt outward from your front door, with the intention to sweep away misfortune. Sprinkle the nutmeg and allspice in front of your door and then sweep it into a tidy line as close to your front door as possible, drawing near you good luck and fortune while chanting this verse:

By the Spirit and the elements four,

Blessings come knocking on my door.

My fortune has now become unstuck.

My life is abundant with my good luck.

Mat Auryn

NOTES:

March 18
Saturday

4th ≈

Color of the day: Black
Incense of the day: Magnolia

Spirit Spring Cleaning

The circle shape is a magical symbol we can call upon. The magic circle is the protective circle we draw when performing a ritual, casting a spell, or sending healing, because a circle represents both spirit and matter.

Our ancestors built houses that were not square but round, because this provided more protection from the elements. A circular design is both flexible and strong, and is safer in severe weather conditions. The circle is also found in nature, from stones and the ovoid shape of eggs to the earth itself. Places like Stonehenge, Avebury, and Newgrange are some of the oldest monuments in the world and have stood the test of time. To the ancients, magic was a part of their lives, and the magic of a circle was a powerful force.

Cleanse your home now and free the spirit of winter or summer (depending on which hemisphere you live in), allowing for the next season's energy to enter. Cleanse and create your own protective space by spraying magic holy water made by adding one tablespoon of salt and two drops of spikenard essential oil to a spray bottle of water.

Go from room to room spraying the water, creating a circle in each room. Imagine you have a golden white light around you as you say these words:

Cleansed and cleaned within this space,
Seasons passing at a pace.
I cast the circle round and round,
Forever protected, safe and sound.
No harm, no negativity, shall pass to me,
For I am safe within my circle round.

Tudorbeth

Notes:

March 19
Sunday

4th ♒

☽ v/c 6:33 am

☽ → ♓ 11:12 am

Color of the day: Orange
Incense of the day: Frankincense

Pain Relief with Airmid

The females in my family are prone to headaches, migraines, and backaches. Several years ago I had surgery to correct one cause of pain, which in turn threw my spine out of alignment and brought on other pain. I explored all healing options, consulted with numerous medical practitioners, and sought relief from Reiki, acupuncture, spinal manipulation, essential oils, crystals, yoga, and meditation. All of that brought only temporary relief.

A permanent reprieve from the aches and pain finally came after I retired from my full-time employment. When I fully realized the extent of my discontent and set my retirement date, I was freed from the constant, chronic discomfort.

You can call upon Airmid, a Celtic goddess of healing, when you need relief from pain:

*Airmid, open my mind to
alternative methods of relieving
pain and discomfort. Bless me with
creative strength at all times.*

Emyme

 ## March 20
Monday

4th ♓

☉ → ♈ 5:24 pm

Color of the day: Ivory
Incense of the day: Hyssop

Spring Equinox – Ostara

Spring Equinox Blessing Basket

We all know spring is about renewal; it's one of the most magical times of the year. In this ritual you will create a blessing basket—a decorative item to display on your altar that represents your magical life. You can also include things you wish to manifest in the coming year. It's like an Easter basket, but instead of candy, put in crystals, tarot cards, candles, etc. Of course, you can certainly add eggs and flowers, too. You can line the basket with decorative moss or just use a napkin or altar cloth.

Next, write your goals and wishes on pieces of paper and tuck them into the basket among the flowers, eggs, crystals, and other items. Or you can hide the papers in little decorative plastic eggs. Keep the basket in a place where you can see it until summer, and then, on a full moon night, dismantle it and bury the papers.

These baskets also make wonderful gifts, especially for those new to magic or anyone who could use some new ritual tools.

Ember Grant

March 21
Tuesday

4th ♓

☽ v/c 11:58 am

☽ → ♈ 12:01 pm

New Moon 1:23 pm

Color of the day: Red
Incense of the day: Bayberry

Mugwort Blessings

Mugwort is an inexpensive herb often associated with psychic power. The most common use for mugwort is cleansing and empowering divination tools. This new moon, treat your tools to a nice reset by creating a simple mugwort brew to clear them of accumulated energy and infuse them with extra psychic power.

To prepare the brew, put three tablespoons dried mugwort in a Mason jar, and pour one cup of boiling water onto it. Let it steep until cooled, then strain through a cheesecloth or strainer into a bowl. Use the liquid immediately, or freeze some in an ice cube tray to thaw and use later.

Dip a soft cloth in the brew and use it to wipe down the surfaces of moisture-resistant tools such as crystals, pendulums, or mirrors. For items that can't withstand water, such as oracle cards, you can sprinkle a handful of dried mugwort over them for the night and let the magical herb do its work. After using mugwort, you'll notice that your readings and divinations are more accurate and easier to interpret.

Kate Freuler

NOTES:

March 22
Wednesday

1st ♈

Color of the day: Yellow
Incense of the day: Bay laurel

Ramadan begins at sundown

Ramadan Sundown

Tonight the star of Venus will appear with the moon and motivate many of us to pray for deep spiritual progress in our lives. The following spell is a universal human prayer for peace.

While standing in your kitchen, anoint a white candle with olive oil and envision the light of thought, science, philosophy, and art as you light the wick with a match. Carry this flame to the center of your home and let it burn as a beacon of hope for the future. Meditate on your own journey and let your soul unfold within your home in a spiritual act of meditation or mindfulness until the candle is safely extinguished.

Commit to volunteer where you are needed to support peace and civil rights and overcome ignorance and fear. If you light your own lamp from within in this way, then you will know peace with yourself and others.

Estha McNevin

March 23
Thursday

1st ♈

☽ v/c 1:13 pm

☽ → ♉ 2:42 pm

Color of the day: Purple
Incense of the day: Jasmine

Charged Nail Polish

Vibrant shades of nail polish are an excellent means of utilizing color magic, and the portable nature of polish makes it easy and practical to use. Consult a list of color correspondences for help in choosing just the right shade to match your intention. Some examples include pink or red for love, white or black for protection, yellow or orange for communication, and green for growth, health, or prosperity.

Once you've chosen a shade of nail polish, light a candle of the same color and hold the bottle of polish in your hands while envisioning that it is infused with a radiant light of the same hue. To seal the charge, say:

Liquid color empowered with light, a magical medium you shall now be.

When painted on nails, release your might; magic unleashed for all to see.

Extinguish the candle, and the nail polish is ready to use.

Michael Furie

March 24
Friday

1st ♉

Color of the day: White
Incense of the day: Orchid

Friday, My Day Spell

Dion Fortune said that "magic is the practice of changing consciousness at will." Friday is my magical day, my day off, the day when I do all of my favorite things. I comprehend the deep and abiding magic that comes from this practice. It changes my consciousness and heals and uplifts me. Even on Fridays when I might have to work, I still practice this spell to great benefit, wrapping myself in the transformative energies of love and passion.

To begin, quickly identify five things you love that don't cost money: walking, with my dog, in nature, by the lake, at dusk. That wasn't so hard. Try it again: laughing, exercise, hugs, smiles, people holding doors. Now tell me five things you are passionate about: ecology, magic, nature, animals, neurophysiology. You know what you love and are passionate about. Can you purposefully choose to spend time today engaged with love and passion?

Dallas Jennifer Cobb

March 25
Saturday

1st ♉

☽ v/c 12:19 pm

☽ → ♊ 8:42 pm

Color of the day: Gray
Incense of the day: Ivy

Garden Gratitude Spell

Spring has arrived in the Northern Hemisphere. March is the time to think about the seeds you want to plant in your herb garden. Consider the types of spells you want to do later in the year. Are you hoping for more success, abundance, love and romance, courage, or something else? The seeds you plant now can help you achieve what you desire in the future. Consider researching herbs you can grow for specific magical outcomes to use in spellwork. Also, trust your inner wisdom about what you want to grow in your personal world. As you plant your seeds, you can say these words:

As I fill my garden with these seeds,

I plant the beginning of my desires, wishes, and needs.

I will tend to these herbs and water them each day.

I am grateful for the blessings that are on the way.

Sapphire Moonbeam

March 26
Sunday

1st ♊

Color of the day: Yellow
Incense of the day: Heliotrope

Smelling the Future

S melling the future…Well, not precisely. However, using an incense with properties that help us open up to the energies of looking forward can aid us while divining the future and using our psychic sight and sixth sense. Thus, the scent can help boost the vision.

So what can we use to smell the future? Well, today's planetary ruler is the sun, and solar herbs have properties that help us illuminate possibilities and look forward. A favorite that most people have on hand, either in resin form or as stick incense, is frankincense. Frankincense resin even has a sunny golden sort of color. Before diving into the week that lies ahead, light some frankincense on your altar and recite:

> Golden tears of the sun,
>
> Shed a light on this week to come.
>
> May my visions bring to view
>
> Insight into this week brand-new!

Now use your favorite method of divination to tap into your psychic senses and divine wisdom. Blessings!

Blake Octavian Blair

March 27
Monday

1st ♊

☽ v/c 9:39 pm

Color of the day: White
Incense of the day: Lily

Self-Confidence Affirmations

With the Sun in confident and determined Aries and the Moon in communicative Gemini today, this is an ideal time to speak words of power into existence. The power of the witch's voice is legendary.

With affirmations, we are speaking words into existence, reprogramming ourselves mentally to think and behave in a certain way, and creating energetic thoughtforms within our energy bodies to assist us in our desires. It's important to speak affirmations from a place of willpower. Even if you don't fully believe the words you're reciting, it's important to suspend those doubts and immerse yourself in a frame of mind where you're saying the affirmations firmly, confidently, and as if they are true because you have spoken them into existence. Say each affirmation to yourself out loud repeatedly while looking yourself in the eyes in the mirror. Here are some possibilities:

I am determined to meet my goals.

I can achieve anything I set my mind to.

I am unstoppable.

Mat Auryn

March 28
Tuesday

1st ♊

☽ → ♋ 6:22 am

2nd Quarter 10:32 pm

Color of the day: Maroon
Incense of the day: Ylang-ylang

Beauty Spring Renewal Ritual

March is associated with Isis, the ancient Egyptian goddess of rebirth, renewal, and fertility, amongst many other things. Use the power of spring by creating a ritual of cleansing and purification. Make a ritual bath with seven drops of rose essential oil in the water, then soak and meditate in the bath. If you do not have a bath, then put seven drops of rose essential oil in your shower gel and shake it up. After your ritual bath or shower, light a blue candle and say these words:

Mother Isis, I ask of you.

Blessed waters of the Nile,

Wash me clean and cleanse my soul,

Pure forevermore, this spring I beguile.

Mind, body, and spirit made whole.

Mother Isis, your blessed waters I beseech.

My life now will be complete.

Isis is the Great Mother and a great goddess of magic, so it is an honour if she works with you. Be respectful and always give thanks by placing a rose or two on your altar when good little things happen to you. Extinguish the candle when done.

Tudorbeth

NOTES:

 ### March 29
Wednesday

2nd ♋

Color of the day: Brown
Incense of the day: Marjoram

honey Bath Spell

Both the Moon and Venus are in their glory today as they travel through their home signs, bringing with them intense emotional and physical desires for things that make us feel and look good. Many of us are no doubt feeling our way through the nuances of love, sex, and pleasure at this time, so why not use the opportunity to enhance our lives by attracting more of what we want?

Draw a bath with your favorite bubble bath, and light a pink candle. Pour a spoonful of honey into the water and stir clockwise as you chant:

By hive and queen, honey and comb,
I draw these blessings to my home!

Take your bath, and as you soak, visualize specific blessings manifesting in your life. Extinguish the candle.

Devin hunter

March 30
Thursday

2nd ♋

☽ v/c 9:45 am

☽ → ♌ 6:31 pm

Color of the day: Turquoise
Incense of the day: Mulberry

Cocoon Spell

Spring is a time of transformation. A cocoon spell helps us burst out of tired winter patterns.

Go to a place where you will be undisturbed for at least thirty minutes. A floor or a bed works well.

Wrap yourself up completely in a blanket or quilt, including over your head. (Make sure you can breathe easily.) Follow your breath until you feel safe and protected. Imagine yourself emerging into spring's beautiful light, where anything and everything is possible.

Slowly expose your head, then each arm and each leg, and remove the blanket until you're lying on top of it.

Close your eyes and breathe in the freedom. Mull over a few options for this new freedom.

When you are ready, slowly return to the present space. Write in your journal about your experiences and what you intend to explore in this season's cycle.

Cerridwen Iris Shea

 **March 31**
Friday

2nd ♌

Color of the day: Pink
Incense of the day: Yarrow

Venusian Love Potpourri

Today is Friday, which is sacred to the goddess Venus and all of her predecessors. It's the perfect day for a little love magic. Not only does this Venusian love potpourri smell good, but it's also a magical charm to create more love in your life.

You will need a small bowl, chocolate pieces, rose petals and/or rosehips, other dried flowers, crushed cinnamon sticks, a rose quartz, and a floral essential oil, such as jasmine.

Place the materials in the bowl, except for the oil, and stir them clockwise with your finger. Whisper romantically:

*Flowers and correspondences
of Venus divine, let love
thrive, and let it be mine.*

Put five drops of the oil into the bowl at the tips of a star. Trace the shape of a pentagram with your finger while reciting the spell to yourself.

Whenever you want to recharge the spell, place five more drops of oil into the bowl and draw the pentagram with your finger again as you recite the spell.

Astrea Taylor

April

This month we move from dark to light, from cold to warm, from brown to green. April is a magical month that starts with April Fools' Day and ends on the eve of May Day, begins with a joke and ends with an outdoor sleep-out. Here in Ontario, Canada, the average temperature at the beginning of April is close to freezing. It's common to have snow on the ground. Throughout April a magical transformation occurs: the temperature climbs as high as 66 degrees Fahrenheit (19 degrees Celsius) and flowers bloom.

Post-equinox, the days grow longer. Between April 1 and 30, the daylight increases from 12 hours and 46 minutes to 14 hours and 8 minutes. As the sun travels northward, it climbs in the sky. Not only do days lengthen, but shadows shorten as well. It is inviting to get outdoors. Like the plants that need sunlight to conduct photosynthesis, we humans need sunlight to help manufacture vitamin D.

This month, make time to enjoy the outdoors. Get out in the daylight, take evening walks in the twilight after dinner, contemplate your garden, and turn your face toward the sun at every chance. With winter coming to an end, now is your time to transform.

Dallas Jennifer Cobb

April 1
Saturday

2nd ♌

Color of the day: Blue
Incense of the day: Rue

April Fools' Day – All Fools' Day

Embrace the Fool

No matter how you feel about April Fools' Day, there's one fool always worth celebrating: the Fool of the tarot. In most tarot decks, the Fool is the first card of the major arcana and has the number zero. The Fool represents spontaneity, new beginnings, travel, and innocence. Pull this card from your deck or print a picture of one. Carry it with you today and let the Fool's journey guide you on your adventures. Embrace your inner Fool and enjoy the day with confidence, grace, and surprise. You never know where you might end up!

Amanda Lynn & Jason Mankey

April 2
Sunday

2nd ♌
☽ v/c 2:03 am
☽ → ♍ 6:57 am

Color of the day: Gold
Incense of the day: Eucalyptus

Palm Sunday

Fae Blessings for the Garden

With today's waxing moon, this is a good time for a spell requesting fae blessings on your garden. If you haven't yet planted your basil and chives, this is a good day to do so, and these are good herbs to use for this spell. A small plant works best, rather than seeds.

Repot your plant in a pretty pot, then water the plant. Slide a copper penny into the soil near the edge of the pot, farthest from the plant. (Copper does not hurt basil or chives). Pour a few drops of milk (any kind) onto the soil and say:

Friends in the fae realm,

I ask your blessing on this plant and garden.

May they thrive under your protection and care,

With my gratitude.

So mote it be.

Care for the plant daily, and enjoy its growth.

Cerridwen Iris Shea

April 3
Monday

2nd ♍

Color of the day: Gray
Incense of the day: Clary sage

Blessing upon an Annoying Task

Whether we are heading to work (it is Monday, after all) or have a really frustrating chore that must be done, most of us have tasks or projects that we are less than enthusiastic to complete. When faced with such situations, I like to use a little blessing magic to help smooth out the unpleasantness and speed up the process of completing the task at hand.

For this blessing, when possible, take a minute to close your eyes and envision yourself happily completing the work with ease, speed, and efficiency. Imagine everything falling perfectly into place, and the dread and annoyance fading away and being replaced by satisfaction. When the feeling is strong, open your eyes and say:

With a fresh new perspective,
I greet this task.

In magical advantage, I now bask.

Completed with ease, efficient and fun,

No longer a chore, the battle is won.

Michael Furie

April 4
Tuesday

2nd ♍

☽ v/c 9:50 am

☽ → ♎ 5:51 pm

Color of the day: Black
Incense of the day: Geranium

Petition for the Right Use of Power

With the Sun in powerhouse Aries and the Moon in fair and just Libra later in the day, this is an auspicious time to request discernment for the right use of power. On a piece of paper, write this petition:

In the name of the Great God and the Great Goddess, through the power of the Universal Spirit, I ask to be granted the wisdom of knowing when and how to use my power and influence in the world for the betterment of myself and others.

I ask for the gift of spiritual discernment to know when to act and speak and when to be still and silent. I ask that my hands, my heart, my voice, and my spirit be used to align with my highest will for the Great Work.

For the highest good of all, (sign your name or magickal name).

Roll up the petition and tie it with string. Place the scroll on your altar and periodically reread it out loud.

Mat Auryn

April 5
Wednesday

2nd ♎

Color of the day: White
Incense of the day: Lavender

Passover begins at sundown

Mini Pilgrimage

Today is National Walking Day in the United States. The goal is to get people exercising; however, it's a good opportunity to explore the spiritual benefits of the celebration. Let's make a mini pilgrimage! Not everyone can make grand pilgrimages to legendary sites afar, but your local spiritual spots are well worth a mini pilgrimage.

Do you have a special site in nature, like a lake, a river, a botanical garden, or even a local monument to somebody you respect? These, too, are sacred sites. Find something walkable, within a few miles of your home, and set out, if you're able, on a walking pilgrimage to the site. Pack a few eco-friendly offerings and some water to drink, lace up your walking shoes, and start walking.

On your journey to and from your site, you can engage in a walking meditation on what the journey and the destination mean to you. While at your site, make your offerings and pay your respects however you see fit. Blessings on your journey!

Blake Octavian Blair

April 6
Thursday

2nd ♎
Full Moon 12:34 am
☽ v/c 8:43 am

Color of the day: Crimson
Incense of the day: Balsam

Libra Releasing Spell

Happy Libra Full Moon, witches! The energy provided today by the cosmos allows us to find harmony and balance. This is a time for rituals of deep healing within and ancestral forgiveness and for relinquishing the chains of the past. Cast this spell to break the chains that bind.

Take the Justice card from your favorite tarot deck and place it before you on your altar. The Justice card embodies the energies of Libra, so allow it to symbolize the Libran frequency. As if speaking before a judge, explain your situation, what you want to release, and why. Using your index finger, tap the sword on the card five times and say:

Justice, be not blind to my plea.

*Bang your gavel and swing
your sword for me!*

As you do this, visualize the sword of Justice cutting through the ties that bind you to what you wish to release.

Devin Hunter

April 7
Friday

3rd ♎

☽ → ♏ 2:29 am

Color of the day: Purple
Incense of the day: Mint

Good Friday

All the 7s Spell

In numerology, seven is a very good, powerful, and protective number. It is often viewed as the number of magic, the number of witchcraft itself, and represents divinity, truth, love, power, success, and protection. Seven is regarded as lucky in many countries, such as in certain regions of Spain and Italy, where they believe that cats have seven lives rather than nine. There were Seven Wonders of the Ancient World, and the opposite faces of a die always add up to seven.

The year 2023 is a magical seven year:

$$2023 = 2 + 0 + 2 + 3 = 7$$

Tap into the magic of seven when casting spells this year by having either seven lines of a spell, seven items, or seven amounts of something, or by repeating the spell seven times. Since seven represents power and success, you could use it to create a promotion or new job spell.

Here is a spell to obtain something you desire, such as a promotion or a specific item. Begin by writing what it is you want on a piece of paper. Then roll up the paper, hold it in your hand, and repeat this spell seven times:

Seven times seven makes forty-nine.

The (thing) I want becomes mine.

As you say the words, imagine how it will feel when you receive your desired promotion or item. See yourself having it, being it, or holding it. Give the universe forty-nine days to manifest the desired outcome or item, and if it hasn't arrived by then, repeat the spell once more.

When the spell is done, bury the paper in the garden, or burn it and dispose of the ashes safely.

Tudorbeth

April 8
Saturday

3rd ♏

Color of the day: Brown
Incense of the day: Pine

Chocolate Cleansing Scrub

Spring is the perfect time to renew your skin. This all-natural scrub removes dead skin cells, nourishes your skin, and invigorates it with antioxidants. It's best to make this scrub just before you want to use it. Combine the following ingredients in a bowl:

  2 tablespoons brown sugar

  1 tablespoon coconut oil

  ½ tablespoon cocoa powder

  1 teaspoon baking soda

  ½ teaspoon salt

Wash up in the shower, rinse, then turn the water off. Speak this verse into the mixture:

Cleanse me to my core,
and nourish me to my soul.

Rub the mixture into your skin while repeating the spell. Let it soak in, then rinse it off. (This scrub is for external use only. Test it on a small area of your skin first.)

Astrea Taylor

April 9
Sunday

3rd ♏

☽ v/c 5:09 am

☽ → ♐ 8:57 am

Color of the day: Amber
Incense of the day: Almond

Easter

Easter Abundance Spell

The celebration of Easter has roots in ancient pagan cultures. It is a celebration of fertility, new life, and the new hope that is ushered in with the arrival of spring. If you have a desire to increase abundance in your life, you can utilize the fertility energy of Easter to accomplish this goal. Use this spell to increase monetary abundance, an abundance of love, or something else.

Obtain an egg. You can use a real one, a plastic egg, or even a drawing of an egg. The most important part of this spell is your own belief that you will indeed manifest abundance in your life. Place the egg in your hand, focus on the thing(s) that you want to increase in your life, and say these words:

This egg that is associated with new
life and spring will multiply the
abundance this season will bring.

Sapphire Moonbeam

April 10
Monday

3rd ♐

Color of the day: Silver
Incense of the day: Neroli

Make a Wish Spell

For this spell you'll need one strip of blue fabric, a pen or marker, and the Three of Wands card from a tarot deck. Begin by writing your wish on the strip of fabric. Take the fabric outdoors and find a shrub or tree that is beginning to leaf out. Tie your wish onto a branch of your chosen shrub or tree. As you tie it, project your energy into your wish as you say:

Let this wish come true,

Let this wish be mine.

Come to me with perfect ease,

Come to me at the perfect time.

Leave the wish tied to the branch. Once home, sit at your altar and hold the Three of Wands card. Meditate on your wish coming to you as you gaze at the card. Do this occasionally until the wish is answered. At that time, dispose of your fabric strip and return the tarot card to the deck.

James Kambos

April 11
Tuesday

3rd ♐

☽ v/c 6:48 am

☽ → ♑ 1:33 pm

Color of the day: Gray
Incense of the day: Ginger

Nesting Manifestations

Every good bird deserves a cozy nest in which to manifest the future. Use the following family blessing this spring to turn your backyard into a family gathering grounds. Gather these items:

- 1 coconut shell, split in two
- 2 handfuls wild grass
- Your hair
- Nontoxic gold leaf paint
- Paintbrush
- Gloves

While wearing gloves, bless the inside of each half of the coconut shell. Inside the coconut shells, paint creative symbols that you associate with your family. Pick an animal, for example, or a heraldry symbol such as the lion rampant of Scotland. Whether the symbol is old or new, paint it in hopes of embracing its values.

Next weave your hair into the wild grass. As you work your magick, imagine the family you came from, as well as the one of your own that you wish to bless. Dress each coconut shell with some of the woven grass, then wedge them in a windowsill or nestle them in a tree or shrub near your home. If a bird takes up residence, Mother Nature will grant your family blessings this spring.

Estha McNevin

NOTES:

April 12
Wednesday

3rd ♑

Color of the day: Topaz
Incense of the day: Marjoram

"Free From" Spell

In honor of Passover, which ends tomorrow, let us cultivate freedom. Moses parted the Red Sea, but you need only a faucet, soap, and a towel.

Run the water cold. Wet your hands, and as you lather them with soap, envision your problems "out there" in the world, at work, in your community or society. Rinse and release those problems down the drain.

Adjust the water so it is tepid. Lather your hands and envision any problems within your home. What needs repairing, cleaning, or fixing? Rinse your hands and release those problems down the drain.

Adjust the water so it is very warm and comforting. Wet your hands. As you lather them, engage your inner knowing. What habits, routines, practices, or thoughts do you need to be free from? Rinse your hands and release those problems down the drain.

While many problems are not easily relieved or released, awareness is the first step in the long journey toward freedom. Turn off the taps. Dry your hands. Get to work. What do you want to be free from?

Dallas Jennifer Cobb

April 13
Thursday

3rd ♑

4th Quarter 5:11 am

☽ v/c 10:14 am

☽ → ♒ 4:42 pm

Color of the day: Green
Incense of the day: Apricot

Passover ends

Rejuvenation Meditation

Imagine you're in a forest, or actually go sit in the woods if you can. Find a place that is quiet, where you can only hear the sounds of nature. If this isn't possible, use headphones and play recorded nature sounds. Breathe deeply and close your eyes. The forest surrounds you. New leaves are emerging, and there are wildflowers everywhere.

Visualize the forest renewing you; see yourself being reborn along with the woods. Your life is like a leaf or flower bud that is slowly opening, unfurling with new purpose and strength. Raise your arms above your head and spread your fingers wide like branches. Return the embrace of the forest. Take in the soothing atmosphere of the forest through your fingers and arms, and feel it spread healing energy throughout your body, forcing out all negativity and stress.

Come back to this place in your mind whenever you need to renew your spirit. Choose a word that helps you access this mental state quickly and say it aloud.

Ember Grant

NOTES:

April 14
Friday

4th ♒

Color of the day: Coral
Incense of the day: Rose

Protection Powder

Nature offers many protective materials to all plants and animals. A broken eggshell found in a bird's nest once protected new life. Rough bark guards the soft heartwood in a tree's center. Shells, seed pods, and nut casings are all forms of protection for plants and animals, shielding them while they develop, grow, and live. They make perfect ingredients for protection spells.

Take a walk in your area and collect some of these items. Combine them all in a mortar and pestle, grinding them into as fine a powder as you can. As you do, focus on their purpose as a protective shield. Keep this mixture stored in a jar.

Sprinkle this protection powder around your home or carry some with you when you need magical protection. You can try burning it on a charcoal disk during protection spells or even use it as a candle dressing.

Kate Freuler

 April 15
Saturday

4th ♒

☽ v/c 11:16 am

☽ → ♓ 6:57 pm

Color of the day: Indigo
Incense of the day: Ivy

Blessing a Windfall

Should you be fortunate to receive a financial windfall from the passing of a relative, keep in mind how the giver spent money during their lifetime. To what causes did they contribute? I was the unexpected and lucky recipient of such a windfall several years ago. The inheritance allowed me to pay off debt, purchase a new car, and treat some family members to a weeklong vacation at the happiest place on earth.

In life, my relative had been generous to an animal shelter. I continued those good works in the form of gift cards at a local pet store. Those cards helped purchase food and supplies for the local animal shelter. Additionally, I donated funds to defray the cost of some adoptions. With every gift, I silently invoked gratitude for abundance.

Emyme

April 16
Sunday

4th ♓

Color of the day: Yellow
Incense of the day: Heliotrope

Peaceful Flower Power Bath Blend

Toxic ingredients in common bath products can take a toll on our health and wellbeing. Making organic bath salts from scratch is cheaper, safer, and way more fun!

The following bath blend can be quickly mixed and stored in a large glass jar with an airtight lid, to be used as needed. It makes a great gift and helps any person feel blessed by the goddess Venus.

- 1 pound Epsom salts
- 1 pound extra fine sea salt
- 1 pound Mochiko sweet rice flour
- 3 cups rose petal powder
- 1 ounce rose absolute essential oil

Estha McNevin

April 17
Monday

4th ♓

☽ v/c 2:57 pm
☽ → ♈ 9:09 pm

Color of the day: Ivory
Incense of the day: Hyssop

Spell to Light a Fire under Your Butt

The Sun and Moon are both in Aries this evening, making this a massive opportunity to do a working for motivation and productivity. Sometimes we need to light a fire under our butts, and this working will help you focus on the work you need to be doing and checking off your to-do list. Take a red chime candle and on one side scratch your name into it with a nail or pin. On another side write "productivity" and on another "motivation." On a cookie sheet, place ground cinnamon to create the shape of a crown of a king or queen. Place the red candle within the crown and light the candle, saying:

> Motivational energy within,
> ignited by fire,
>
> To accomplish the tasks that I desire.
>
> As the candle burns and
> the wax melts down,
>
> I wear the productivity crown.

Let the candle burn down and don't leave it unattended.

Mat Auryn

April 18
Tuesday

4ℏ ♈

Color of the day: Red
Incense of the day: Ylang-ylang

Sacred Spaces and Gratitude

April is a great time for getting out of the house and reconnecting with a favorite spot you haven't visited in a while. There are many different ways to tap into a specific place's energy. Our favorites involve meditation and offerings (always compostable!).

Find a comfy place in your favorite spot and close your eyes. Feel the energy of that place wash over you and attempt to tap into it. When you can feel the energy truly pulsating around you, visualize or verbalize what about the space you are most thankful for, and send your gratitude out into the universe. Let the natural energy of the space fill you with peace and contentment.

When you are done with your meditation, leave your offering in an out-of-the-way spot as a gift to the land and the spirits that dwell there. Alternatively, you can pick up any trash around your spot.

Amanda Lynn & Jason Mankey

 April 19
Wednesday

4ℏ ♈

Color of the day: Brown
Incense of the day: Lilac

Drop the Baggage Clearing Spell

Today both the Sun and the Moon are in the beginning stages of shedding their Aries form, taking with them the little lies and deceits that we tell ourselves to justify our actions and internal thoughts. Specific, right? Well, the other planets are lending their energies to this process as they each do their own thing, putting us in the unfortunate position of having to deal with ourselves, along with the weight of our decisions and sacrifices, for the first time in quite a while. What should you do about it? A cleansing!

Burn together over a charcoal some rosemary, rose, copal, and mugwort. As you do this, say:

I accept my part and release the fear,
of this baggage, my path be clear!

Devin Hunter

April 20
Thursday

4th ♈

☽ v/c 12:13 am

New Moon 12:13 am

☽ → ♉ 12:30 am

☉ → ♉ 4:14 am

Color of the day: Turquoise
Incense of the day: Carnation

Solar Eclipse

New Moon Spell to Relieve Anxiety

For this spell, seek out a flat stone in nature or obtain a tumbled stone such as quartz, amethyst, or moonstone. At night, light a gray candle and speak to the moon in your own words. Ask for relief from anxiety, tension, and stress, and request that the stone be enchanted as a charm to draw out and cast away any anxiety that attempts to emerge. While holding the stone in your dominant hand, say:

Great Mother Moon, grant unto me the ease of my anxiety.

As you say these words, will that the stone now becomes a magical charm.

From this point on, whenever you feel ill at ease, hold the stone so it can absorb the tension. Wash the stone weekly to clear it of the anxious energy it has retained.

Michael Furie

 April 21
Friday

1st ♉

☽ v/c 11:41 pm

Color of the day: Rose
Incense of the day: Thyme

Ramadan ends

Nothing to See here Spell

Home is where we should feel safe to work our magic. However, from time to time, we all must entertain guests who don't feel the same way we do about witchcraft. The next time guests surprise you by knocking on your door, take a moment to cover sensitive items and do this spell to hide your magic in plain sight.

When visitors arrive, say, "Just a moment!" Lightly spray a few rooms in your home with cinnamon room spray while saying to yourself in a pleasant voice, "Nothing to see here." You could also add other relevant words, such as "move along" or "get the job done." Then take a deep breath, open the door, and greet your guests while thinking, "There's nothing to see here."

To dismantle the spell, open a few windows and run fans to disperse the aroma. Wash your hands and say, "I release the spell."

Astrea Taylor

April 22
Saturday

1st ♉

☽ → ♊ 6:11 am

Color of the day: Blue
Incense of the day: Patchouli

Earth Day

An Earth Day Ritual

This ritual serves to remind us how the seed and the earth are connected, and how it has been so for eons. You'll need a pot, some potting soil, and some easy-to-grow seeds that are tolerant of cool weather, such as dill or lettuce. If you have a garden, you may sow your seeds directly into it. Begin by filling the pot with potting soil or prepare a small plot of the garden for outdoor planting. Plant your seeds according to package directions. Water the seeds and say:

The seed is the child,

The earth is its mother.

I return the seeds to the mother's womb,

The seed and the earth are bound together forever.

As you observe Earth Day, remember this endless cycle of life. Seeds sprout, plants grow, and more seeds are produced and return to the earth again. As you tend your seeds, indoors or outside, be mindful of this cycle.

James Kambos

 ## April 23
Sunday

1st ♊

Color of the day: Orange
Incense of the day: Marigold

Willow Healing Talisman

We are in the Celtic tree month of Willow now, so working with willow for healing is even more powerful now than in other months.

If you have access to a willow tree, pick up a small twig from the ground (do not cut it from the tree), or find a photo of a willow tree that speaks to you and print it out. This is your willow talisman.

Hold the talisman in your hands as you sit quietly. Follow your breath. Feel the healing energy of the willow fill you from the point of contact throughout your body. Memorize the sensation, so you can call it up whenever you are in pain.

Sleep with the willow talisman under your pillow for thirteen consecutive nights, and meditate while holding it during the day. Then keep the talisman in a safe place and use it as needed in healing work.

Cerridwen Iris Shea

 ## April 24
Monday

1st ♊

☽ v/c 8:15 am

☽ → ♋ 2:58 pm

Color of the day: Gray
Incense of the day: Narcissus

Magical Rainwater Spell

Gardens are beautiful, and they can be anything from wild to ordered, small or large. They can be an array of colours or even just a lawn, some trees, or a few patio plants. Whatever type of garden you have, including an indoor garden, the flora need a boost every now and again from magic. Rain from April showers is a power boost, especially when it's had a spell cast over it.

When there's a forecast of rain in April, try to capture as much of it as you can by putting out rain barrels, buckets, or old pots and pans. Afterward, pour the April rain into a watering can. Then hold the can in your hands as you say this spell:

April showers bring forth May flowers,

*Let my garden bloom for
months, not hours.*

Blessed water falling from the sky,

*Bless this garden with colours
sensual to the eye.*

Alternatively, if you have a water barrel that is full of April rain, place both your hands in the water and cast the spell. Imagine your energy flowing into the rainwater and visualize your garden in full bloom in June. Make sure to wash your hands afterward. Use your magical rainwater to water all your plants, including your houseplants, and watch them bloom and thrive.

Tudorbeth

NOTES:

April 25
Tuesday

1st ♋

Color of the day: Scarlet
Incense of the day: Basil

Rain Spell

Weather changes and goes through many transitions, just like our lives. The element of water is connected to fluid emotions. You can tap into the power of water/rain and use it to help wash away inner turmoil and pain. This spell works by visualizing rainwater washing over you and your energy. Utilize the healing power of rain to help you work on healing yourself and getting a fresh new start. Safely burn a white candle for illumination, transformation, and the purity of your intentions. Chant these words:

Let it rain, let it rain, let it wash away my pain.

May the water wash my spirit clean so I can start again.

If this spell resonates with you, it can also be used on a sunny day by visualizing the rain washing over your spirit as you chant the words.

Sapphire Moonbeam

April 26
Wednesday

1st ♋

☽ v/c 7:41 pm

Color of the day: Topaz
Incense of the day: Honeysuckle

Listen to the Elders

Take some time here at the start of this Mercury retrograde period (which began on the 21st) for some midweek pampering. Schedule a full spa manicure and pedicure, and treat an elderly relative to the same. Everyone needs occasional foot and hand pampering. Side-by-side chairs provide a time for just the two of you to bond. Coax some wisdom and/or juicy stories out of your relative and be prepared to take notes. You may find out facts about your family's past that will astound you. Incant:

To the keeper of family history, I offer this physical indulgence in exchange for stories, recording the facts that have formed our family to this place and time.

Emyme

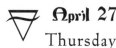

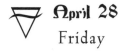

April 27
Thursday

1st ♋

☽ → ♌ 2:30 am

2nd Quarter 5:20 pm

Color of the day: White
Incense of the day: Nutmeg

Cold Water Transformation

Cold water immersion can improve cardiovascular circulation, facilitate weight loss, reduce inflammation, and promote the natural healing capacity. It has been repopularized recently, but its benefits have been known and practiced throughout the northern countries for centuries. I live on Lake Ontario in southern Canada. I go into the lake once a month through the winter and daily through the spring, summer, and fall. My body's natural healing capacity has awakened.

Share the magic of a cellular reset with me using a cold shower, an ice bath, or a dip in a lake, river, pond, or stream. Be safe and take a buddy.

Strip off your warm clothes and step into the water, aware of the increased sensation you feel. Move quickly to get deep enough to dip. Quickly squat or duck or dive under, immersing the crown chakra. Arise, feeling the signals of reset and transformation triggered throughout your body.

Dallas Jennifer Cobb

April 28
Friday

2nd ♌

Color of the day: Purple
Incense of the day: Violet

Tree Breath Communion

Today is Arbor Day. This is one of my favorite holidays, as it celebrates our tree siblings. Try to spend at least part of the day out among the trees, whether in your own yard, a city park, or forest bathing on conservation land.

We know that we share breath with the trees. They breathe out the oxygen we need to inhale, and we exhale the carbon dioxide that the trees breathe in. Our relationship with the trees is truly vital to life on this planet. It's a delightful symbiosis. However, we know that energetically we can be energized by sharing energy exchange with trees, and we can spiritually share breath with them as well.

Today, during your time among the trees, stand with your back against a tree and close your eyes. Visualize yourself breathing with the tree and sharing breath as your energetic fields merge and mingle. Enjoy the connection with these wise and life-sustaining beings, the trees. When finished, thank your new friend for the shared connection. Happy Arbor Day!

Blake Octavian Blair

April 29
Saturday

2nd ♌

☽ v/c 6:53 am

☽ → ♍ 2:59 pm

Color of the day: Black
Incense of the day: Sage

Protection Spell Bottle

This spell bottle is an easy-to-make magical charm for protecting your home. You can make the bottle as simple or as elaborate as you want, depending on your mood.

Materials:

• A bottle or jar with a tight lid

• Black tourmaline

• Frankincense

• Dried rosemary leaves

• A piece of your hair (or hair belonging to someone in your household whom you wish to protect)

When you're ready to assemble the bottle, hold the black tourmaline in your hand and say:

Black stone to protect the body.

Visualize yourself experiencing physical safety in your home. Place the crystal in the bottle.

Next add the rosemary and say:

Rosemary to protect the mind.

Visualize yourself experiencing the peaceful existence of a mind unaffected by negative influences.

Add the frankincense, saying:

Frankincense to protect the spirit.

Imagine your spirit, or energy body, surrounded by a shielding layer of armor.

Add your hair to the protection mixture and put the lid on. Place the bottle anywhere in your home.

Kate Freuler

NOTES:

 April 30
Sunday

NOTES:

2nd ♍

Color of the day: Amber
Incense of the day: Eucalyptus

Well Blessing

Use this ritual to bless a well or other water source. If you have a well that provides your water, decorate the area around it with flowers. If not, draw some tap water to serve as a symbol as you offer a blessing for the water.

We must always appreciate the access we have to clean water. Not everyone in the world is as fortunate. Water is essential for life. We honor water for what it symbolizes, as one of the four elements, but we can't forget its practical value as well.

Recite this chant over your well or symbol of your water source:

*Abundant and clean, let
this water remain,*

With every drink, our lives to sustain.

Complete the ritual by drinking some water and contemplating how essential it is. Be grateful for it.

Ember Grant

May

Welcome to the famously merry month of May! Though it was originally named after the Greek fertility goddess Maia, the Catholic Church has since designated this month as sacred to the Virgin Mary, even referring to her as "the Queen of May" during this time. Day one of this flower-filled month is the beloved holiday of Beltane, during which the veil that usually conceals the world of the fairies fades, and our power to make contact with them reaches its yearly peak. Indeed, May's birth flower is a fairy favorite: the lily of the valley. As for our skies, this month they host the Eta Aquariids meteor shower, which reaches its peak around May 6 and is most visible before the sunrise.

May is also the month when the light half of the year begins to assert itself in earnest, and we sense the days lengthening, the sun growing warmer, and the leaves filling out the trees. This allows us to gaze bravely into our own brilliance and to courageously release anything that has been holding us back from being our most radiant, expansive, beautiful selves. Indeed, May's bright presence reminds us to claim the vital prosperity that is our birthright and our natural state.

Tess Whitehurst

May 1
Monday

2nd ♏

☽ v/c 7:53 pm

Color of the day: White
Incense of the day: Rosemary

Beltane

Beltane Ribbon Mini Maypole

You might not be able to dance around a maypole, but you can make your own mini maypole!

You will need:

- A ½-inch dowel, 2 feet long

- 9 ribbons in different colors representing different wishes, each 3 feet long

- A thumbtack

- Red thread

Hold the dowel vertically. Place the ribbons so that the top of each ribbon folds across the top of the dowel, and the ribbons cascade down all sides of the dowel. Drive the thumbtack through the ribbons deep into the top of the dowel, holding all ribbons in place.

Braid three sets of three ribbons each, speaking the wish of each ribbon as you braid it into the others. Fasten off the braids with red thread.

Now there are three braids of three ribbons each hanging from the dowel. You can twirl this mini maypole in your sacred Beltane dance or hang it in your home. Release each braid as the wishes manifest.

Cerridwen Iris Shea

NOTES:

May 2
Tuesday

2nd ♍

☽ → ♎ 2:09 am

Color of the day: Maroon
Incense of the day: Cedar

Love Spell Box

If you want the love of your life to find you, consider doing this love spell. Love spells help communicate your desire to the universe. It has been said that your true love will find you when you stop looking, so this spell will help you with that.

Use a box or any type of container with a lid. Obtain an old-fashioned compass, or draw a compass on a piece of paper, and place it in the box. Place additional items in the box, such as hearts, the word *love*, etc., along with a photo of you. Write down the following words on a piece of paper, then say them aloud and place the paper in your love box with the other items:

Guide my true love.

Help him/her find me.

I will be ready when my true love arrives.

This is a love that is meant to be.

Close the box, keep it closed, and trust that your true love will be guided to you.

Sapphire Moonbeam

May 3
Wednesday

2nd ♎

Color of the day: Yellow
Incense of the day: Bay laurel

Silver Tongue Brew

Enchant your morning brew (coffee, tea, etc.) with a little spark of magic to enhance your communication skills. Simply gaze into your cup and visualize yourself being eloquent and articulate. See people hanging on your every word as you impart wisdom and wit, intelligence and imagination.

Chant these words over your drink:

With each sip

That crosses my lips,

That passes my tongue,

Like words being sung—

With each word I say,

Things go my way.

I infuse this drink

With magic today.

Drink every drop. Repeat the words as often as desired. You can use this spell for any beverage at any time of the day.

Ember Grant

May 4
Thursday

2nd ♎︎

☽ v/c 5:17 am

☽ → ♏︎ 10:32 am

Color of the day: Purple
Incense of the day: Balsam

A Morning Dew Spell

Morning dew is a very powerful cleanser and purifier. If you need clarity or are going through a difficult time, this spell may help.

In the early morning when you won't be disturbed, go outside while the dew lies heavy on the grass. With your issue clearly in your mind, kneel upon the earth. Bend forward so your forehead and both palms touch the dew. A few seconds is long enough. Feel the cleansing qualities of the dew being absorbed into your forehead and hands. Stand up. Feel any toxic energy drain through your feet and into the earth. Mother Earth will neutralize this energy.

Now return to your daily frame of mind. Your issues will soon begin to fade, and solutions will begin to come to you. Do this each morning until you feel you no longer need to.

Magical tip: This ritual also works well with frost or snow on the ground.

James Kambos

 May 5
Friday

2nd ♏︎

Full Moon 1:34 pm

Color of the day: Rose
Incense of the day: Vanilla

Cinco de Mayo – Lunar Eclipse

Altar Purification

If you enjoy burning incense at your altar, you'll be familiar with the pile of ashes that always accumulates. Think of how long those ashes have been sitting in your magical space and the energy that has gathered in them over the days or weeks. During that time they've absorbed feelings and experiences, which you don't necessarily need anymore, especially if you've worked through a problem. While tidying your altar, include the ashes in this cleansing spell. You will need some ashes from incense, a glass of water, and a spoon.

After tidying your altar, put the ashes in the glass of water. Using the spoon, stir the water to create a swirling motion. Say:

This cleansing water washes away the lingering energy of the past. I move forward clearly and with focus.

Go outside and pour the water and ashes onto the earth.

Kate Freuler

May 6
Saturday

3rd ♏

☽ v/c 10:38 am

☽ → ♐ 4:04 pm

Color of the day: Blue
Incense of the day: Rue

Discover Your Phoenix

New job, school, town? Reinvent yourself! I did this when I moved from one job to another and knew no one. To that rote question "How are you?" I answered every time, "Can't complain." Some of my fellow workers became annoyed and said, "Of course you can," to which I replied, "I have my spouse and my child. All my family members are healthy. I am making a decent wage. My home is secure," and so on.

Some people inevitably walked away in a huff. Others saw that they, too, were blessed. "Can't complain" became my own personal incantation. It was true then and remains true now, and acknowledging the change as permanent created a new me. My phoenix had transformed.

Look inside and find your own phoenix. Create a simple affirmation as a constant reminder of the future.

Emyme

May 7
Sunday

3rd ♐

Color of the day: Gold
Incense of the day: Hyacinth

Petals of Purpose

Rose petals have the ability to bless a path with love and light. Sprinkling them on someone's route or leading a person to you with a path of petals is a truly romantic and emotive way to let flowers guide our hearts to deep levels of trust and discovery. If you feel so inclined today, gather some rose petals and leave a trail for someone you love, to guide them on a path of purpose and hope. The trail can end at their car or mailbox or anyplace where you leave a sweet treat or loving note.

Making someone feel loved and cared for is as simple as blessing their path with intentional care. Romantic gestures aren't just for Valentine's Day, and roses are more than an apology flower. If you care deeply for someone, take the time to share the power of this original flower of love and bless the path you are on together. Shatter every cliché and scatter flowers to discover how much magick is to be found in shared moments of loving tenderness. Uplifting the ones we love begins with blessing them.

Estha McNevin

May 8
Monday

3rd ♐

☽ v/c 4:28 pm

☽ → ♑ 7:33 pm

Color of the day: Lavender
Incense of the day: Hyssop

With Every Step Travel Spell

With the return of warm weather in the Northern Hemisphere, my favorite mode of travel becomes more comfortable. I love to go backcountry camping, carrying all my gear and food on my back. With such a load, it is crucial to be sure-footed, so I don't get injured. Even if you live in a city or hate camping, this spell can be used when you walk, hike, or run.

As you lace up your hiking boots (or running shoes), say:

Bless these boots that I may be injury-free. I know these boots support me.

Stand up, aligning head over shoulders, hips, and feet, and say:

Bless this body that is energized and able. Let me be balanced, aligned, and stable.

Take a few steps consciously, aware of your footfalls, and say:

Bless these feet that carry me. Let the highest magic protect me with every step. So mote it be.

Dallas Jennifer Cobb

 May 9
Tuesday

3rd ♑

Color of the day: Red
Incense of the day: Geranium

Beauty Bath of the Sirens

With the Sun in Venus-ruled Taurus now, spells for beauty, enticement, pleasure, and glamour are enhanced. This simple spell is a bath to cast a glamour upon you. Think of glamour magick as the energetic equivalent of dressing nicely and wearing makeup and perfume. It's an energetic self-grooming that enhances how others perceive you. In this spell we will also call upon the power of the sirens from Greek mythology, whose songs were so alluring that no one could resist or ignore them if heard.

Bath spells should never be about physical cleaning. You should already be clean on a physical level first. Simply add two cups of rose water to your bath while reciting this verse:

Water of roses, water of spout,

Beauty within and beauty without.

An aura that glows like golden treasure,

Enhancing my splendor without measure.

By song of sirens from the enchanted sea,

Enticing all those who gaze upon me.

Put on some music that is sexy to you. Relax and soak in the beauty. Air-dry if possible.

Mat Auryn

NOTES:

May 10
Wednesday

3rd ♑

☽ v/c 7:52 pm

☽ → ♒ 10:05 pm

Color of the day: White
Incense of the day: Lavender

Planter/Garden Blessing Spell

Earth energy is off the charts today, making this a fantastic time to bless and consecrate a garden plot, a planter, or pretty much any area or anything in which you can grow a plant. To do this, make a tea from hyssop, lavender, and thyme, and set it aside to cool to room temperature. Strain the tea into a small cup or bowl, and add the leftover organic matter to the compost pile. Using the fingers of your dominant hand, sprinkle the desired area or item with the tea as you recite this blessing:

Carry the blessings of the earth; hold these blessings, the land gives birth.

As they grow, so too shall I; as they grow, I touch the sky.

Free from pest and fungus, protected they'll be tall and mighty, a sight to see!

I consecrate this vessel and all therein; against all odds, this magic shall win!

Devin Hunter

May 11
Thursday

3rd ♒

Color of the day: Turquoise
Incense of the day: Myrrh

Safe hollow Tree Magic

A lot of older spells exist in which items are either tied to tree branches or left in the hollows found in some trees. Though this can be effective magically, many things can harm the health of the tree or endanger small animals that may call the tree home. For this magic all you need is a single leaf from a tree.

Hold the leaf, pressed lightly between your hands, and strongly envision your magical goal. Build this in your mind and mentally send this energy down through your hands into the leaf, charging it with power. When you feel the charge is complete, go to the tree and place the leaf in a hollow while asking the tree to aid you in achieving your goal. Thank the tree quietly and walk away without looking back.

Michael Furie

May 12
Friday

3rd ♒
4th Quarter 10:28 am
☾ v/c 11:15 pm

Color of the day: White
Incense of the day: Thyme

Golden Opportunities Spell

If you are looking for new ways to manifest success in your life, you might consider using colors to assist you in a form of sympathetic magic. Sympathetic magic is a way to utilize the power of a color and its magical meaning to achieve a desired result.

The color gold is associated with riches and wealth. Wearing gold in your clothing or jewelry can help attract what you want. You can wear gold eye shadow to empower yourself to "see" golden opportunities more easily. Wearing gold-rimmed or golden-colored sunglasses can be used for this same purpose. To further enhance the magic and to remain open to opportunities, you can chant these words:

May the golden color help me see the opportunities that are meant for me.

May the golden energy light up my view and help me see the opportunities that are new.

Sapphire Moonbeam

May 13
Saturday

4th ≈

$\mathcal{D} \rightarrow \mathcal{H}$ 12:39 am

Color of the day: Indigo
Incense of the day: Magnolia

Clear Your Space,
Clear Your Mind

Today's planetary ruler is Saturn, and it is a good day to do a little hearth and home magic. We often hear people say that our outside environment mirrors our inner life. Well, often there is some level of truth to that. Each can influence manifestations in the other.

Think about an area of your life where you've been feeling stagnant, disoriented, or scattered. Do you feel like you never get quality time with those you live with? Perhaps clean up the common space, such as the living room, or clear the clutter off the dining room table so you can have a communal meal, movie night, or game night. Feeling swamped with work, whether for your job or school? Clean off your desk or your home office space. If you're literally buried in papers and stacks, you'll probably feel that way internally!

As you clean, see the situation improving and visualize a happy resolution. When you're finished, do a nice cleansing by spritzing some holy water and/or wafting the smoke of the incense of your choice.

Blake Octavian Blair

NOTES:

May 14
Sunday

4♄ ♓

☽ v/c 10:56 pm

Color of the day: Yellow
Incense of the day: Juniper

Mother's Day

Mother's Day Gratitude Spell

Mothers come in all shapes and sizes; they are not just the women who gave birth to us. Instead, mothers can be friends, sisters, lovers, and those who have raised us and looked after us in our darkest moments. The greatest mother of all is, of course, our beautiful Earth, and although we haven't been the most responsible of her children, we do still care for her.

On this Mother's Day, show your gratitude to our wonderful Mother Earth. Go outside and stand barefoot on the grass, then stretch and raise your hands to the sky. Now turn your hands palms down and slowly crouch down upon the ground with your palms touching the earth. Then recite this gratitude spell:

Thank you, Mother Earth,
for your gifts.

Thank you for the summer rain.

Thank you for the winter sun.

Thank you for easing
spring chills and pain.

Thank you for the autumn
colours that stun.

I am grateful and I am
blessed in every way.

Thank you to all on this Mother's Day.

Show your appreciation of the earth by doing something beneficial for her, such as watering the garden, picking up plastic from the beach, or picking up litter from the countryside or forest. You could invite friends and family to appreciate Mother Earth by starting a tradition of having a Mother's Day picnic followed by planting a tree, picking up litter, or engaging in a garden activity.

Tudorbeth

May 15
Monday

4th ♓
☽ → ♈ 3:56 am

Color of the day: Silver
Incense of the day: Narcissus

I Also Bloom Spell

In many areas, May is when flowers bloom and their sweet scents perfume the air. Even if flowers aren't in bloom near you, you can still celebrate your inner unfolding with this soul-affirming spell. It requires fresh flowers. Anything from the fanciest rose to a common dandelion will do, but organic flowers are best.

You will need a spray bottle, some natural or purified water, sunshine, and fresh flowers in a vase.

Fill the spray bottle with water, then place it in the sunshine to make sun water. After a few minutes, mist the flowers with the sun water until they're soaked. Lift one flower and anoint yourself lovingly with it. Brush the wet petals upon your cheeks, forehead, heart, throat, and anywhere else you wish. In a loving and confident voice, say:

Just like these beautiful
flowers, I also bloom.

When done, mist the flowers one last time and set them outside so they can be enjoyed by butterflies and bees.

Astrea Taylor

 May 16
Tuesday

4th ♈

Color of the day: Scarlet
Incense of the day: Bayberry

A Godparent Spell

A godparent and a godchild usually form a special loving bond. To be asked to be a godparent is an honor. This ritual was performed frequently in the Appalachian region at one time.

To perform this ritual, the godchild should still be an infant. To begin, the godparent carries their godchild outside. Then the godparent continues holding the child and walks the infant around their house three times. During this time, the godparent whispers secret hopes and wishes to the godchild. To end the ritual, the godparent returns the child gently to the crib. The godparent must never repeat what they said to their godchild, or the enchantment will be broken.

James Kambos

May 17
Wednesday

4th ♈

☽ v/c 5:10 am

☽ → ♉ 8:28 am

Color of the day: Brown
Incense of the day: Marjoram

Emerald Luck and Love Spell

Emerald is the gemstone for the month of May. Emeralds are known as a stone of successful and abundant love, good fortune, and the ability to open the heart chakra. The ancient Egyptians believed the emerald was a source of eternal life. To increase good luck and love in your life, use the energy of the emerald to work toward manifesting lasting success.

On a flat surface on your altar, place clear quartz crystals in the shape of a heart. In the middle of the heart shape, safely light a small green candle to represent an emerald, and say:

> May the green candle represent
> the emerald well, to enhance
> the power of this spell.
>
> May good luck, abundance,
> and love be mine. I trust it
> will arrive right on time.

You can repeat this spell several days in a row to increase luck, abundance, and love in your life over time. Extinguish the candle.

Sapphire Moonbeam

May 18
Thursday

4th ♉

Color of the day: Green
Incense of the day: Carnation

Candle Spell for a Raise

For this spell you will need a green pillar candle, essential oil for abundance (optional), and a recent pay stub.

On the front of your candle, using a pin, etch the symbols for Earth (⊕), the planet Jupiter (♃), and a dollar sign ($) in a vertical line. On the back of your candle, etch your name and arrows pointing up. Anoint the candle and each corner of the pay stub with the oil (optional). Place the candle on the pay stub and charge it with the energy of you getting the raise that you need and deserve. As you safely light the candle, chant:

> Money, money, come to me.
>
> Give the raise that I need.
>
> I work hard and this is earned.
>
> Bring the raise that I deserve!

Just before the candle has burned down, take your pay stub and fold it up. Seal it closed with a bit of candle wax. Carry the stub with you until you get your raise. Extinguish the candle.

Amanda Lynn & Jason Mankey

May 19
Friday

4℔ ☿

New Moon 11:53 am

☽ v/c 1:51 pm

☽ → ♊ 2:48 pm

Color of the day: Pink
Incense of the day: Yarrow

New Moon Snake Magic

For this new moon, use the symbolism of the snake to represent transformation and renewal. First, forget any negative associations you have with snakes. They're remarkable creatures that we need in the environment, but unfortunately many people have been conditioned to dislike and fear them. We should certainly respect them and use caution around them since there are, of course, poisonous ones, but snakes can be a powerful magical symbol.

Find an image of a snake that you find pleasing—a statue, drawing, photo, tattoo, or even a piece of jewelry. Spend some time meditating on it. One of the reasons snakes are so prominent in myth and folklore is because of their ability to shed their skin. Use this as a metaphor for your own renewal and transformation.

Light some incense and watch the smoke curl and rise upward, like a snake. See yourself like the snake, shedding an old "skin" to emerge renewed, transformed, healed, or whatever you need to have a fresh start. Here's a chant you can repeat as you meditate:

Shed old skin, start again.

Strength is within; it's time to begin.

Ember Grant

NOTES:

May 20
Saturday

1st ♊

Color of the day: Gray
Incense of the day: Sandalwood

Fruiting Vines for Sustainability

A living wreath is a vine that binds values of love, fidelity, loyalty, or fertility into a home. Displaying a living jasmine wreath is a wonderful way to explore aquaculture. Clipping and cloning jasmine is easy. As long as the water and containers are kept clean, new plants will thrive from each clipping.

To make a wreath, you will need:

• Green string

• A small vase

• A 12-inch bamboo embroidery hoop

• 1 mature jasmine plant

• Rooting solution

• A jade stone

• Fresh water

Using the green string, begin by making a loop from which to hang your wreath. Next bind the small vase and the bamboo embroidery hoop so they both hang and the vase is suspended inside the center of the hoop. Using bonsai or pruning shears, cut the longest shoot vine from the mature jasmine plant. Dip the cut end in rooting solution, then nestle it in the vase by adding a jade stone and fresh water.

Weave the vine. Try looping patterns or pentagrams. Display your living wreath in a bright window. Fertilize it monthly with organic plant food, and continue weaving it as it grows. Repot the shoots to create a set of sister plants when the new roots are long and verdant.

Estha McNevin

NOTES:

May 21
Sunday

1st ♊

☉ → ♊ 3:09 am

☽ v/c 6:12 pm

☽ → ♋ 11:28 pm

Color of the day: Gold
Incense of the day: Frankincense

Ginger Love Spell

Spicy ginger is associated with fire and passion. It's considered a hot, quick-acting magical herb, known to speed things up and bring pizzazz to any spell. This working is designed to reignite the spark in a relationship after a dull period.

Materials:

- A 1-inch square piece of paper and a pen
- A piece of fresh ginger root, about the size of your thumb
- A knife
- 1 foot of red thread

Write the names of you and your partner on the paper and fold it up as tiny as possible. Using the knife, create a slit in the ginger root without cutting it completely in half. Shove the paper into the slit you have made, then wind the red thread around it several times. Tie a knot in the thread.

As the liquid of the ginger root permeates the names, infusing them with spicy juices, the fire will also return to your relationship. Keep this love charm in a safe place until the ginger dries out, disposing of it afterward.

Kate Freuler

Notes:

May 22
Monday

1st ♋

Color of the day: Gray
Incense of the day: Clary sage

Victoria Day (Canada)

Biological Diversity

International Day for Biological Diversity is a United Nations–sanctioned day for the promotion of biodiversity issues currently held on May 22. This is a very large initiative, with too many topics to address here. Using STEM (science, technology, engineering, and mathematics) enables deeper knowledge of the four elements: air, earth, fire, and water. By combining ancient earth-based beliefs with modern methods, cooperation of nations will bring about solutions to save and improve the quality of life here on Mother Earth. If this is an issue or cause that appeals to you, your local community government is a good place to begin.

Emyme

May 23
Tuesday

1st ♋

Color of the day: Maroon
Incense of the day: Cinnamon

Healing a Childhood Wound

With the Sun in communicative Gemini and the Moon exalted in nurturing Cancer today, this is an ideal time to communicate with your inner child. Write a letter to your childhood self with words of encouragement and love for a very difficult time in your childhood. Don't hold back. Compliment them. Tell them what you wish someone had told you but never did.

Fold the paper up and hold it to your chest. Focus on all the love, strength, and comfort as an energetic force running through your body and into your hands and infusing the letter with those feelings. Open up the letter and read it out loud as if you were reading the letter to your childhood self (and a part of you is).

Burn the letter in a safe manner, such as in a fireplace, a fireproof cauldron, or a bonfire. While your message may not be sent to the past, it's sent to that part of yourself that is still a child who is holding on to that experience.

Mat Auryn

May 24
Wednesday

1st ♋

☽ v/c 5:12 am

☽ → ♌ 10:35 am

Color of the day: Topaz
Incense of the day: Lilac

Invoking Safety and Ease

When we are stressed, our parasympathetic nervous system, which regulates our body functions, can be overwhelmed by our sympathetic nervous system, which wants to fight, flee, or freeze. Want to quickly invoke a sense of ease and peace and send messages of safety to your nervous system? Dr. Peter Levine invented Voo Breathing to ease hyperarousal and give your brain and body a break.

Take a breath in, and as you exhale, incant:

Vooooooooooooooooooo.

Use your voice, feel your belly rumble, and vibrate with the sound. Again, breathe into the belly and the chest, then express the air and chant:

Vooooooooooooooooooo.

Making the exhale a little longer than the inhale stimulates the vagus nerve, and that helps to slow and regulate the heart rate and blood pressure. Vooooooo, the deep rumble in the belly, literally massages the vagus nerve and promotes relaxation, invoking a sense of safety and ease.

Dallas Jennifer Cobb

Notes:

May 25
Thursday

1st ♌

Color of the day: Crimson
Incense of the day: Mulberry

Shavuot begins at sundown

Thumbtack Candle Magic

To determine the correct path to take when faced with an important decision, gather a white votive candle and one thumbtack for each of the potential choices, marking the tacks with a dab of paint, ink, or nail polish to differentiate them. Stick the thumbtacks into the candle, each at the same level, being careful not to crack the wax. Light the candle and say:

For good of all and with true aim,

First tack to fall in magical precision.

Witch's power and candle's flame,

Bring to light the correct decision.

As the wax melts, the tacks will loosen, and the first to fall will reveal the best choice.

Michael Furie

May 26
Friday

1st ♌

☽ v/c 2:38 am

☽ → ♍ 11:05 pm

Color of the day: Coral
Incense of the day: Cypress

Reclaim Your Energy Spell

The novel *Dracula* was first published on this day in 1897. Since we often deal with energy vampires, here's a spell to reclaim your energy.

Gather these supplies:

• 1 orange candle

• Citrus incense or essential oil

• A small bowl of water

• 2 stones

Sit comfortably where you won't be disturbed. Light the candle. Light the incense or anoint yourself with the essential oil. Dip your fingers in the water, then hold one stone in each palm.

Follow your breath.

With each exhale, imagine the energy vampire's tentacles detaching from your aura.

When you feel free and serene, take three full breaths.

Now, as you inhale, imagine the energy of earth, air, fire, and water restoring the energy of spirit, replenishing your energy, and forming a shield against future energy vampires. Continue until you feel refreshed.

Ground and center. Bury the stones in your yard or a pot of earth. Let the candle and incense burn out safely.

Cerridwen Iris Shea

Notes:

May 27
Saturday

1st ♍

2nd Quarter 11:22 am

Color of the day: Brown
Incense of the day: Sage

Wish upon a Star

The warm and pleasant weather often found in May makes it a great month for stargazing. For this spell, wait until the sun goes down and then venture outside to do some stargazing. Instead of the usual glance, really look at the sky, taking in everything above you.

Once you've taken a thorough look at the heavens, settle in and pick a favorite star for that evening. You don't have to know what star it is; the star should just resonate with you. As you look up at your star, feel its power and contemplate all the years it took for the light and energy of that star to reach planet Earth.

Tap into the energy of the star shining down upon you and say whatever it is you wish for. Let your intentions mix with the star's energy to make your dreams a reality and say:

By starlight, my will be done!
Amanda Lynn & Jason Mankey

May 28
Sunday

2nd ♏

Color of the day: Orange
Incense of the day: Marigold

Remember a Little Rosemary

The solar energy of Sunday always makes me want to seize the day and make the most of it, even if that means relaxing and taking it easy. Even easygoing days can include simple magic. Today is a good day to visit your magical home apothecary and remember to use a little rosemary, as it is associated energetically with the Sun. Rosemary is considered the herb of remembrance, and its energies are said to be excellent for workings to spark the memory. Some lore also claims that rosemary tea can help you fall asleep. Today, use rosemary in cooking (or a tea if you desire) and say the following charm:

By fragrant herb and ray of sun,

*To rosemary's spirit this
prayer has begun.*

May happy memories come to me

And recall easily when in need of glee.

May rest come easily when I need,

*As energy of rosemary calms
and does its deed.*

Blessed be.

Blake Octavian Blair

May 29
Monday

2nd ♏

☽ v/c 5:46 am

☽ → ♎ 10:51 am

Color of the day: Ivory
Incense of the day: Lily

Memorial Day

Forgotten Soldier
Memorial Working

Today is Memorial Day here in the United States, a day when we honor our nation's fallen warriors. It is a time to reflect not only on their lives and bravery but also on the cost of war and its heavy toll.

Not all fallen soldiers have family or loved ones to remember them. As we celebrate the lives of those who fought to protect our country, let us also remember those whom others have forgotten. All you need is a white candle, a small bell, and a few moments of your time. At your altar, safely light the candle and ring the bell three times before saying:

*Three times I ring this bell for
the forgotten soldier, who fell in
battle and was denied the chance
to grow older. May they rest in
peace and find their way; the
heaviest price was theirs to pay.*

Extinguish the candle or allow it to safely burn out completely.

Devin Hunter

May 30
Tuesday

2nd ♎

Color of the day: Black
Incense of the day: Ginger

Hermes Vehicle Blessing

The Greek god Hermes is associated with safe travels, good fortune, and work. One of the ways his blessings were bestowed was with a laurel branch dipped in water. Laurel is a common tree, but if you can't find one, use bay leaves. They can be found in the spice section of most markets.

For this blessing you will need a vehicle, some incense, a lighter, a laurel (bay) branch, and a bowl of water.

Stand before the vehicle and light the incense. Cleanse yourself and the vehicle with the smoke. Dip the branch in the water. Say:

Hermes, great god of travel and luck, I call upon you with reverence in my heart. I ask you to bless this vehicle with safety and good fortune.

Allow the water to drip upon the vehicle. Continue until the water is gone. When done, lay the branch in a natural place. Say:

Hermes, a gift for you, and a humble thanks for your blessings.

Astrea Taylor

May 31
Wednesday

2nd ♎

☽ v/c 10:53 am

☽ → ♏ 7:45 pm

Color of the day: Yellow
Incense of the day: Honeysuckle

Invitation to the Universe Spell

Divination is not an easy thing to learn, as we can easily misinterpret the images we are given. It can take years for a witch to master this part of the craft, and not all can do it. However, it is a wonderful part of magic to learn and is very useful when we are confronted with a crossroads in life. Try this divination spell to enhance the images and sensations that come through to you from the universe.

You need to make sure you are not going to be disturbed, so turn off your phone and all other electrical devices. Lie down or sit in a comfortable place, close your eyes, and focus on your breathing. Other ways of entering a meditative state include visualizing a special place or focusing your gaze on an object, such as the flame of a candle. When you are content that you are now in a peaceful state, say this spell:

Great Spirit, help me to be wise and true,

Let the right action come through.

Help me to listen to your voice.

I will listen now that I am free.

Speak words of instinct and of wisdom.

Show me the path that is right for me.

Afterward, sit or lie down and listen to your inner voice coming through. Think of a problem you have and what you should do about it. You must let yourself be totally relaxed. Listening to your instincts does take a while to learn, so don't be too disappointed if you receive no ideas; you must continue with the meditation ritual and exercise the spirit. Remember, magic is not always easy. Some parts of it are difficult, while other parts come naturally. If you are likely to forget the images and feelings that come through, have a pen and notebook next to you so you can write them down immediately.

Tudorbeth

June

The month of June is a time that inspires warmth, love, passion, and deep appreciation of beauty. Agricultural festivals in old Europe acknowledge and celebrate the many flowers and fruits that become abundant at this time. It is no coincidence that these plants—such as roses, raspberries, strawberries, wildflowers, and those that feature red or pink flowers or fruit—are associated with the planet Venus and the goddess Aphrodite. June is also the traditional month for weddings, and the term *honeymoon* refers to the beverage mead, made from fermented honey, that was traditionally given to the bride and groom as an aphrodisiac.

June brings the start of summer, and for thousands of years the summer solstice has been a prominent festival in many cultures. This celestial festival signifies the beginning of warm weather and abundant growth yet also reminds us of its opposite calendar festival: the winter solstice. All hail the Holly King! Spells done in June are often connected to love, romance, growth, health, and abundance.

Peg Aloi

June 1
Thursday

2nd ♏

Color of the day: Green
Incense of the day: Clove

Love Line Clearing

With the Moon in Scorpio right now, we are all feeling our feels a bit more than usual and little inconveniences may seem like heavy burdens. Chances are your relationships, especially those of a romantic variety, are experiencing their own type of communication breakdown caused by insecurities and a need for control or direction. Luckily, the Sun is in Gemini and can ease this stress.

Rub fresh parsley or lavender on your hands, and once you smell the herbaceous aroma rise up, take a deep breath and then blow it in the direction of the rising sun. Say:

Gemini, lend your might,
so we can avoid a fight.

Put our heads on right and
our hearts in sight!

Open the lines of communication,
clear away the debris.

Illuminate the darkness
with conversation, and let
us bond with revelry.

Devin Hunter

June 2
Friday

2nd ♏

☽ v/c 8:51 pm

Color of the day: Pink
Incense of the day: Thyme

St. Elmo's Day Energy Spell

St. Elmo's fire was not just a film from the 1980s that defined a generation; it is an actual weather phenomenon. St. Elmo's fire emits a blue or violet glow around a tall object and is often seen around the tall masts of ships at sea. Sailors came to view it as an omen of protection, but it can also be seen during times when there is a buildup of energy, such as before an earthquake or a volcanic eruption. It is commonly seen during violent electrical thunderstorms, but it is also seen dancing around tall objects such as chimneys, church spires, and other tall buildings. It emits a strange buzzing or humming sound, like an electrical field buzzing round it.

This weather phenomenon is named after St. Erasmus, who was also known as St. Elmo and is the patron saint of sailors. But it is that energy that makes it explode in an array of beautiful splendour. That energy lives inside of us when we start a creative project and we want to explode and show everyone its power. If you have been working on something dear to

your heart but are frightened to show it off, call upon the fire of St. Elmo and use his energy today to show the world your talent, no matter what it is. Have your project close to you and safely light a purple candle. Stare into the flame and then close your eyes and see the flame in your mind's eye still burning bright—this is your talent and your potential. Feel the power in your project and believe in yourself, then recite this spell over it:

> St. Elmo's fire, this energy abounds,
>
> Lift my talents off the ground.
>
> Make my magic soar and zoom,
>
> Make my project go boom.
>
> Igniting all who see,
>
> Inspiring all, not just me.

Then concentrate on your magic and imagine what you want to happen with your project. Do you need to send it to an agent, a publisher, or someone else? Then do it. Send it off, and as you do so, blow out the candle and imagine the rising smoke taking your project to the person who needs to see it. Good luck.

Tudorbeth

June 3
Saturday

2nd ♏

☽ → ♐ 1:03 am

Full Moon 11:42 pm

Color of the day: Indigo
Incense of the day: Magnolia

Communicating Clearly

With the sun in Gemini and the moon in Sagittarius today, there's an abundance of expansive communication energy, which can paradoxically confuse clear intentions. To help focus your ability to communicate a specific point, write out exactly what you want to say on a piece of paper. Read it over, making certain it's exactly what you wish to say, rewriting it if necessary. Once complete, read it aloud as if you were speaking directly to the person with whom you are trying to communicate. Fold the paper in half and then in half again, making each fold toward you. Finally, place an orange candle (a color of Mercury) in a holder over the paper. Light the candle and say:

> Powers of clarity, pierce through the haze, sharpen my focus and intention.
>
> Making my point with skill and ease, message received with retention.
>
> Forces of Jupiter and Mercury, empower the magic, so mote it be!

Michael Furie

June 4
Sunday

3rd ♐

☽ v/c 11:24 pm

Color of the day: Orange
Incense of the day: Juniper

Money-Drawing Tea

Many magical herbs are safe to ingest, which means there are endless witchy teas that you can make. When you consume magical tea, you symbolically absorb what you desire into your body and life. Create and drink this money-attracting tea when you need some extra cash.

Materials:

- A cup for drinking
- 7 coins
- 1 teaspoon dried ginger root
- 1 teaspoon dried peppermint
- 3 cloves
- A tea ball or reusable tea bag (optional)
- 1 cup boiling water

Place your cup on a flat surface in direct sunlight if possible, and place the coins around it in a circle. Put the herbs or tea ball in the cup. Boil the water and pour it over the herbs. Notice how the sun glints off the coins, warming them and intensifying the prosperous energy they carry, which infuses the tea as well. Allow the tea to steep for about five minutes as you visualize your goals. As you drink the tea, feel it warming your insides, filling you with the prosperous energy of the herbs and the sunlight.

If you don't have a tea ball or bag, you can pour the water directly over the dried herbs, then strain the tea through cheesecloth or a strainer into a mug before drinking.

Kate Freuler

NOTES:

June 5
Monday

3rd ♐

☽ → ♑ 3:31 am

Color of the day: Lavender
Incense of the day: Hyssop

Sweet Life Spell

Vanilla extract may just be one of the most magical items in your spice cabinet. It evokes sweetness, emotional healing, and sensual enjoyment. This spell for tasting life's sweetness is enhanced with vanilla extract, sugar, and your willpower. The more willpower you use, the more effective it is. Use sparkling water or moon water for enhanced enjoyment.

You will need a fancy glass, some purified water, vanilla extract, sugar (optional), and a spoon.

Place the fancy glass before you. Ceremoniously add the water and then drop a tiny bit of vanilla extract and sugar (if using). With the spoon, stir the mixture clockwise and say, "I will a sweet life," again and again, until you say it with conviction.

Drink the water to claim your sweet life. Savor the sweetness! When the glass is empty, strike the side of the glass gently with the spoon and let the resounding sound clear the air.

Astrea Taylor

 June 6
Tuesday

3rd ♑

Color of the day: White
Incense of the day: Basil

Cooking Up Momentum

We all have to eat, so how about integrating some kitchen magic into mealtimes? Sometimes Tuesday arrives and we feel we've had a sluggish start to our week. Well, the planetary ruler of Tuesday is Mars, and he's a mover and a shaker! So let's harness some Martian energy today and cook up some momentum for the rest of the week.

Using herbs and spices that correspond to Mars is a great way to add the energy of action and momentum to our own spirit. Cumin is a staple resident on most spice racks and is a common ingredient in favorite dishes like tacos and chili. Instill a dash of magic in your meal by adding cumin to taste in either dish while stirring in the form of a pentagram and chanting:

Spirit of cumin, bring to me

Some Martian momentum and energy.

By pot, spoon, and planet,

So mote it be!

Enjoy a magical dinner aligned with today's planetary energies and then rest well tonight for a better tomorrow!

Blake Octavian Blair

June 7
Wednesday

3rd ♑

☽ v/c 12:40 am

☽ → ♒ 4:42 am

Color of the day: Brown
Incense of the day: Marjoram

A Wedding Band Spell

To bless a pair of wedding bands, begin this spell at least three days before the ceremony. Place the bands in the center of a square piece of red or pink fabric, or use a handkerchief that's a family heirloom. Then tie the four corners of the fabric together to form a bundle. Hold it as you say these Words of Power:

Bands of silver or bands of gold,

May our love never grow old.

And as these bands are round,

Our hands and hearts
are forever bound.

Set the bundle on your altar for two days. Untie the bundle. Place the wedding bands in a safe place. Keep the fabric as a keepsake. Your wedding bands are now blessed.

Tip: For extra power, it's nice if you and your partner say the Words of Power together.

James Kambos

June 8
Thursday

3rd ♒

Color of the day: Purple
Incense of the day: Apricot

Salt and Sun Cleansing Potion

This is a simple cleansing water that harnesses the power of salt and sunlight. Simply add nine grains of sea salt to one cup of warm water and allow it to sit in full sunlight for at least four hours. A glass container would be best. Visualize the salt, sunlight, and water creating a powerful purifying potion. If you'd like, chant these words as you prepare it and before using it:

By salt and sun,

Defilement undone.

Sprinkle drops of the potion anywhere you need cleansing or add to a bath. Use it within a month's time.

Ember Grant

June 9
Friday

3rd ≈≈

☽ v/c 12:24 am

☽ → ℋ 6:14 am

Color of the day: Rose
Incense of the day: Orchid

Invoking Pentagram Garden Spell

The invoking pentagram is a traditional magickal technique that brings in positive energy most often focused on growth. The most common invoking pentagram is that of earth (perfect for a garden spell!), which is drawn by beginning at the top of the pentagram and moving downward to the left.

To use an invoking pentagram to help your garden grow, stand in front of your garden (or whatever you are growing plants in) and visualize your plants green, healthy, and abundant. Using very large motions, draw your pentagram in front of you in the air, and visualize powerful growing energy moving out through the pentagram and into your garden. As you do this, say:

Energies of earth,
manifest and flow.

May your powers help
my garden grow.

So mote it be!

Repeat this spell anytime you want to add a little extra magickal energy to your garden and the plants you are growing.

Amanda Lynn & Jason Mankey

NOTES:

June 10
Saturday

3rd ♓
4th Quarter 3:31 pm

Color of the day: Gray
Incense of the day: Ivy

Bibliomancy Prayer

With the Sun in Gemini (ruled by Mercury) and the Moon in psychic Pisces today, this is a perfect time to unite words with divination to gain some clarity. Bibliomancy is one of the oldest forms of divination in the world, and also one of the easiest methods to perform. Simply relax and clear your mind and still your emotions as much as possible. Say a prayer of guidance. I like to use this petition to my own higher self:

I call upon my higher self to reveal to me
The answers that I need to read.
Guide my hands and guide my eyes
To find some guidance true and wise.
Show me the answer that I require
To this question that I inquire.

Mat Auryn

 ## June 11
Sunday

4th ♓
☽ v/c 9:20 am
☽ → ♈ 9:20 am

Color of the day: Yellow
Incense of the day: Heliotrope

Spell for Tolerance

We have all encountered those who insist on being one up on us. When you share a photo of your child/spouse/home/car/anything, that person points out that they have it bigger and better. You mention a job you had in the past, and they have had a bigger and better one. You mention a spot of good fortune, and, yes, they have experienced something bigger and better.

Most of us get used to this and find ways to avoid including those people in conversations. Possibly more annoying is the person who has had it worse. Fender bender? They have totaled a vehicle. Illness? They have been so much sicker.

Try to be patient with these types, minimize time spent with them, or weed them out of your life if necessary. At the very least, here is a spell for tolerance:

Tolerance requested and
tolerance given; out of my sphere
may negativity be driven.

Emyme

June 12
Monday

4th ♈

Color of the day: White
Incense of the day: Rosemary

Pay It Forward

Embrace the future today by donating old, unused computers and phones to a worthy charity. Once you have reset the hard drive and scrubbed the memory from the device, try this tech-safe disinfecting and detachment solution to ensure that any old devices are clean and ready for a new user.

Into an eight-ounce spray bottle, combine the following ingredients and shake the solution vigorously for five minutes. Visualize pure light emanating sharply from the fluid within.

- A 2-inch stick of palo santo
- 8 frankincense tears
- A ¼-inch piece of black tourmaline
- 3½ teaspoons isopropyl alcohol
- 2 teaspoons extra strong mint tea

Estha McNevin

 June 13
Tuesday

4th ♈

☽ v/c 2:27 pm

☽ → ♉ 2:31 pm

Color of the day: Red
Incense of the day: Geranium

Autonomic Resilience Spell

The benefits of autonomic flexibility (where the nervous system can easily return to a state of regulation following a stressful incident) include reduced inflammation, control of the immune response, emotional regulation, resilience to stress, inhibition of distractions, and an increased capacity for friendship and connection. In addition, with higher levels of autonomic flexibility, we have a perception of wellbeing and social acceptance and increased compassion.

Polyvagal theory holds that as we become more able to regulate ourselves, the negative impacts of stress and trauma are reduced in severity and duration, and we can consciously change our internalized state, and experience, at will. Autonomic flexibility is very powerful magic indeed.

Easy self-regulation can be promoted by stimulating the vagus nerve. Sit comfortably. Breathe in deeply so the rib cage lifts and the diaphragm is stretched. Breathe out much more slowly. Again, short inhalation, stretching the diaphragm, followed by slow, slow exhalation. Repeat. Feel your heart rate slow, your shoulders relax, and the effects of stress dissipate.

Dallas Jennifer Cobb

NOTES:

June 14
Wednesday

4ħ ♉

Color of the day: Topaz
Incense of the day: Honeysuckle

Flag Day

Your Personal Flag

Today is Flag Day in the US, so create your own personal flag. Start today and take as much time as you wish. Choose three to five symbols that resonate with you and represent who you are or what you're working toward, such as a Celtic knot, a star, a dragon, etc.

Choose a piece of fabric for the background of your flag in any color. Cut and shape it to your wishes. Sketch the placement of your symbols first. Attach your symbols to the background in other fabrics and colors that are appropriate to your goals. Trace the designs onto the fabric, then cut them out and sew or glue them in place. Or you can use fabric paint to draw them. Finish the edges of the flag with a hem or pinking shears. When complete, bless and consecrate your flag by breathing on it and then holding it to your heart and saying:

I fly this flag, introducing myself to the world with peace and compassion.

Hang the flag in your home and/or bring it with you to festivals.

Cerridwen Iris Shea

 ## June 15
Thursday

4ħ ♉
☽ v/c 9:36 pm
☽ → ♊ 9:46 pm

Color of the day: Crimson
Incense of the day: Jasmine

New Ideas Wind Spell

June 15 is known as Global Wind Day. It is a time to celebrate the power of the wind, and encourages us to think about ways that wind can provide sustainable energy for the world. Since wind is associated with the element of air, you can access the power of air to help you acquire new ideas. You can use this spell in June or at any time of the year on a windy day.

Visit an area in nature where you can breathe in fresh air. While the wind blows, take a deep breath, raise your hands in the air, and say these words:

May the power of the wind bring me a perspective that is new and help me discover a new point of view.

As the air circulates with the winds that blow, bring new ideas to me with ease and flow.

Sapphire Moonbeam

June 16
Friday

4ﬔ ♊

Color of the day: Coral
Incense of the day: Vanilla

Triple Gemini Trance Oil

We have a major Gemini situation today in that the Sun, Moon, and Mercury are all hanging out with the divine twins—and you know they all talk. Take advantage of this energy by performing divination and trance work or by bottling it up with the following magical condition oil. Once made, this oil can be used in any spell or working where you need the strength of Gemini and its properties of psychic and mental clarity.

Into a half-ounce bottle, blend the following oils and allow to charge on your altar overnight:

13 drops fern essential oil

11 drops clary sage essential oil

9 drops lemongrass essential oil

The next day, fill the rest of the bottle with the carrier oil of your choice. (Fractionated coconut, olive, and grapeseed work well.) Label the bottle and store in a cool place.

Devin hunter

 ## June 17
Saturday

4ﬔ ♊

Color of the day: Blue
Incense of the day: Rue

Tessellation in Nature and Dwellings

Today is World Tessellation Day, created to honor the birth of artist M. C. Escher, who is sometimes referred to as the "father of modern tessellations." Tessellation is where one repeated geometric shape (or tile) covers a flat surface, with no overlaps or gap. This repeating pattern can also be found in three dimensions, such as honeycombs, known as tessellation of space. Tessellations were found in ancient art and in buildings. Tiled tessellated floors often show up in homes, especially in bathrooms.

Should you wish to explore this concept further, create an altar cloth or small quilt in a tessellated pattern. You could create artwork using a star pattern, similar to a pentagram, or choose a honeycomb pattern to honor bees and their contribution to life.

Emyme

June 18
Sunday

4th ♊
New Moon 12:37 am
☽ v/c 2:24 am
☽ → ♋ 6:58 am

Color of the day: Amber
Incense of the day: Hyacinth

Father's Day

A June New Moon Prosperity Spell

A June new moon is a powerful time to work prosperity magic. You'll need a gold or orange candle and a dollar bill. Place the candle on your altar and lay the dollar in front of it. Safely light the candle. Meditate on prosperity as you gaze at the flame. See the candle's glow increasing in your mind's eye. Now slowly draw the dollar toward you. "See" money coming to you from different directions. Visualize the dollar's value increasing.

Return to an everyday state of mind. Safely snuff out the candle. You may use it for prosperity magic again. Hide the dollar in a safe place; don't spend it. Watch how your finances may increase.

James Kambos

June 19
Monday

1st ♋

Color of the day: Gray
Incense of the day: Neroli

Juneteenth

Juneteenth Affirmation for Compassion

On Juneteenth in the United States, we commemorate the emancipation of African American slaves. Today, spread compassion by word and deed. There is still much pain and suffering in the world. Participate in a community service project or make a donation to charity today. Do what you can to spread compassion and love.

Light a candle today for the sorrow of the past and present and for hope for the future. Chant these words over the candle:

May the light from this flame fill the world with compassion.

May understanding and love inspire all of our actions.

Allow the candle to burn out.

Ember Grant

June 20
Tuesday

1st ♋

☽ v/c 5:43 pm

☽ → ♌ 6:04 pm

Color of the day: Maroon
Incense of the day: Cinnamon

Solar Candle Blessing

With the sun's energy nearly at its peak today, it's a great time to charge and bless your candles. This spell infuses your candles with fierce solar power, which increases that aspect of any magic they're used in. It can be done outside in full sunlight or with sunlight coming through a window or a skylight. You will need some candles, matches, and a chime candle (red, orange, or yellow).

Place the candles on their sides in the sunshine. Light a match. Say:

Sun, Great Star, I thank you for your light and your warmth. I ask for your blessing upon these candles.

Light the chime candle, and allow the wax to drip onto the other candles. After a few minutes, rotate the charging candles. Continue to drip wax onto the charging candles while repeating the spell. If the candles start to melt, move them to shade. When you're done, give thanks to the sun and extinguish the chime candle.

Astrea Taylor

 June 21
Wednesday

1st ♌

☉ → ♋ 10:58 am

Color of the day: Brown
Incense of the day: Lavender

Litha ~ Summer Solstice

Solar Fire Blessing

The sun is at the height of its power on the Summer Solstice, being the longest day of the year. You can tap into this energy to boost your own inner fires. Stretch your arms up toward the sun and say:

I call forth the sun for the fires of wisdom.

With your magickal imagination, scoop the sunlight in your hands and place your hands on top of your head, infusing it with all that solar power. Stretch your arms back up toward the sun like before and say:

I call forth the sun for the fires of passion.

Scoop the solar light into your hands and place them on your heart, infusing it with the energy. Repeat this process again, scooping the solar energy with your hands and placing them on your belly, infusing it with this fire, and say:

I call forth the sun for the fires of vitality.

Mat Auryn

June 22
Thursday

1st ♈ ♌

☽ v/c 1:01 pm

Color of the day: Turquoise
Incense of the day: Nutmeg

Magical Sunscreen

Since all forms of sunscreen are meant to protect the skin, we can add to that inherent quality and make them magically protective as well. For this spell, you can use any type of sunscreen, whether chemical or mineral.

Gather a white candle and some frankincense incense. Light the candle and incense, placing the incense in front of the candle. Hold the container of sunscreen in both hands and envision that white light is streaming from your hands into the cream. Focus on the idea that the cream, when used, will protect the wearer not only from solar radiation but from harm in all forms. When you feel ready, say:

Simple cream of modern design,
shield of power you now become.

Deflect danger, neutralize, unwind,
blocking all harm under the sun.

Extinguish the candle when done.

Michael Furie

NOTES:

 # June 23
Friday

1st ♌

☽ → ♍ 6:35 am

Color of the day: Purple
Incense of the day: Rose

Wind Chimes Invocation Spell

Wind chimes are a symbol of magic, often used to ward off evil spirits. The earliest wind chimes from ancient Rome had bells attached to them to create the sound, and in Eastern societies bells were also used, hung in corners of the house to guard against evil. However, in Asia, wind chimes are believed to be good luck and they are used in feng shui with the belief that they maximise the flow of chi. Nowadays they are made of glass, bamboo, shells, stone, wood, metal tubes, or porcelain, and there is a new trend of using recycled utensils or even cookie cutters!

In Eastern Europe, wind chimes are used as indicators of when spirits are around. That is why many of us have wind chimes in the house: when they inexplicably move with no draught or window open, we know there are "guests" around.

Create your own wind chime made of items that are important to you. If you are a water sign (Cancer, Scorpio, or Pisces), you could make it from shells, or if you have a number of crystals around, you could use them

too. It can be quite basic in design. Use a round piece of metal, wood, plastic, or even strong cupboard; it should look like a large ring, as you are going to tie the items to it. You can use ribbon, string, or twine to attach your items to the ring. Cut some different lengths of ribbon, but also some the same length so that the items can touch each other when the wind blows. Then hang the chimes in your house or garden.

If you would like the elementals to feel welcome in your house, say these words as you put your wind chime up:

Tinkling sounds,

Items of my heart.

Blessed elementals,

Merry meet and merry part.

Enter free in my witch's den.

And then depart freely again.

Tudorbeth

June 24
Saturday

1st ♍

Color of the day: Indigo
Incense of the day: Sage

Sun Water Spell

Moon water is all the rage in Witchcraft circles these days, but sun water is also an effective magickal tool. To make sun water, pour fresh water into a clean bowl and set outside in the sun. To give your sun water a little extra magickal *oomph*, add garden flowers, crystals, or a stone such as carnelian to the water. You can also add a drop or two of essential oil, especially an oil that reminds you of sunshine, such as lemon or orange.

Before the sun sets, gather your water and pour it into a clean jar or bottle, straining out any extras that you may have added (or that may have accumulated throughout the day). Sprinkle your sun water on any item you want to charge with solar energy, or use it to anoint yourself for extra strength, endurance, and vitality.

Amanda Lynn & Jason Mankey

June 25
Sunday

1st ♍

☽ v/c 6:24 pm
☽ → ♎ 6:57 pm

Color of the day: Gold
Incense of the day: Almond

Magical Flower Dollies

Fairy folk flower dolls are an old British tradition of child magick from times when toys were rare. Gaelic culture teaches us that children and fairies are closely linked. Gifting a child flowers is a way to protect and inspire them to explore their own fairy magick.

Today is a fine day to craft a springtime flower dolly, tussie-mussie bouquet, or flower crown and gift it to a child. Old Irish legends give a lot of power to flower rings, believed to ward and protect us from bad fairies. Dollies, brooms, and corsages draw guardian spirits and good fairies to a child so that they are never lost or forgotten. While whimsical, fairies are oddly formal. Curtsy to them if you know what is good for you. But to be truly fairy blessed, one must dance and prance around wildly as the fairies do, gifting flowers on the way to Tír na nÓg, the Celtic Otherworld.

Estha McNevin

June 26
Monday

1st ♈︎ ♎︎

2nd Quarter 3:50 am

Color of the day: Silver
Incense of the day: Narcissus

happy herbs

The waxing moon is a good time to make a big batch of happiness herb mixture to keep on hand for any time you need a dash of positivity. Perform this spell in the daytime when the sun is out.

Materials:

+ A bowl

+ 3 tablespoons dried catnip

+ 3 tablespoons dried lavender

+ 3 tablespoons dried calendula flowers

+ 3 dandelion seeds

Set the dandelion seeds aside, and put the rest of the herbs together in the bowl. Mix the herbs with your fingers while thinking of something that genuinely makes you smile, whether that's a person, a memory, or even a funny joke.

Now hold one dandelion seed toward the sun and say:

I wish for joy.

Add it to the herbs.

Repeat this with the remaining two seeds, saying "I wish for peace" and "I wish for contentment."

Keep a little bit of these herbs with you to smell or sprinkle around when you need to boost your mood.

Kate Freuler

NOTES:

 June 27
Tuesday

2nd ♎

Color of the day: Black
Incense of the day: Ylang-ylang

Morning Brew Meditation

Today is National Coffee Day in Colombia, one of many coffee-producing nations. Although this is a Colombian celebration, coffee is enjoyed worldwide, and that makes it a good day to consider the process involved in getting these beloved beans to us in the United States.

Today, if you're a coffee drinker, set your coffee to start brewing by whatever means and then begin a meditative journey in your mind, thinking about the country where your coffee was grown and the environment there. Is it in danger? How is climate change affecting it? Consider the treatment of the workers involved in the farming process and how the beans got to the place where you purchased them. Visualize these contemplations as a journey.

End your meditation when your coffee is finished brewing. You might have to do some research before and certainly after this meditation to suss out the facts! It's always good to try to be an informed consumer and to shop ethically.

Blake Octavian Blair

 June 28
Wednesday

2nd ♎

☽ v/c 4:19 am
☽ → ♏ 4:55 am

Color of the day: Yellow
Incense of the day: Lilac

Drain Your Worries

Light an assortment of votive candles in holders around your bathroom. Choose all white or a riot of colors. Prepare the bathwater to your preferred temperature, and use your favorite oils or bubble bath.

Slide into the bath, close your eyes, and relax. Let the candles and water soothe you. Let your tensions dissolve into the bath. Let your mind wander. If you start worrying about something, take a deep breath, splash in the water, and let it go.

When you are ready, step out of the bath and wrap yourself in a soft towel. Open the drain of the tub. Take your hand and flick water toward the drain, imagining the drops as your worries. Watch the water and your worries drain away.

Look at yourself in the mirror and say:

I am beautiful. I am enough.

Extinguish the candles and return to the world.

Cerridwen Iris Shea

 June 29
Thursday

2nd ♏

Color of the day: White
Incense of the day: Myrrh

Sacred Embodiment

In the Northern Hemisphere, late June is filled with light, warmth, and abundance. Strawberries ripen invitingly. My body softens to the sun, the earth, the water, and the warm air. With the sun in Cancer, the sign of the sacred mother, this is a good time to practice sacred embodiment.

Know your length. Stand with your feet hip-distance apart. Breathe up, lengthening your spine and creating space between the vertebrae. Exhale down into the earth and feel grounded.

Know your width. Breathe widely, feeling the width of your collarbones, rib cage, belly, and hips. Expand sideways in space.

And know your depth. Within you, cultivate your passion and power. Invite who you love, what you cherish, what stirs and moves you, and what you are passionate about to bloom within you. Feel the length, width, and depth of your body. As you inhabit your body consciously and fully, claim it and hold it as your own sacred space.

Dallas Jennifer Cobb

 **June 30**
Friday

2nd ♏

☽ v/c 10:20 am
☽ → ♐ 10:59 am

Color of the day: Rose
Incense of the day: Alder

Knock on Wood

Trees are a magical presence in our lives. It is considered a good idea to say "knock on wood" during a conversation when we hope future events will unfold for us in a favorable way and to ward off any misfortune. You can connect with the wisdom, beauty, and magic of trees when you visit a wooded area. Find a big beautiful tree and spend some quality time with it. Be silent and stand still. View the sights, colors, smells, and movements nearby. Watch the leaves as they turn gracefully in the wind. Think of a wish or dream that you have, then knock on the wood three times to get the protection and blessing of the tree. You can also say or think these words:

As I stand silently and knock on this tree, please provide protection and luck for me.

Sapphire Moonbeam

July

In 46 BCE, when Julius Caesar decided to reform the Roman lunar calendar, the names of the months were numbers. He moved the first of the year back to January, and, being the egoist he was, he renamed the fifth month (the month of his birth) for himself: Iulius (Julius, today's July). He also gave it a thirty-first day. (Then he named the next month after his heir, Augustus.)

July (the month of my birth, too) is high summer. In many places, it's the hottest month of the year. It's the month in which everything blooms until the heat of the sun makes flowers—and people—wilt and nearly melt.

What do I remember from my childhood Julys? Rereading my favorite books. Dragging the big old washtub out on the side lawn, filling it with cold water, and splashing all afternoon. Helping my father tend his flowers—roses, columbines, tulips, and hydrangeas. Climbing to the very top of our neighbor's huge weeping willow tree. Chasing fireflies before bedtime and putting them in jars to glitter and wink throughout the night. Sleeping in the screened porch with all the windows open to catch every possible breeze. What are your favorite July memories?

Barbara Ardinger

July 1
Saturday

2nd ♐

Color of the day: Blue
Incense of the day: Sandalwood

Canada Day

Yes-or-No Tea Leaf Reading

Sometimes you just want a quick yes-or-no divination technique. While tea leaf reading, or *tasseography*, can certainly provide far more insight and guidance than this spell, it can also be used to get a fast answer to a burning question.

Materials:

• Your favorite loose leaf tea

• A teacup with a handle and a saucer

• 1 teaspoon food-grade rose water

Make yourself a cup of loose leaf tea as you normally would, allowing it to steep to your desired flavor. Just before your drink it, add a teaspoon of rose water. Say:

Nature's herbs and roses know
if the answer's yes or no.

State your question aloud and then drink the tea. When you're done, point the handle of the cup toward you. Turn the cup upside down onto the saucer to drain the excess liquid, then flip it back up and look inside.

If most of the leaves are stuck to the right of the handle, the answer is yes. If they're on the left, the answer is no.

Kate Freuler

NOTES:

 July 2
Sunday

2nd ♐

☽ v/c 9:33 am

☽ → ♑ 1:20 pm

Color of the day: Yellow
Incense of the day: Eucalyptus

Rock Out!

Music is a powerful conductor of magickal energy and can help us clear out emotional baggage and make a fresh start. All you need for this spell is the music of your favorite artist and perhaps a little privacy.

Start the music and let loose! Allow the music to move through you and embrace it. Don't be scared to sing along, dance, or even scream. Remind yourself why you love your favorite artist, and embrace all the emotions that come with the music. If the music makes you feel good, lean into that and embrace the positive vibes.

If the music makes you sad or melancholy, embrace that too! Music often brings up old memories, happy and sad. If the music makes you feel like crying, go ahead and cry–let out those emotions! When you feel like all your emotions have been released, turn off the tunes and feel cleansed and refreshed.

Amanda Lynn & Jason Mankey

 July 3
Monday

2nd ♑

🌕 Full Moon 7:39 am

Color of the day: Gray
Incense of the day: Clary sage

Full Moon Power

For this full moon, rediscover your personal magical power. It's easy to lose confidence in your personal magic, forgetting that you are the source of it, not your tools or spells. Go out tonight beneath the full moon. If it's cloudy, just remember the moon is still there. If you can't get outside, visualize the moon instead. Then chant:

Moon rising high, let the magic begin.

I may look to you, but it comes from within.

You are the guide, a light in the dark.

Renew my strength, let all doubt depart.

Your magic is inside you, not in the moon. Let the moon inspire you. It has an influence on our lives, but the magic is within. Think of the moon as recharging your magical energy. Visualize its light penetrating you and awakening your personal power.

Ember Grant

July 4
Tuesday

3rd ♑

☽ v/c 12:45 pm

☽ → ♒ 1:30 pm

Color of the day: Scarlet
Incense of the day: Cedar

Independence Day

Fourth of July Transformation

Since July 4 is the celebration of independence in the United States, this holiday is a great time to break free from a stagnant or negative situation in your life. If you have been feeling stuck or frustrated or if you want to break free from something, this spell will assist you.

Fireworks and the fire element can be used to express your desire for intense and explosive transformation. Just make sure you are actually ready for big, powerful changes. Whether you see fireworks in person or watch them on a screen, you can use the power of your mind and visualization.

Make a list of the top three things that you want to change in your life. As you watch the fireworks explode, sparkle, drift, and glide across the sky, say these words:

May my situation change.
Help me break free.

May the fiery explosions ignite
transformation for me. So mote it be!

Sapphire Moonbeam

July 5
Wednesday

3rd ♒

Color of the day: Topaz
Incense of the day: Bay laurel

Summer Syrup for Sipping

It can be a challenge during the hot days of summer to stay motivated and hydrated, but nothing nourishes like mango-infused honey syrup. Filled with medicinal spices and succulent fruits, honey infusions are a delicious way to stay healthy one spoonful at a time.

You will need:

- 1 vanilla bean, split lengthwise
- 1 cinnamon stick
- 1 teaspoon annatto seed powder
- 3 teaspoons cardamom powder, freshly crushed
- 2 cups mashed mango
- 4 tablespoons lemon juice
- 4 tablespoons orange juice
- 2 cups honey
- A 33.75-ounce glass bottle with a rubber swing top

In a medium saucepan, combine all the ingredients. Cook on medium high heat until the syrup begins to reduce and reaches 230 degrees F. Then remove the thick elixir from the heat and let it cool to 190 degrees F. When

ready, decant the syrup (including the vanilla bean and the cinnamon stick) into the glass bottle. Store in the pantry and add the syrup to any smoothie, lemonade, or carbonated water to celebrate vitality with all things mango this summer.

Estha McNevin

NOTES:

July 6
Thursday

3rd ♒

☽ v/c 9:42 am

☽ → ♓ 1:33 pm

Color of the day: Green
Incense of the day: Mulberry

Fresh Water Blessing

During the season of Cancer, the water sign in which the summer solstice occurs, I always create time for a fresh water blessing, investing spirit and energy in this life-giving force. Regardless of where you live, take a moment today to conduct a water blessing. Whether you go to a remote lake or an urban pond or pull a glass of water from your tap, pause and connect. Touch the water with your body. Dip a toe in, or a finger, or even your tongue. As your body touches the water, send thoughts of gratitude to the water:

Thank you.

Imagine the water meeting you in relationship:

I love you.

Pledge to serve and protect the water:

I will work to keep you safe.

Ask now what the water needs from you, and listen. Through the coming year, remember to honor and serve the water.

Dallas Jennifer Cobb

July 7
Friday

3rd ♓

Color of the day: Purple
Incense of the day: Violet

Silver and Gold

Jewelry has been associated with magical powers since ancient times. Silver carries the energy of the moon, intuition, rest, emotions, and psychic ability. Gold corresponds with the sun, action, success, and prosperity. Use this spell to charge your jewelry with the energies of these heavenly bodies. The best times to do so are the full moon and the summer solstice, but any time will do.

You will need some silver or gold jewelry and moonlight or sunlight.

Place your jewelry on a windowsill or in a safe location outdoors in the light of the sun (gold) or the moon (silver). Say:

*Sun/Moon, with great love, I ask
you to charge this metal. Imbue
it with your powers. May it be
a little piece of your brilliance
that I can carry with me.*

Leave the jewelry in the light as long as you safely can. Give thanks, and if the jewelry isn't too warm, wear it.

Astrea Taylor

July 8
Saturday

3rd ♓
☽ v/c 2:22 pm
☽ → ♈ 3:19 pm

Color of the day: Black
Incense of the day: Patchouli

Clay Figure Manifestation Spell

Today's astrology features a very passionate set of placements, divided almost entirely between the elements of water and earth. These energies lend an intuitive sense of what is needed in our lives at the moment, but also of what others need, as both the Sun and Mercury are sailing through sensitive Cancer. This spell can be done for yourself or others to help manifest that thing that is most needed. All you need is a bit of self-drying clay. (Play-Doh will do the trick!)

With the clay, sculpt a miniature of something that symbolizes the thing you are manifesting. As you do so, visualize it coming to be and say:

*From clay to figure, figure to life,
I conjure what's needed to end the strife!*

Place your sculpture to dry in the direction of the rising sun. Once that thing has manifested, place the figure in water for a few days, and it will return to being soft and reusable.

Devin Hunter

July 9
Sunday

3rd ♈

4th Quarter 9:48 pm

Color of the day: Gold
Incense of the day: Juniper

Neighborhood Love Spell

For this spell you can use real pink cotton candy or you can imagine it. Sit quietly, close your eyes, and follow your breath. When you feel centered, open your palms facing each other, creating a sphere of energy between them. Imagine this sphere filled with the energies of love, acceptance, and friendship, with the energy looking like pink cotton candy. Feel it grow in your hands.

Move your hands apart, then spread your arms until they are fully extended. Turn the palms up, visualizing the energized cotton candy balanced on the palms.

Open your eyes. Imagine the energy filling your room, your home, your block, your neighborhood (in a fun, positive way).

Release the energy and shake your hands to disengage it. Place your hands on the floor to ground and center.

You'll notice the difference the next time you go out. Greet your neighbors with friendship and respect.

Renew the spell as needed.

Cerridwen Iris Shea

NOTES:

July 10
Monday

4th ♈

☽ v/c 7:11 pm

☽ → ♉ 7:55 pm

Color of the day: White
Incense of the day: Lily

Letting Go of a Relationship Spell

Relationships are crucial for a healthy life, and we have so many of them throughout our lifetime, as we are social beings. Although some relationships last for years, others are fleeting, and as soon as that person comes into our lives, they are gone. Relationships can be with work colleagues, friends from school or college, lovers, and even family.

The hardest part, I always find, is saying goodbye and moving on from a relationship, even if it has been a negative one. We tend to question our actions and wonder if we could have done something different. Yet negative or toxic relationships are damaging to us, as they hinder our growth both spiritually and mentally. Nevertheless, we must let that person go and say goodbye to the relationship.

If you have formed a negative relationship and need to let go, try this spell. If you have a picture of that person, then look at it while performing this spell. If not, you can picture them in your mind as you send them on their way from your heart and mind.

Sprinkle some salt on a flat surface, such as a table, tray, or plate, and with your index finger, draw their initials in the salt. Look at their picture or imagine their face, then say this spell out loud:

> Bless this person in time and space,
>
> Remove the memory of their face.
>
> Their actions hurt my heart,
>
> And now we are forever apart.
>
> I say goodbye and free myself,
>
> Never to meet again, but time will tell.

Imagine the person going their own way and you going yours. Afterward, throw the salt away; do not use it for anything again, as it has absorbed the person's negative actions and has cleansed your heart. You can dissolve the salt in water and then simply pour it down the drain.

Tudorbeth

July 11
Tuesday

4th ♉

Color of the day: Gray
Incense of the day: Bayberry

A Sand Divination

During the Ottoman Empire, some seers divined the future by using sand. This ritual is based on that method. You'll need some sand, which you can find at garden centers, and an old metal tray. (If you're planning a trip to the beach, that would also be a good place to perform this ritual.)

First, spread the sand over the tray, and cover it completely. Then think of a question. As you do so, run your hands through the sand. Feel it. Play with it. When you feel ready, stop and look at the sand. Do you see any images? Do you see any patterns or figures? "Read" whatever you see.

When done, smooth out the sand. Keep your tray of sand where it won't be disturbed, ready for next time. If you do this ritual at the beach, let the tide wash away your reading.

James Kambos

July 12
Wednesday

4th ♉

Color of the day: Yellow
Incense of the day: Marjoram

Simplify Your Spells

A religious official in another faith system once said that taking the name of a deity in vain can be considered a simple prayer. For example, you stub your toe and invoke a deity in pain, and the deity assists in your healing or in dispelling your anger.

Spells do not have to be elaborate. There are many ways to simplify worship. For example, light a candle, visualize and speak your intention, meditate on that intention for a minute or two, extinguish the candle, and off you go. Here is a template:

I invoke (choose a deity) to provide (choose an item or characteristic) for my family and me on this (choose a celebration) day.

Emyme

July 13
Thursday

4th ♉

☽ v/c 2:11 am

☽ → ♊ 3:26 am

Color of the day: Turquoise
Incense of the day: Apricot

Protect Your Selfies

It's nearly impossible these days to avoid having your image available either on the internet or simply on the cameras and mobile devices of others. This need not be a source of magical fear, however, if certain precautions are taken. We can seal ourselves and disconnect all images of us at once using a single selfie.

For this spell, all you need is an image of yourself (it can be on your phone) and your athame. Gaze at the image and see a thin, glowing cord linking the image to your body. With the athame, make a smooth cutting motion, severing the cord so that the image can no longer be used to magically influence you in any way. Next, encircle the image with the athame in a counterclockwise circle and envision that every image of you instantly loses its cord as well.

Michael Furie

July 14
Friday

4th ♊

Color of the day: Pink
Incense of the day: Orchid

Animal Companion Collar of Protection

Animal companions are an integral part of the family, and when something bad happens to them, it can be as devastating as when something happens to anyone else in the household. While the Sun is still in family-focused Cancer, it's a more than perfect time to include them in your family spells.

This spell is incredibly simple. A lot of witches I know like to put pentacle charms on their animal companion's collar for protection, and you can include that in this spell if you desire, but all you need is the animal's collar itself. Hold the collar in your hands while conjuring all your desire to protect your animal companion, and declare:

By the power of this charm,

I protect (name of animal companion) from all harm.

By this charm which I fix and adorn,

Protect this creature while it is worn.

Simply place the collar on your animal companion. Be sure to give them lots of pets and scratches.

Mat Auryn

July 15
Saturday

4th ♊

☽ v/c 8:35 am

☽ → ♋ 1:13 pm

Color of the day: Indigo
Incense of the day: Ivy

Bury It!

Sometimes we need to recognize what no longer serves us and give that energy back to the earth so we can start fresh. For this spell you will need a flat rock, a marker, and possibly a shovel or trowel for digging so you can bury your rock.

Start by writing down whatever you want to cast out of your life on your rock. Your writing doesn't have to be specific, but as you write, imagine exactly what it is you wish to rid yourself of. After you have made your inscription, push that energy of what you're getting rid of into the rock.

Now bury your rock in a spot where it won't be disturbed. As you do this, ask the earth to take away the unwanted energy. As an alternative to burying your rock, you can also throw it into a body of water.

Amanda Lynn & Jason Mankey

July 16
Sunday

4th ♋

Color of the day: Amber
Incense of the day: Hyacinth

Dance Like Nobody's Watching

We've all heard the famous quote "Dance like nobody's watching." Well, today happens to be the birthday of famed Irish dancer Michael Flatley. I say we take a cue from this occasion, and a little wisdom from this quote, and combine them into a bit of inspiration to express our spirit!

Not all of us feel we're great dancers, but that doesn't matter. Give yourself five minutes alone in a room, and put on a song (even using headphones or earbuds) that reflects your mood, then just dance and move as your spirit leads you! It's not about you being Lord of the Dance, but rather allowing yourself to fully express how your spirit is feeling. At the end of your song, sit for a few minutes to rest and lightly meditate or journal on how you feel now as compared to before your soulful dance.

Blake Octavian Blair

July 17
Monday

4th ♋
New Moon 2:32 pm
☽ v/c 11:06 pm

Color of the day: Ivory
Incense of the day: Neroli

New Moon Pearl Spell

Tonight, as the new moon rises, perform this pearl spell to honor the balance of light within the depths of our own emotional waters and to safeguard our intuition with lunar equilibrium.

Gather these items:

- Silver jewelry thread and needle
- 1 string of black pearls
- 1 string of white pearls
- A glass punch bowl
- 3 tablespoons salt
- 8 cups rainwater

Bead a 34-inch necklace, alternating black and white pearls. Tie it off with intention and place the necklace in the bowl. Add the salt and water, then lift the bowl up toward the night sky. Chant the following eight times:

Light from within me, journey upon the waves; draw love and hope in these darkest of days.

Fill me now with an inner delight, and with your ageless wisdom bring me lunar insight.

Finally, try to carefully dump the water over your head so that the string of pearls flows into place around your neck. So mote it be.

Estha McNevin

NOTES:

July 18
Tuesday

1st ♋

☽ → ♌ 12:39 am

Color of the day: Red
Incense of the day: Ginger

Islamic New Year begins at sundown

Four Directions Cleansing Spell

Everyone and everything that enters your space brings energy with them, and sometimes it's not the good kind. This simple spell requires only chalk and a stick of incense to grab on to and disperse any negative energy that other people bring into your room or home.

On your front step or just inside your front door, use the chalk to draw an X on the floor. Add an arrow shape to the end of each arm of the X. It should look like four arrows pointing outward, which will direct energy to the north, south, east, and west.

Light your stick of incense and hold it above the symbol. Move it in clockwise circles around the symbol, empowering it with the smoke. Say:

This symbol grabs all negative energy that passes over it and sends it far away. So mote it be.

Anyone who passes over the symbol will be cleansed of negative energy before entering your personal space.

You can place a doormat over the symbol to keep it hidden. This spell can be repeated as needed or integrated into part of your housekeeping.

Kate Freuler

NOTES:

July 19
Wednesday

1st ♌

Color of the day: White
Incense of the day: Lavender

Resilience Spell

This spell can be used to increase your resilience in the face of hardship. Frankincense is one of the most powerful aromas for courage and protection. It is also uplifting and can increase optimism. For this spell, either burn the resin as incense or use the essential oil of frankincense in a diffuser. Just be sure you can breathe in the aroma.

Focus on being strong and overcoming whatever obstacles you face. See yourself recovering easily from any setback and gaining new strength and stamina anytime you face adversity. Use this chant as you visualize and breathe in the fragrance:

I can adapt, I can persist.

In the face of adversity I can resist

The temptation to give in to defeat.

Any challenge I face I will firmly meet.

Ember Grant

July 20
Thursday

1st ♌

☽ v/c 10:08 am

☽ → ♍ 1:13 pm

Color of the day: Purple
Incense of the day: Clove

Friendship Toast Spell

True friends are the people in your life who understand you and love you just as you are. It's important to let them know how much you appreciate them from time to time. This spell uses a toast to show your appreciation. It's best to practice it a few times so you can say it with confidence and warmth.

The next time you have the opportunity to get a coffee or a drink for a friend, order two of the same kind and pay for both of them. If possible, make them special drinks to raise the bar, like mochas instead of drip coffee.

When the drinks arrive, raise your glass and gaze at your friend. Say:

A toast! To a friendship that is wonderful and wise through the lows and the highs. To us!

Clink your glasses and take a sip to seal in the magic of the spell.

Astrea Taylor

 ## July 21
Friday

1st ♍

Color of the day: Coral
Incense of the day: Yarrow

Friday De-stress Spell

It's Friday, the end of the workweek for many and a day when most people are in high spirits. However, if your week has been challenging, stressful, or difficult, you might need a little help dissolving the heavy energy of the recent challenges. Friday evening is a great time to relax and find a way to let it all go. Grab a candle so you can work with the transformational energy of fire to change your thoughts and your personal energy. Safely light the candle and repeat these words as many times as you need:

*As this candle burns, help
my stress melt away.*

Don't allow it to affect me in any way.

As you gaze at the candle flame, allow yourself to ease into a more peaceful state. When you are done repeating the words, snuff out the candle.

Sapphire Moonbeam

 ## July 22
Saturday

1st ♍

☉ → ♌ 9:50 pm

Color of the day: Gray
Incense of the day: Pine

Got My Back

This simple magical practice for creating increased cues of safety in the body, even in uncertain situations, can transform our ability to respond effectively to situations.

Sit with your spine stacked over the sitting bones. Feel your head sitting atop the spine. Now use your nose to draw micro circles in front of you—tiny, subtle, and in both directions. Notice the movement in your first (atlas) vertebra, which sits just below the skull in the neck. Now trace miniscule figure-eight shapes with your nose and attune to your second (axis) vertebra. As you move through Atlas and Axis, your eyes scan your surroundings. Gently draw your head back a tiny amount, noticing the response of the muscles in the back of the body. Feel it? That muscular contraction is a reminder that you have your own back and are now empowered to respond, not react. These small, subtle cues from the body carry deep reassurance to the mind and emotions. Now you know how to support yourself.

Dallas Jennifer Cobb

July 23
Sunday

1st ♏

☽ v/c 12:06 am

☽ → ♎ 1:54 am

Color of the day: Orange
Incense of the day: Marigold

Reading Candle Wax

Ceromancy is the art of interpreting the results of hot candle wax that has been poured into cold water. To do this, light a taper candle, hold it over a bowl of water, and let the wax drip freely into the water. An alternative method is to place a votive candle in a shallow glass jar lined with sand and to let that burn for a few minutes until a puddle of wax has formed at the top of the candle. As you pour the wax into the cold water, ask whatever question you wish. Be sure to pour a decent amount of wax into the water; one or two small drops is not enough for good results!

To interpret the shapes in the water, let your mind wander and trust your intuition. Things might not make sense immediately, and that's okay. Be patient as your mind figures out what the drippings might mean.

Amanda Lynn & Jason Mankey

July 24
Monday

1st ♎

Color of the day: Lavender
Incense of the day: Hyssop

Fires of Creativity Oil

Today the Sun and Mercury are both in Leo, the sign of the artist and the performer. It's a great time to be creative, to work on a project that's important to you. Creativity is heightened when we're relaxed and not pressuring ourselves. Lavender is a fantastic ally for creativity because it's a Mercury-ruled plant that induces relaxation. Fiery Sun-ruled cinnamon helps speed things up and blasts through blockages, while frankincense helps you tap into your inner realms. You can use any carrier oil, but I recommend almond oil due to it being ruled by Mercury as well. Combine:

- 6 drops lavender oil
- 1 drop cinnamon oil
- 4 drops frankincense oil
- 2 drams almond oil

Dress an orange candle (orange is the color of Mercury and a secondary color of the Sun) with your creativity oil and say:

Creativity, creativity,

Come to me with clarity.

Mat Auryn

July 25
Tuesday

1st ♎

☽ v/c 11:05 am

☽ → ♏ 12:55 pm

2nd Quarter 6:07 pm

Color of the day: White

Incense of the day: Cinnamon

Prosperity Sandwiches

Now is a good time for some easy summertime kitchen magic. Craft an edible spell to increase your own prosperity using bread or fresh produce that is naturally aligned to the energies of growth and abundance. Breads containing wheat flour are linked to prosperity, as are tomatoes, zucchini, alfalfa sprouts, mayonnaise, and peppers. Cheese is related to success, happiness, and transformation. Using a few or all of these items along with some of your own favorite ingredients, build a sandwich. When it is ready, hold both hands over it and mentally charge it with gold light while envisioning yourself as prosperous and happy. Before you take the first bite, say:

> *May this food nourish my body,*
> *mind, and spirit, the sacred three,*
> *and fill my life with prosperity.*

Eat the sandwich and let your body absorb the magic.

Michael Furie

 July 26
Wednesday

2nd ♏

Color of the day: Yellow

Incense of the day: Lilac

A Threshold Protection Spell

To protect the entry of your home from negative energy or to cleanse the entry after a negative person has left your home, try this spell. You'll need salt and a clove of garlic.

While thinking of your intent, sprinkle salt along the threshold of your main entry, then rub a crushed clove of garlic over the salt. Leave the clove of garlic outside your front door overnight to absorb as much negative energy as possible. The next day, remove the garlic clove. Carry it away from your front door and dispose of it. You may compost it or throw it in the trash. Lastly, sweep any remaining salt away from your front door.

James Kambos

July 27
Thursday

2nd ♏

☽ v/c 6:36 pm

☽ → ♐ 8:24 pm

Color of the day: Crimson
Incense of the day: Jasmine

Family Protection Spell

The Yggdrasil, or Tree of Life, is symbolic of the interconnectedness of all. It is the World Tree of all creation, yet it also links us to the spiritual world, the cosmic centre that lies within everyone and exists everywhere all at once, just as family and friends are attached to our lives.

If you have an Yggdrasil tree anywhere in your garden, then you can create a family or friend tree. Make little cards for your family and friends, with their picture on one side and their name and birth date on the other. Laminate the cards and attach them to the tree. Ancient Celtic ancestors used to tie ribbons round the trees when asking for protection for their loved ones, and each ribbon used represented a member of the family, as they didn't have photographs.

Here is a specific spell of protection for your family or friends for you to perform. Write out the names of your family and friends, or use your family tree scroll if you have one. Have pictures or the names of your nearest

and dearest in view as you safely light a white candle and say these words:

Bless my family, bless my friends,

May their friendship never end.

I send to them the gift of love,

Graced with protection from above.

Now blow out the candle and waft the photos or names through the rising smoke, sending your request of protection to the universe.

Tudorbeth

NOTES:

July 28
Friday

2nd ♐

Color of the day: Rose
Incense of the day: Mint

R-E-S-P-E-C-T Spell

There is an explosion of Leo energy today, as the Sun, Mercury, and Venus are all traveling through this sign and giving off major big-cat vibes. This is a time when you are likely to feel a bit territorial about your areas of expertise and may expect others to fall in line behind you on things you feel passionate about. Obedience isn't so much the objective as is respect, so cast this spell to make sure you are getting the respect you deserve.

For this spell you will need a physical picture of yourself and a gold marker. Draw a crown above your head and then outline yourself with the marker in the photo to create a golden aura. Say:

Golden aura from my sovereign crown,

I demand respect and ooze renown!

Make them see what I bring to the table.

Let them see I am more than able!

Keep the photo with you or in your book of shadows.

Devin Hunter

 ## July 29
Saturday

2nd ♐

☽ v/c 7:51 pm

☽ → ♑ 11:44 pm

Color of the day: Brown
Incense of the day: Rue

Tiger Day Inspiration

Is the tiger an animal that inspires you? If so, then today you are in luck, for it is Global Tiger Day, often called International Tiger Day. This celebration is held every year on July 29 and was created at the Saint Petersburg Tiger Summit in Russia in 2010. The objective of this annual observance is to promote a global system of raising public awareness of tiger conservation issues and protecting tigers in their natural habitats.

Even if the spirit of the tiger is not something you work with in your magic, please take a look at some statistics and offer up a spell of goodwill and positive energy for this most majestic of animals. For inspiration, read William Blake's poem "The Tyger" and Frank Stockton's short story "The Lady, or the Tiger?"

Emyme

July 30
Sunday

2nd ♑

Color of the day: Yellow
Incense of the day: Heliotrope

Celebrate Yourself!

Deity feast days get a lot of attention. Create a feast day for yourself! Today works for this spell because it's before the first harvest (Lammas) and comes after the more social Summer Solstice.

When you wake up, take a moment to just be, and then state:

Today I celebrate myself.

Build a unique altar to yourself using significant items, photos, craft materials, artwork, baking, etc. Then do what gives you pleasure. Take a luxurious bath, take a long walk, read a book, or write a song. Eat whatever you want. Be as social or enjoy as much solitude as you wish.

Create a graphic to share with others on social media that today is a self-celebration. Or say nothing. Make plans or be spontaneous.

Before bed, light a candle and state:

Today was the Feast of Me.

I am worth celebrating!

Let the candle burn down safely.

Cerridwen Iris Shea

July 31
Monday

2nd ♑

☽ v/c 10:13 pm

☽ → ♒ 11:58 pm

Color of the day: Silver
Incense of the day: Rosemary

The Pit of Prosperity

Today is National Avocado Day. Not only is this fruit delicious and nutritious, but magically it packs a punch for prosperity magic.

Next time you partake of the deliciousness of avocado, save the pit. Avocado pits are excellent inclusions in prosperity spells. In fact, you can use a pit all on its own to make a prosperity charm. While the pit is fresh and somewhat soft, carefully carve prosperity symbols into it Choose symbols that resonate with you, then say the following charm over it:

Green and prosperous fruit I eat,

Pit of prosperity, an extra treat.

Attracting plenty toward me,

As it is carved, so mote it be.

Set the magical pit on a napkin or towel and let it dry on your altar. Then leave it on your altar or carry it in a charm bag.

Blake Octavian Blair

August

S ummer is at its height of power when August rolls in, bringing with it the first of the harvest festivals, Lughnasadh (or Lammas), on the first of the month. Lughnasadh is a festival of strength and abundance, a reflection of August itself. Lugh and the Corn God are highly celebrated during this month and are particularly good to work with in spells or rituals for abundance, prosperity, agriculture, marriage, or strength. The Earth Mother in her many forms is ripening and overflowing with abundance. While we often see the first harvest as being associated with corn, there is much more that has been harvested by this point. We must remember not to overlook anything or take anything for granted in our lives, and the harvest is an excellent reminder of that. It is a time to begin focusing on expressing appreciation and giving thanks for all that we have.

The full moon this month is most often called the Corn Moon, but also goes by the Wyrt Moon, Barley Moon, or Harvest Moon. The stones carnelian, fire agate, cat's eye, and jasper will add extra power to your spells and rituals at this time. Use the herbs chamomile, St. John's wort, bay, angelica, fennel, rue, barley, wheat, marigold, or sunflowers in your spells. The colors for August are yellow, gold, and the rich green of the grass and leaves.

Kerri Connor

August 1
Tuesday

2nd ♒

🌕 **Full Moon** 2:32 pm

Color of the day: Maroon
Incense of the day: Basil

Lammas

A Lammas Full Moon Spell

When the August full moon rises on Lammas, the moon will cast a golden glow upon a lush, bountiful Earth ready for the harvest. This is a time to give thanks.

You'll need a small piece of bread or cornbread. If possible, when the moon rises, go to a place outdoors where you won't be disturbed. Bring the piece of bread as an offering. Sit on the ground holding your bread. Raise the bread toward the moon and say:

Mother Earth and Mother Moon,

Summer's end is coming soon.

We still have the sun and August heat,

And the earth's bounty is at its peak.

*Thank you for the harvest
that is at hand,*

*Thank you for the bounty
that is upon the land.*

End by leaving your bread on the ground as a sign of thanks to Earth and the moon.

James Kambos

August 2
Wednesday

3rd ♒

☽ v/c 5:15 pm

☽ → ♓ 11:05 pm

Color of the day: Brown
Incense of the day: Bay laurel

Magical Air Conditioning

The one thing about summer that is most prominent in my mind is that it is hot. Whenever I have the chance to be in front of an air conditioner in the summer, I take it. Why not add a little magic to such an integral part of the summer season?

Most types of air conditioner units have removable filters, and these can be charged with a symbol, such as a pentagram for protection, a heart for love, a clockwise spiral for health, or even a dollar sign for prosperity. Using your index finger or athame, trace your chosen symbol over the air filter, then put it back in the air conditioner. Turn on the unit and the magic will pour into the room along with the refreshingly cool air.

Michael Furie

August 3
Thursday

3rd ♓

Color of the day: Green
Incense of the day: Balsam

Love, heart, Relationship

With the Sun and Venus both in fun and flirty Leo now, this is a great time to do a spell to spice things up in the bedroom. For this spell you will need a red sachet bag, the silkier the better. In the bag you will place four equal parts of dried rose petals, dried lavender petals, dried jasmine petals, and cinquefoil (five-finger grass). The flowers bring in love, lust, sensuality, and seduction. Cinquefoil is used in magick to grab things with its "five fingers." Put the ingredients in the bag and say:

Flowers three for sensuality

And cinquefoil to bring to me

Enhanced fun, lust, and play,

Whether it be night or day.

Close and tie the bag and say:

For the highest good and harming none,

As I tie this bag, the spell is done.

Place the bag somewhere near your bed. You could hang the bag above your headboard or place it between your mattresses, under your pillow, or under your bed.

Mat Auryn

August 4
Friday

3rd ♓

☽ v/c 9:21 pm

☽ → ♈ 11:19 pm

Color of the day: Coral
Incense of the day: Rose

Farmers' Market Bounty

From the largest city to the smallest village, farmers' markets are everywhere. Take this opportunity to partake in the goodness of the earth. Invite friends and family over to prepare a salsa or a chutney using fresh ingredients from the market. Both salsa and chutney are considered a garnish, and both can be smooth or very chunky. Salsa is Mexican and has a tomato base, even when prepared with fruit. Chutney is from India and tends to be sweeter and not hot. Under the umbrella of relish, there can never be too many options. Every guest can leave today with a full jar and the recipe. As you prepare your salsa or chutney, incant:

Bless the fruit of the earth.

Bless those who create from the fruit of the earth.

Bless those who partake of the fruit of the earth.

Emyme

August 5
Saturday

3rd ♈

Color of the day: Indigo
Incense of the day: Sage

Sunflower Determination Spell

Sunflowers are known for their vibrant color and their bright yellow petals as they reach for the sun. As the flowers grow taller, they carry the energies of hope and determination. If you have been lacking hope in your life, you can utilize this flower to empower your personal energy.

For this spell you can use a sunflower, visualize a sunflower, or even paint or draw a sunflower for your altar. Use the method that works best for you. You can also use a white candle for the purity of your heart and a yellow candle for joy to enhance the potency of this determination spell. Safely light the candles and say these words:

May the energies of the sunflower help me see that there is always hope that surrounds me.

As I reach for my goal with determination and power, may my manifestation and success grow hour by hour.

Remember to extinguish your candles.

Sapphire Moonbeam

 August 6
Sunday

3rd ♈

Color of the day: Orange
Incense of the day: Eucalyptus

Harvesting the Sun

It is time to harvest what we have been growing in our gardens and to consciously harvest the power of the sun. Take five minutes to sit quietly in the sunlight. Close your eyes, yet see the light of the sun within. Focus on the solar panels in your skin. Feel them warm and generate energy as you harvest the sun. We can take vitamins from a bottle, but our skin is the most efficient tool for producing vitamin D. Outdoor sunlight provides ultraviolet radiation that the skin uses to produce vitamin D_3. There are thousands of tissues and systems in the body regulated by vitamin D_3, including those connected to natural immunity and mental wellbeing, so harvesting the sun is not just pleasurable but also life-sustaining.

Tell yourself:

As I soak in the sun, I know that the earth and I are one. I am a photo synthesizer.

Dallas Jennifer Cobb

August 7
Monday

3rd ♈

☽ v/c 12:13 am

☽ → ♉ 2:25 am

Color of the day: Ivory
Incense of the day: Narcissus

Sweet Dreams Pillow Spell

For restful sleep and to dispel nightmares, place a small amethyst stone and a small sprig of rosemary inside your pillowcase. If desired, add a few drops of lavender or bergamot essential oil to a cotton ball and insert that as well. Say these words as you place the objects:

No nightmares plague my rest,

No disruption of my sleep.

I wake refreshed and energized

From dreams peaceful and deep.

Visualize waking from a deep, soothing sleep with memories of only the sweetest dreams.

Ember Grant

 ## August 8
Tuesday

3rd ♉

4th Quarter 6:28 am

Color of the day: Black
Incense of the day: Bayberry

Goodwill with Dill

For millennia, people have worked with dill in their magic. It's associated with love, protection, abundance, and repelling negative energy. In North America, this is about the time of year when the fragrant dill flowers turn into seeds. Many believe the seeds are the most potent form of dill, because they're concentrated and flavorful. This spell uses dill seeds to spread your goodwill to the places you visit most.

Purchase or harvest several dill seeds. Hold some in your hand and say:

With dill and goodwill,
I reap luck and no ill.

Sprinkle the dill seeds wherever you want more love, luck, and abundance in your life. That could include your shoes, your garden, your desk, and your purse or pocket. Eat a couple of seeds to ingest the benefits. You can even put them in your food for the next few days to extend the spell.

Astrea Taylor

August 9
Wednesday

4th ♉

☽ v/c 6:39 am

☽ → ♊ 9:05 am

Color of the day: Topaz
Incense of the day: Lavender

Try Something New Spell

August is the time of Lugh, the Celtic god known for his variety of skills. What have you always wanted to try but have never had the time or opportunity to do? Let Lugh bless it!

Pick one thing and block out regular time (daily or weekly) to work on it for the next three months. Before you start, perform this spell.

Gather these items:

• A yellow candle

• A small dish

• A citrine crystal

• Sunflower petals or seeds

• A small bag

• A journal and pen

Light the candle. Say:

Lugh, bless me as I learn (add skill).

Give me the strength, patience, and time to explore it.

So mote it be.

Pour a little candle wax into the dish to create a disk. Carve your initials into it. Place the wax disk, the citrine, and the sunflower petals or seeds in the bag. Keep the bag with you as you learn your new skill, and track your progress in your journal. Let the candle burn down safely.

Cerridwen Iris Shea

NOTES:

August 10
Thursday

4℞ ♊

Color of the day: White
Incense of the day: Carnation

holiday Meditation by the Sea

Holidays are what many of us work for, those days or weeks somewhere different, and many of us choose a vacation by the sea. The smell of the ocean and a changing tide when you are at the beach is wonderful. There is something different about the air near the coast, possibly because of the extra ions in the sea air. This accelerates your body's ability to absorb more oxygen, which balances your serotonin levels. It is no wonder that ancestors in the past, such as the Victorians, believed in the healing effects of being by the sea or ocean.

When we are by the sea, our senses are alive as we look at, feel, and smell all the wonderful things around us. This energy can be harnessed into positive action, and a changing tide is a great way to restore, reaffirm, or rearrange a plan, a project, or your life.

Next time you are at the sea and the tide begins to change, go down to the water's edge and dip your feet in the water and let the tide wash over your toes. Keep your hands at your sides, with palms open, and say three times:

Changing tide,

Bring about change,

Manifest dreams and rearrange.

Stand for a while in the changing tide and imagine the waves taking away your negativity attached to a project or something that you no longer want in your life. The incoming waves bring enthusiasm, energy, and determination to your chosen idea of what you truly want. Feel inspired, and when you leave the water, thank the sea for its strength and renewal of your plan.

Tudorbeth

NOTES:

August 11
Friday

4th ♊

☽ v/c 1:27 pm

☽ → ♋ 6:52 pm

Color of the day: Pink
Incense of the day: Thyme

Elemental Balance
Self-Care Working

Astrologically speaking, things are pretty relaxed right now. The planets and elements are in balance, making life a little easier than it has been for a while. Take advantage of this natural sense of balance to rejuvenate with a little R&R magic. All you need is your favorite lotion and a few minutes of mindfulness and intention.

This working is done by placing four strategic dabs of moisturizer on your body or face. Each time you apply one of these dollops of moisturizer, do so in the name of one of the elements, like this:

In the name of (element), I bless this skin and the body therein.

After you have done one for each of the four elements, proceed to rub the moisturizer into your skin and say:

In the name of Spirit, I bless this vessel and the soul within!

Devin Hunter

August 12
Saturday

4th ♋

Color of the day: Blue
Incense of the day: Pine

Elephantine Spell
for Good Fortune

It's World Elephant Day, a day dedicated to the preservation of these majestic animals and their habitats. Elephants really are wonderful creatures and are revered in many cultures as symbols of wisdom, strength, protection, and good luck. They are also seen as harbingers of good fortune.

Today, in honor of the elephant, and perhaps to attract a bit of good fortune, place an image of an elephant near your main entry to welcome the blessings of good fortune into your home. Alternatively, you can invite the spirit of the elephant to bring good fortune to your career by placing one on or near your desk.

The best magic involves reciprocity, however, and we often get back what we put into the world. So consider making an offering in the form of a donation to an organization that is assisting the effort to protect these creatures and preserve their habitats. This is magic that benefits both you and the beloved elephant!

Blake Octavian Blair

August 13
Sunday

4th ♋

Color of the day: Gold
Incense of the day: Almond

Left handers Day

International Left Handers Day is observed annually on August 13 to celebrate the uniqueness of left-handed individuals. In my family, left-handedness is inherited, from my father to my sister to her son. As being left-handed was long thought to be a sign of evil or bad luck, for hundreds of years left-handed children were often punished to drive out the devil. My father did not have to endure beatings, but he was forced to learn to write with his right hand. However, writing was the only thing he changed; he played sports left-handed, including bowling, golf, and softball. Now one can find many items created specifically for left-handers, scissors being one example. I cannot use my sister's scissors; they just do not work for a right-hander.

Take a moment today to honor the diversity of left-handers. Celebrate the unique qualities of everyone in your immediate and extended family with a short, personal blessing.

Emyme

NOTES:

August 14
Monday

4th ♋

☽ v/c 3:46 am

☽ → ♌ 6:36 am

Color of the day: White
Incense of the day: Lily

Enchanted Extracts

When it comes to baking, many recipes call for various flavor extracts. Some popular ones are vanilla, mint, and lemon. Like essential oils, extracts contain the magical properties of the plants they're derived from. If you enjoy baking, consider the magical properties of the different extracts in your pantry. As you add them to your treats, be sure to acknowledge the energy being stirred in that will spread to all who eat them.

Mint: Attracts prosperity and health and wards off evil

Cherry: Increases physical attraction and sexuality

Vanilla: Promotes love and tenderness

Lemon: Used for cleansing, purification, and clearheadedness

Almond: Brings success and wisdom

Try empowering your extracts ahead of time, so that when you bake with them they're ready to go. When you realize that these extracts contain the power of the plants they come from, the door to creative kitchen witchery opens!

Kate Freuler

NOTES:

August 15
Tuesday

4th ♌

Color of the day: Red
Incense of the day: Ylang-ylang

A Lion's heart within the Tiger's Eye

The heart of a lion is a tough quality of leadership. Standing up for others and doing what we know is right means facing the fear of being beaten back for holding a line of integrity. Leadership when it is in self-less service to the greater good is one of the most charming and admirable aspects of a willing hero.

This spell is designed to help you lead by example and requires that you find an elder to place a heart-shaped tiger's-eye charm in a secret location, which you must discover using question-and-answer riddles.

The elder you pick should want to have fun with puns and wordplay, set a challenge, or map a physical hike for you. In retrieving the charm, solving the riddles, or following your elder, you will earn self-respect and delight someone you look up to with a fun game of wits. Take a moment today and let someone you admire and respect help you feel inspired as you prove to yourself that love is the law of the lion's heart; the tiger's-eye surely sees you.

Estha McNevin

 August 16
Wednesday

4th ♌
☽ v/c 5:38 am
New Moon 5:38 am
☽ → ♍ 7:14 pm

Color of the day: Yellow
Incense of the day: Marjoram

Release the Past New Moon Spell

The new moon is a great time of the month to set new intentions and release past energies. New moons are like an energetic threshold: out with the old and in with the new. You can use the new moon energy and burn sage or incense (whatever you have on hand) to cleanse your living space and help usher in a new meaningful phase in your life. If you don't have access to these magical supplies, remember that the most powerful component of any spell is always you. You can close your eyes and visualize the smoke dancing in the air. Once you have decided what you need to leave behind, chant these words:

I burn this sage/incense to release the past. The situation I experienced was not meant to last.

Please help clear the way for a new path for me. As I will it, so mote it be!

Sapphire Moonbeam

August 17
Thursday

1st ♍

Color of the day: Crimson
Incense of the day: Jasmine

Self-Love Affirmation Spell

Most of us need a little help with self-love now and again. This spell helps bring awareness to just how amazing we are so that we can love ourselves without reservation. You will need a pink or white candle in a candleholder, rose oil, a rose quartz, and a mirror.

Before the spell, cleanse yourself in whatever way works for you, then anoint yourself and the candle with rose oil. Light the candle and set it safely in front of your mirror. Turn off any lights in the room so you can only see yourself in the candlelight. Stand in front of the mirror and look yourself over from head to toe, placing the rose quartz on each body part as a blessing. Finish the spell by saying something you love or appreciate about your body while looking at yourself in the mirror. Extinguish your candle when finished.

Amanda Lynn & Jason Mankey

August 18
Friday

1st ♍

Color of the day: White
Incense of the day: Violet

The King's Gold Door Wash

During Leo season, it's a perfect time to call upon financial abundance fit for royalty. It's ideal to perform this spell during the planetary hour of the Sun while there's still daylight out if you want to enhance it even more. This spell is a door wash designed to wash away financial hardships and draw in financial abundance and prosperity. In a bucket, combine these ingredients:

- Castile soap (Peppermint scented is ideal.)
- 5 drops bay essential oil
- 5 drops frankincense essential oil
- 5 drops peppermint essential oil
- 5 drops lemon essential oil

Fill the bucket with warm water. Now wash your front door on both sides, including the door handle and, if you have one, the door knocker. Focus on your intent of washing away your financial hardships and replacing them with an attraction of financial abundance. While washing, chant the following spell:

By golden mane and lion's crown,

An abundance of money to go around.

To cover my needs and then some more,

Prosperity always flowing to my door.

Mat Auryn

NOTES:

August 19
Saturday

1st ♍

☽ v/c 4:51 am

☽ → ♎ 7:53 am

Color of the day: Brown
Incense of the day: Rue

Back to School Spell

It's back to school time, which can give anyone the jitters. This spell will cleanse your aura and give you the confidence to succeed. You'll need an herb bundle and a feather. Begin by crumbling about a tablespoon of the herb bundle into a heatproof container, and safely ignite it. It'll probably just smolder. Using the feather, fan the smoke about you. Visualize yourself as calm and confident. Think of this image when you go off to school. When the herb ashes cool, scatter them on the ground.

James Kambos

August 20
Sunday

1st ♎

Color of the day: Amber
Incense of the day: Frankincense

Venerating Trailblazing Women

Today is the anniversary of the 2012 death of comedian Phyllis Diller, one of the first female stand-up comedians who was known for her rather rambunctious personality. Today, let us celebrate women in historically male-dominated professions who have broken boundaries and trail-blazed a path to success for future generations. We all owe them a great deal.

Gather a yellow candle in a holder and a pen and paper. Make a list of female trailblazers who have made a difference in your life, your line of work, your faith, your hobbies, or in any area of your life. Then light the yellow candle in honor of the inspiration these women have provided, read your list, and thank them for all they've done. Place the list under the candle, and supervise it until it burns out. Blessed be.

Blake Octavian Blair

August 21
Monday

1st ♎

☽ v/c 4:31 pm
☽ → ♏ 7:22 pm

Color of the day: Lavender
Incense of the day: Clary sage

The End: A Binding Spell

I'm a recovering addict, and the last day I got high was August 21, 1990. Every year I call to mind the dirty, gritty, and hopeless reality of my last using day so that I am regularly in touch with the pain that led me into recovery. Use this binding spell to bring things to an end. You need a pen, paper, and a string.

Sit quietly. What do you want to end? Write it on the paper. Say:

I call your name, I know your game. I no longer want to play.

Fold the paper and say:

Out of sight, you cannot fight. Away you now will stay.

Tie the string around the paper, wrapping it around and around, and say:

Around and around, you now are bound, and you will stay that way.

Tie the ends of the string in a knot and say:

A knot of one and now you're done. You shall forever stay away.

Dallas Jennifer Cobb

 August 22
Tuesday

1st ♏

Color of the day: Scarlet
Incense of the day: Geranium

Grace, Power, and Mystery

Today, the moon is in Scorpio and the sun is at the very end of its yearly journey through the sign of Leo, poised to enter the sign of Virgo tomorrow. This combination of energies creates the perfect environment for a spell to enhance your own allure, abilities, and inner strength.

For this spell you'll need a mirror and your favorite incense. Choose whatever scent makes you feel powerful. Settle in front of the mirror, positioning it so you can look into your own eyes. Light the incense so the smoke drifts in front of the mirror. Gaze into your eyes in the mirror and envision yourself filled with strength, calm, and a mysterious aura. Build this feeling, and when it's at its peak, say:

Power, mystery, and grace found within pour through my gaze.

Those whose eyes are caught by mine, new strength and allure they shall find.

Michael Furie

August 23
Wednesday

1st ♏

☉ → ♍ 5:01 am

Color of the day: White
Incense of the day: Lilac

Malachite Money Spell

For this spell you'll need a small piece of malachite, a dollar bill, and prosperity water. To create prosperity water, add three drops each of orange, lemongrass, bergamot, and frankincense essential oils to one cup of spring water. Use this water to cleanse and charge the malachite. As you sprinkle the stone with the water, visualize all the wealth you need coming to you. Next, wrap the malachite in a dollar bill as you say these words:

Money, money, come to me,

For good of all, so mote it be.

You may wish to tie a green string around the dollar bill to keep it closed. Carry this talisman with you in your pocket, purse, or wallet for as long as you desire. You may wish to recharge it periodically by sprinkling it with the prosperity water.

Ember Grant

August 24
Thursday

1st ♏

☽ v/c 1:10 am

☽ → ♐ 4:07 am

2nd Quarter 5:57 am

Color of the day: Turquoise
Incense of the day: Myrrh

Lavender Salt Bowl

Lavender blossoms and salt come together in this elegant, cleansing salt bowl. Salt neutralizes negativity, and lavender flowers promote restoration. It's the perfect place to charge and cleanse items (except for metal, which rusts).

Gather these materials:

- A bowl
- Sea salt
- Epsom salt
- Baking soda
- Lavender blossoms
- A crystal

Choose a bowl that looks attractive with the other colors, and set it on your altar. Add the sea salt, then the other salts. Sprinkle the lavender blossoms on top, and then stir them widdershins (counterclockwise) with your dominant finger.

When the bowl appears to be well mixed, place both of your hands on the bowl and say:

*Lavender and salt, I charge
you to cleanse and charge the
items I place within you.*

Now put it to use. Test the bowl by placing a crystal within it. It should feel cleansed and charged within a day or so.

Astrea Taylor

NOTES:

August 25
Friday

2nd ♐

Color of the day: Purple
Incense of the day: Vanilla

Fairy Bread Fertilizer

For crofters in Scotland, soil repair is a point of cultural pride. From peat roofs to cow patty logs, the farmer feeds the earth near as much as the animals in the northern climates.

Over the centuries, this idea of feeding the soil has evolved into many recipes for fairy bread. Left out in late summer to entice the fairies to return next spring, this sweet promise offers the earth spirits the seeds and bulbs within. Fairy bread is fun to make and easy to pack into fun shapes for gifting. You will need:

- 12 cups mud
- 1 cup wildflower seeds
- 3 tablespoons molasses
- 3 tablespoons Shaggy Mane mushroom spores
- 12 crocus bulbs

Mix everything but the bulbs in a large bucket, then pack more mud around the bulbs in a ball or press them into silicone craft molds and garnish them with spores, clay, or sand. Finally, let them dry for one week and then plant or gift them.

Estha McNevin

August 26
Saturday

2nd ♐

☽ v/c 7:56 am
☽ → ♑ 9:05 am

Color of the day: Blue
Incense of the day: Ivy

Carpet of Calm

This spell can be done anytime and anywhere you need a few minutes of peace in a chaotic day. It also works if you have disruptive neighbors, especially on a floor above or below you.

Follow your breath. Close your eyes if it is safe so to do.

Imagine beneath you a thick, pale blue carpet infused with calming vibrations. Steep yourself in the calm. Let your muscles relax, your head clear, and your breath flow.

Imagine the calm energy of the carpet flowing through and over the chaos below and around you, and all of it quieting down.

Notice how the chaos is muffled, slows, and then stops.

Take a deep breath, exhale, open your eyes, and return to your day.

Cerridwen Iris Shea

August 27
Sunday

2nd ♑

Color of the day: Yellow
Incense of the day: Juniper

Aurora Australis Enchantment

The *aurora australis* is the southern lights found in the Southern Hemisphere, similar to the *aurora borealis* of the Northern Hemisphere. And just like their Nordic cousins, the southern lights look like multicoloured angel wings streaking across the sky. The *aurora australis* is best seen in August and September, around the time of the spring equinox, which in the north would be Mabon or the autumnal equinox. These amazing lights bring the potential for creativity and signify individuality. They show us the beauty and fragility of us all and help to remind us that we are here for such a short time, just like the lights of the *aurora australis*.

If you want the lights to appear and you are under southern skies, cast a spell of appearance and ask them to appear. Due to the rarity of the lights, it is a great time to do magic and spellwork, as anything in magic that is a one-off or once-in-a-lifetime event brings such power to it that the energy can be harnessed and stored for future work. Capture this energy by simply drawing it into some salt and/or water in a bowl underneath the rare celestial event.

Here is an appearance spell for the *aurora australis*. Go outside at twilight and raise your hands to the sky, forming a Y shape with your arms and body, and say:

Blessed lights of southern skies,

Appear to me before my eyes.

Upon this night and for a week,

Shine your beauty for all to seek.

Afterward, meditate for a while and imagine the lights streaking across the sky. When they do appear, remember to harness all that energy.

Tudorbeth

August 28
Monday

2nd ♑

☽ v/c 7:49 am

☽ → ♒ 10:32 am

Color of the day: Silver

Incense of the day: Rosemary

Mother Earth Balance Spell

Sometimes there are moments or events in our lives that can throw us completely off balance. When life throws you a curve, this is a time to reconnect with the core of your being. If you want to feel more grounded, consider doing this spell.

Find a place to sit comfortably on the ground. Place your hands on the earth. Take a moment, close your eyes, and imagine your hands and your personal energy radiating into the ground. Visualize your hands connecting with the nurturing heartbeat of Mother Earth. In order to focus this energy, chant these words:

I send my energy into the ground, where the stability of the earth can be found.

Restore my balance, bring peace to me. As I will it, so mote it be!

Spend time connecting with Mother Earth anytime you need to integrate more harmony into your spirit.

Sapphire Moonbeam

NOTES:

August 29
Tuesday

2nd ♒

☽ v/c 11:04 pm

Color of the day: Gray
Incense of the day: Ginger

Retrograde Remedy Spell

As you may have noticed, Mercury is retrograde right now in Virgo, a sign it rules. This means that this particular retrograde period is likely to be more problematic than others. Have no fear—we have you covered!

To help counteract the potential negative influences brought on by this retrograde, make this special incense blend. Combine and powder equal parts of copal, rosemary, and lavender. Burn a little over charcoal each morning during the retrograde (August 23 to September 15) to soothe any disturbances or mercurial upsets.

Devin Hunter

August 30
Wednesday

2nd ♒

☽ → ♓ 9:56 am

Full Moon 9:36 pm

Color of the day: Topaz
Incense of the day: Honeysuckle

Once in a Blue Moon

When we cleanse and charge our magickal tools, we often focus on the ones we use the most. But what about the other tools we use? For instance, maybe there's a special kitchen knife you use in your spellwork, or perhaps you have a statue where you leave offerings. The rarity of a blue moon is a good time to think about those other tools and give them a jolt of lunar energy.

Start by thinking about some of the more nontraditional and overlooked tools you use in your spellwork. Gather those up and place them on a clean cloth either outside (if the weather is nice) or inside near a window with access to moonlight. As you lay out your items, speak over them with the intention that the moon will cleanse and charge them for your upcoming magical workings:

Fill this tool (or item) up with lunar energy and the first stirrings of autumn. So mote it be!

Leave your items in the light of the moon until morning.

Amanda Lynn & Jason Mankey

August 31
Thursday

3rd ♓

Color of the day: Green
Incense of the day: Nutmeg

No-Nonsense Purification Bath

Fragrant and luxurious baths have become popular in the witchcraft world, but ritual baths aren't always pretty, colorful, and smelling of flowers. Sometimes a ritual bath is a major cleansing of bad energy, and for that, you need to take serious measures.

This cleansing bath is not your average flowery concoction. The ingredients are chosen for their protective and cleansing properties over their scent, to scare away whatever plagues you. (Please note that if you have plant allergies or skin sensitivities, this spell might not be right for you. Proceed with caution.)

Materials:

- 4 cloves garlic
- 3 drops clove oil
- 3 whole dandelion roots
- 3 tablespoons salt
- 1 handful goutweed

Make the bath as hot as you can comfortably submerge yourself in. Put the ingredients in the water. Notice the weedy, pungent scents and how they act as a deterrent. As you sit in the tub, imagine that the water is drawing all the negativity from you. This might look like bugs crawling out of your body, drowning, and disappearing into the water.

When the bath starts to cool, drain the tub. (To avoid clogging, place a drain strainer over the drain. These are available at most dollar stores.) Rinse yourself thoroughly with fresh water from the shower to complete the ritual.

If you don't have a tub, you can make this brew in a bowl or pitcher. Let it cool to a safe temperature, then stand in the shower while pouring it over your head. Rinse off afterward.

Kate Freuler

September

The equinox happens toward the end of this month, heralding the beginning of autumn in the Northern Hemisphere and the start of spring in the Southern Hemisphere. An equinox happens when the sun crosses the celestial equator, an imaginary line in the sky not unlike our Earth's own equator. It's on the equinox that the sun rises due east and sets due west. This is why people often go to famous landmarks to watch the rising or setting of the sun on the equinoxes and solstices. In our ever-changing world, it's nice to know there are at least some constants!

Astrologically, the autumnal equinox is when the sun sign of Libra begins. It's fitting, as this is the time when day and night are of equal length, and Libra is the sign of the scales. The full moon that corresponds with this event is called the Harvest Moon or the Corn Moon. The few days around the equinox and the full moon bring a period in which everything is ripening and full of energy. It all seems to be coming into fullness, preparing either for the coming of winter or the start of the growing season.

Charlie Rainbow Wolf

September 1
Friday

3rd ♓

☽ v/c 6:36 am

☽ → ♈ 9:25 am

Color of the day: Pink
Incense of the day: Cypress

Void-of-Course Curse Removal

Don't panic! You aren't experiencing a disconnect. The Moon is just void-of-course for a while this morning, and Mercury is still retrograde. Our magic is likely to feel a little off, and the energy we intuitively sense in magic can be unreliable at this time. However, workings related to the removal of curses benefit from this chaotic breakdown of normally stable energy. Perform this working if you feel you have been cursed or jinxed.

Combine one cup of salt with one large pinch each of thyme, mint, and bay leaf. Mix well, then lay a line of it on the ground, going north to south. Standing with the line to your left shoulder, say:

I can cross the line, but you can't follow.
All your power's gone and hollow!

Then hop over the line and immediately say:

So must it be, for the good
of all but mostly for me!

Sweep up the salt mixture and throw it away.

Devin Hunter

September 2
Saturday

3rd ♈

Color of the day: Indigo
Incense of the day: Magnolia

Healing Spell for Relationships

Often in life we experience heartache and regret over a lost relationship—not only romantic breakups, but friendships that have become distant due to gradually losing touch over time. If you have a relationship you'd like to rekindle or heal, begin by meditating on the reason for the distance between the two of you. Light a pink or white candle and place a rose quartz stone beside it. Visualize the light filling the stone and turning it into a beacon for the person you intend to reach. Say these words:

We may have gone our separate ways
And haven't talked for many days;
But if there's hope that we can mend,
Let's find a way to meet again.

Allow the candle to burn out safely. Keep the rose quartz on a windowsill for as long as you wish, sending your call to the intended recipient.

Ember Grant

September 3
Sunday

3rd ♈

☽ v/c 7:57 am

☽ → ♉ 11:00 am

Color of the day: Amber
Incense of the day: Hyacinth

Lucky Lunch Box Kabbalah

If you are ready to explore Pagan history and culture daily, begin to deepen your habits and routines to include tarot and Kabbalah. This afternoon, embellish your lunch box. Draw the key code of the Tree of Life either as spheres with twenty-two paths, a cube with its many cards, or a verdant tree with great roots. Hand-draw or paste this image inside your lunch box and begin using your lunchtime as a portal of mystic nourishment.

Not only will the images and geometry of the Tree of Life bless the food you place inside the box, but each time you open it you will be reimagining and reexperiencing the expansive cube of space, that mystic experience for which the Tree is the root code. Picking a tarot card for the day or committing a Kabbalistic tarot deck to use along with your lunch box will yield profound results even in the most mundane of places. In joy we learn.

Estha McNevin

September 4
Monday

3rd ♉

Color of the day: Gray
Incense of the day: Hyssop

Labor Day (US) – Labour Day (Canada)

A Blessing for Fair Labor

Today is Labor Day in the United States and Canada, a day to honor workers and all the good that has been gained from labor movements and trade unions. Today, dedicate some time to remember and honor the hardworking people who have fought to achieve these accomplishments and also some time for rest and relaxation. Even if you must work today, you owe it to yourself to set aside even a few quiet moments for this simple bit of celebration.

Find a quiet place where you can have a few moments to yourself. Contemplate those who came before you, the efforts you are making in the present day, and your hopes for future generations. Then recite a blessing such as the following:

A blessing on those who work for fair labor.

To look out for each other is only being a good neighbor.

May we rest and rejuvenate so as to do our work in good favor.

So mote it be.

Blake Octavian Blair

NOTES:

September 5
Tuesday

3rd ♉

☽ v/c 12:46 pm

☽ → ♊ 4:07 pm

Color of the day: Black

Incense of the day: Cedar

A Time to Settle Accounts

Now in September, the fingers of dusk draw across the land earlier in the day. You know the season has turned toward autumn and closure. It's time to settle accounts. It's time to assess where we are in life and where we're going.

Tonight, take time to decide on your goals and hopes. To do this, create some quiet time. Sit by a window at dusk, and have a pen and paper with you. Focus on the mellow light of dusk creeping in. Think of what you've accomplished this year. What do you still want to do? Begin to write a list of your hopes and concerns, then cross off anything that you feel is unrealistic. What is left on your list? Concentrate on these goals. Lay the list on your altar. Over the next few days, read your list. Now begin a practical plan to make them happen.

James Kambos

September 6
Wednesday

3rd ♊

4th Quarter 6:21 pm

Color of the day: White

Incense of the day: Lilac

Spell for a Broken Heart

Goldenrod, a common plant that grows wild in many areas, is also called woundwort due to its healing properties. It makes sense that a plant with so much healing power can also help mend a broken heart.

Materials:

- A small heart-shaped container
- Enough goldenrod flowers to fill the container
- A blue cloth

Pack the container with goldenrod, noting that the empty heart is now filled with warmth and healing yellow flowers. Say:

Goldenrod flowers, heal the cracks in my broken heart.

Woundwort, fill my heart with vitality.

Wrap the heart in the blue cloth and keep it under your bed or pillow. If you are allergic to goldenrod, you can place the charm safely outdoors. Once you begin to feel better, dispose of the goldenrod and reuse the materials if you wish.

Kate Freuler

 September 7
Thursday

4th ♊
☽ v/c 6:22 pm

Color of the day: Purple
Incense of the day: Carnation

Candle Spell for Clarity

The stresses of modern living can make the outside world and everyday activities difficult to manage, especially if we find ourselves needing to focus on something specific. This spell is designed to clear the mind and provide a moment of clarity.

Etch an eye into the center of a pillar, chime, or taper candle, and then anoint with the cleansing oil of your choice. (We recommend diluted peppermint or rosemary oil.) Before lighting the candle, hold it before your nose and inhale the fragrance, allowing the scents to open up your mind. Bring the candle to your third eye and make sure the etched eye is placed on your forehead. With your eyes closed, say aloud your intention regarding clarity and focus.

When you feel the candle has been properly charged, set it down and light it. Let the candle burn for as long as you need until your mind is clear and your focus is sharp. Extinguish the candle and repeat the spell as necessary.

Amanda Lynn & Jason Mankey

 September 8
Friday

4th ♊
☽ → ♋ 1:00 am

Color of the day: Coral
Incense of the day: Alder

Calm Over Chaos Bottle Spell

With the moon in Cancer today, you have a greater connection with your emotions. This bottle spell takes advantage of that energy to help you rise above chaotic feelings and choose calmness (when it's appropriate).

You will need a bottle with a cap, a marker, some moon water, an amethyst, some copal, some lavender oil, and some hops. Set the bottle on your altar. Write "Calm" on the bottle, and add the ingredients one at a time. For each one, say:

May this help me choose
calm over chaos.

When you've added all of the ingredients, cap the bottle. Tip it gently from side to side while feeling your inner calmness. Once you've felt that, shake the bottle roughly. Can you still find your inner calm even when the waters are turbulent? Sometimes you have a choice, even in chaotic circumstances. Whenever you want to choose your emotions more wisely, shake the bottle and find your inner calm.

Astrea Taylor

September 9
Saturday

4th ♋

Color of the day: Blue
Incense of the day: Patchouli

Letting Go of the Past

If there's something from the past that you're struggling to release, using magic to achieve that goal can be helpful. You'll need a piece of paper, a pen, a cauldron or heatproof bowl, a black candle, and some powdered slippery elm.

To begin, write a letter to yourself explaining exactly what you wish to let go of, as if you were your own wise elder or guide. Allow yourself to gain a new perspective on your past, showing yourself the compassion that you may normally reserve for others. Light the candle and read the letter. When done, burn the letter in the cauldron. Sprinkle the slippery elm on the ashes and say:

What's done is done, but
these ties no longer bind.

The power fades and new
freedom and peace I find.

For good of all, including me,
as I will so shall it be.

Extinguish the candle and flush the ashes down the toilet.

Michael Furie

 September 10
Sunday

4th ♋
☽ v/c 8:47 am
☽ → ♌ 12:36 pm

Color of the day: Gold
Incense of the day: Frankincense

Grandparents' Day

The first Sunday after Labor Day is Grandparents' Day here in the United States. Choose this day to honor any and all grandparents, great-grandparents, and ancestors. Take them out to lunch or dinner, or invite them over to your home for the same. Go through old pictures while you can and write down the names of everyone in each photo and what was happening at the time. Makes copies of the photos and the stories and create books for relatives. When the people have passed, their tales will go with them, so gather your family lore while you can. Incant:

We wish you love, light, and
longevity. Share with us the
knowledge of the past.

Emyme

September 11
Monday

4th ♌

Color of the day: White
Incense of the day: Lily

Psychic Attack Frankincense Bath Soak

September 11, 2001, was a day when the world held its breath and watched events unfolding in New York. The internet was still in its infancy, and I remember getting my first home computer that day and I couldn't get online. It was only later in the evening that I learned what had happened.

Many practitioners reached for the frankincense that day, as this is one of the most sacred oils and is used in many cleansing, anointing, remembering, and protection rituals. It is used as an offering to the gods and goddesses at certain times of the year. However, it can also be used for spells concerning clairvoyance and divination.

Further, frankincense is good for protection magic, both for family and loved ones and also for work and career. It is particularly beneficial if you have been under psychic attack and need rebalancing or have been involved with negative and toxic people. The antiseptic qualities of frankincense cleanse and release the toxic residue buildup mentally, physically, and spiritually.

Frankincense is probably one of the oldest goods ever traded. This aromatic compound was used from ancient times as incense in India and China and in Christian worship. The ancient Egyptians used it to prepare rejuvenating face masks. However, it was also used in food, especially desserts such as frankincense ice cream, Turkish delight, and hard-boiled sweets. (Never use undiluted pure essential oil in food, and always check the label.)

If you think you have been under psychic attack, then create a frankincense bath soak with Epsom salts. Using a mortar and pestle, crush together one tablespoon of frankincense with five tablespoons of Epsom salts. Place in a sealable glass jar and label it. Add a scoop of the mixture to a bath or foot soak. Psychic attack can happen at any time and to anyone, and generally the victim will feel tired and weak. If symptoms persist, seek a doctor's advice.

Tudorbeth

September 12
Tuesday

4th ♌

☽ v/c 11:06 am

Color of the day: Maroon
Incense of the day: Basil

Healing Bath

With the Sun in Virgo, the sign of the healer, and with Mercury, its ruling planet, also in Virgo, this is a great time for spells related to healing and well-being. Here is one of my favorite healing bath salt recipes.

In a bowl, mix:

- 1 ½ cups Epsom salt
- 1 ½ cups coarse sea salt

Then add these oils:

- 2 drops lemon essential oil
- 3 drops rosemary essential oil
- 3 drops peppermint essential oil
- 6 drops lavender essential oil
- 6 drops eucalyptus essential oil

Stir the mixture together thoroughly while saying:

Like the spinning of a wheel,

I stir in powers that can heal.

Store the salt in a small Mason jar. When you're ready to take your bath, add a handful or two of the salt to the tub water and say:

I conjure forth a bath of healing

To improve how I am feeling.

Soak in the tub, and when you are done, drain the water while chanting:

I wash away all the pain

As it goes down the drain.

Mat Auryn

NOTES:

September 13
Wednesday

4th ♌

☽ → ♍ 1:18 am

Color of the day: Yellow
Incense of the day: Marjoram

Nature Peace Wind Spell

When life feels overwhelming, you might be having trouble processing stressful, worrisome thoughts. This peace wind spell can help. Allow yourself time for some self-care and consider going on a nature walk. Nature restores us and helps us get back on a more grounded spiritual path.

Visit a park or nature preserve away from the sounds of the city. If you can, go to an area that has a lot of trees. Find a comfortable place to sit and tune in to the sights and sounds of the forest. This simple chant can help you connect with the universe and work on releasing your troubling thoughts:

Help me release my thoughts
with ease as the wind blows the
leaves high up in the trees.

May my overwhelming thoughts begin
to cease. Help me regain harmony
and restore my inner peace.

Sapphire Moonbeam

 September 14
Thursday

4th ♍

New Moon 9:40 pm

Color of the day: Green
Incense of the day: Basil

New Moon Chalkboard Spell

New moons are great for fresh starts, and a chalkboard spell is a fun way to get going.

You will need:

- A small, inexpensive chalkboard
- Colored chalk
- An intention for the moon cycle

Bless your chalkboard using your breath. Exhale on it, saying:

I bless and consecrate this
as my intention board.

With the chalk, write your intention at the top of the board. Beneath it, make a simple line drawing of your intention. Beneath the drawing, list three actionable steps you will take during this moon cycle to fulfill your intention.

Set the board where you will see it every day. As you complete each step, put a checkmark beside it on the list. (Do not cross it out.)

At the next dark moon, give thanks and erase everything on the board so it's fresh for something new, or keep working on this intention.

Cerridwen Iris Shea

September 15
Friday

1st ♍

☽ v/c 9:49 am

☽ → ♎ 1:44 pm

Color of the day: Rose
Incense of the day: Yarrow

Rosh hashanah begins at sundown

Sweet Celebration

Rosh Hashanah, the celebration of the Jewish new year, begins today at sundown. This is a time for feasting and celebration, a time to look back at the year past and to look forward to the year ahead. Traditionally, sweet foods are consumed at Rosh Hashanah, because they help to usher in a sweet, productive, and abundant new year. Make this simple, traditional food to mark this day and bring sweetness to your life.

Core and slice crisp, tart apples. Prepare a small bowl of honey. Dip the apples in the honey, thinking about how sweet life is and how many good things there are in store for you this new year. With each dip, bring more oozing sweetness to your life.

L'Shana Tova. Happy New Year.

Dallas Jennifer Cobb

September 16
Saturday

1st ♎

Color of the day: Black
Incense of the day: Sandalwood

hand-Washing Protection Spell

Paying attention to cleanliness has become even more important in recent years. Use this spell each time you wash your hands as an extra layer of protection. Visualize yourself being protected as you say these words:

As I wash my hands with care,

Let me always be aware.

Guard me with a magic shield.

If I'm harmed, be quick to heal.

Wash me clean and keep me well.

With this act I cast the spell.

Ember Grant

September 17
Sunday

1st ♎︎

☽ v/c 9:06 pm

Color of the day: Yellow
Incense of the day: Heliotrope

Athena Organization Working

Both the Sun and Mercury are traveling through Virgo now, making magic related to organization a breeze! Appeal to the goddess Athena for help in tackling big organizational projects, and ask for her guidance when searching for systems that will facilitate these changes for the long term. Here is a working that will do just that, and all you need are some fresh flowers, a black pen, a 3-by-3-inch white piece of paper, a lighter, and a fireproof dish.

After offering fresh flowers to Athena, draw a simple owl on your piece of paper. On the other side of the paper, write your request for assistance to Athena and then say:

Mighty Athena, great goddess of wisdom and skill, I beseech you to aid me as I climb this hill. Hear my plea and be my guide; impart your grace as I turn the tide.

Then burn the paper in a fireproof dish. Work on organizing each day, and once you are finished, make another offering of fresh flowers.

Devin Hunter

September 18
Monday

1st ♎︎

☽ → ♏︎ 12:58 am

Color of the day: Silver
Incense of the day: Clary sage

Moon Tarot Mysteries Revealed

In the major arcana of the tarot, the eighteenth card is the Moon. This card signifies mysteries, hidden meanings, secrets, and sometimes even deceptions. It's a great card to focus on when trying to figure out a mystery in your life.

Take the Moon card from your favorite tarot deck and place it on the center of your altar. Position yourself so you can look at the card comfortably for an extended period. As you look at the card, think about a situation you are experiencing that might not be what it seems or that you feel has some mystery behind it. Close your eyes and feel the energy of the Moon card radiate out toward you. When the energy hits you, ask for the mystery you've been thinking of to be revealed. You should then see the answer in your mind's eye.

Amanda Lynn & Jason Mankey

September 19
Tuesday

1st ♏

Color of the day: Red
Incense of the day: Ylang-ylang

Leaf Punch Craft

Hearth charms like punched leaves can help us bring warmth and joy into the home as we learn dot matrix art and balancing magick this season. Punching shapes is the first step in learning other crafts like embroidery. Looking at the holes we punch, we let the light in through all those seemingly unrelated imperfections. The bigger picture always reveals a theme, and crafting with leaves is fun when we employ Pagan, planetary, and zodiac images.

All you need is a few freshly fallen leaves and an embroidery needle. Poke holes in oak and maple leaves in patterns that are meaningful to you and reflective of your hopes and goals. You can keep the leaves between the pages of a book or two sheets of glass for later use, although the best use of punched leaves is to weave them into seasonal decor or craft them into paper lanterns and eventually burn them during Samhain season.

Estha McNevin

September 20
Wednesday

1st ♏

☽ v/c 6:21 am
☽ → ♐ 10:06 am

Color of the day: Topaz
Incense of the day: Lavender

A Kitchen Protection Spell

This spell will protect the heart of the home: the kitchen. You'll need a few drops of olive oil and some sprigs of basil. First, dab the tip of a finger with the olive oil. Bless each kitchen appliance with the oil. You may trace a holy symbol (such as a pentagram or a cross) on each appliance. Next, rinse the basil sprigs in water. While they're still wet, shake a few drops of water in each corner of the kitchen. Shake a few drops in front of all kitchen windows and doors, too. This seals the room with protection. End the ritual by saying:

> I protect my kitchen, every
> tool, every pot.
>
> I protect every appliance,
> those that chill
>
> And those that keep my
> food nice and hot!

You may enhance the spell by cooking with the basil or drying it for later use.

James Kambos

September 21
Thursday

1st ♐

Color of the day: Turquoise
Incense of the day: Mulberry

UN International Day of Peace

Compassion for the Naysayers

Some people do not like it when you surpass their expectations of you. Perhaps you get a part in the play, win the lottery, win at love, get a promotion, and so on. These are the people who find fault with your achievement or ignore it, or maybe even no longer speak to you, only about you.

Do not let their reactions take the shine off your achievements. Bowing to such pressure can only diminish you. Instead, this is a time to be compassionate. Yes, reject the hurt and privately offer up positive energy for the naysayers. Say or think a specific sentence articulating your wish. Concentrate on that as often as you feel the need, then go about accepting that award, make plans for the lottery win, or enjoy the promotion, all with a light heart.

Emyme

 September 22
Friday

1st ♐
☽ v/c 3:32 pm
2nd Quarter 3:32 pm
☽ → ♑ 4:20 pm

Color of the day: Purple
Incense of the day: Rose

Coffee Potion for Love

This sweet and slightly spicy cup of coffee is filled with not only the flavors of the unfolding season but also the magical energy of love.

You will need:

• A coffee cup

• 1 tablespoon pure maple syrup

• ⅛ teaspoon cinnamon

• 1 cup freshly brewed coffee

• Milk or creamer, to taste (optional)

Spoon the maple syrup into an empty coffee cup and stir in the cinnamon. Pour in the hot coffee and stir to mix. Pick up the coffee cup, and as you smell the aroma, say:

Potion of power, energy, and love,
fill me now with your magical glow;
that joy and esteem radiate from
me, attracting those whom I should
know; compatible people drawn to
me for loving adventures, blessed be.

Sip the coffee and savor the magic.

Michael Furie

September 23
Saturday

2nd ♑

☉ → ♎ 2:50 am

Color of the day: Brown
Incense of the day: Sage

Mabon – Fall Equinox

Pumpkin Spice Prosperity Spell

The equinox is an auspicious time for magick, and now that it's autumn, it's the perfect time to break out the pumpkin spice. These aromatic spices are delectable in desserts and beverages, and they're also associated with wealth, power, prosperity, and magick. This prosperity spell uses these high-powered ingredients and the ample magick available at this time of the year.

You will need a bowl, spices (cinnamon, ginger, allspice, nutmeg, and cloves), coins, honey, water (preferably sun water), and a spoon.

Combine the spices in the bowl. Smell the aromas and adjust the spices until they smell perfect. Add the coins and several drizzles of honey to the bowl. Stir everything together to coat the coins. Bury the coins outside or in a pot of soil. Level the soil, then draw a money symbol on the surface. Say:

Buried money, grow for me.
Increase my wealth and prosperity.

Water the coins and give thanks.

Astrea Taylor

 September 24
Sunday

2nd ♑

☽ v/c 4:05 pm

☽ → ♒ 7:29 pm

Color of the day: Orange
Incense of the day: Eucalyptus

Yom Kippur begins at sundown

Falling in Love with Your Life

Today the Sun is in Venus-governed Libra and Venus is in confident, fiery Leo. This is the perfect time to cast a spell to fall in love with yourself and your life, and to do so in a balanced and healthy fashion.

For this spell take a simple pink chime candle and scratch your name into the side of it with a small nail or pin. Pink is a secondary planetary color for Venus, and in one of the traditions I'm initiated into, it is the color used for the magick of healing related to self-love. Place the pink chime candle on a plate, and under the plate place a picture of yourself. Light the candle and focus on the feeling of falling in love with yourself and your life as you say:

Venusian power, glowing bright,

Internal passion I ignite.

A love of self, a lust for life,

In healthy ways and balanced right.

Extinguish the candle when done.

Mat Auryn

September 25
Monday

2nd ≈

Color of the day: Ivory
Incense of the day: Neroli

Selenite Energy Refresher

Selenite is a luminous white crystal known for simultaneously cleansing and charging any object it comes in contact with. It creates clean, fresh energy that can be clearly felt. A selenite wand is perfect for this clearing ritual.

Sit or stand somewhere private. Feel how the selenite connects with your own energy field. Pass the wand under each foot, a couple of inches away from your skin. Using a sweeping motion, move it up one leg, then the other. Notice that everywhere the selenite passes, there's a streak of pure, clean energy, like a broom sweeping up dirt. Pass the wand over your abdomen, back, chest, up both arms, over both hands, and up your neck. Pay special attention to passing it over your mouth, eyes, and ears.

Hold the crystal at the crown of your head and envision the renewed energy it has created all around and within your body. It has gathered up any vibrations that were creating imbalance. Now you can continue your day feeling refreshed.

Kate Freuler

 ## September 26
Tuesday

2nd ≈

☽ v/c 8:38 am

☽ → ♓ 8:18 pm

Color of the day: White
Incense of the day: Ginger

Pavlov's Parallel to Magic

Today is the birthday of famous Russian physiologist Ivan Pavlov, the man behind the famous "Pavlov's dog" experiments. We have a magical parallel to Pavlov's classical conditioning experiments that we can examine.

Pavlov found that whenever the dogs saw an object or witnessed an event associated with being fed, they would begin to salivate. Well, the same thing happens to us during our preparations for ritual and magic. When we establish a routine of lighting a certain incense or repeating specific opening prayers and invocations, it sends us into our magical mindset.

Today, examine if you already have any of these routines, and maybe outline them in your Book of Shadows. If you don't have any such routines, today is a good day to think about beginning to develop them.

Blake Octavian Blair

September 27
Wednesday

2nd ♓

Color of the day: Brown
Incense of the day: Bay laurel

Sighing Meditation

A sigh is a long out-breath that you can hear. Sighing can mean many things. It could be a sigh of exhaustion, a sigh of frustration, a sigh of relief, a sigh of contentment, or a sigh to relax. The magic of sighing is that it resets us physiologically and can reduce tension, stress, and irregular breathing in the body. Sighing inflates the alveoli (the little balloons in the lungs) and increases oxygen levels.

Pause for a moment and become still. Close your eyes. Be aware of how your body feels right now. Are there any aches or pains, any tightness or strain?

Take a deep breath and sigh it out. As you sigh, feel the release of all that strain.

Again, breathe deeply and sigh it out, letting go of tension and achiness.

Take one last deep breath and let out a long, loud sighing exhale.

Scan your body again and notice the difference a sigh makes.

Ahhhhhhhhhhh.

Dallas Jennifer Cobb

September 28
Thursday

2nd ♓

☽ v/c 4:58 pm

☽ → ♈ 8:17 pm

Color of the day: Green
Incense of the day: Clove

The Mask Spell

The face of the Green Man looms in trees here in the West, while in Asia the contented face of the Buddha beams across the land on temple walls. In Egypt the mystical face of Tutankhamen peers through space and time, the epitome of ancient Egypt. There is indeed something magical about all these faces—but all these faces are masks.

We like to look at these symbols, these faces of time and tradition. They bestow something upon us, and when gazing at these faces, we find peace, knowledge, and reverence. We honour the cultures and their peoples every time we look into these faces and masks, many of which have magic and myths associated with them. It is said that if you look upon the face of Tutankhamen, you will never want for anything, while gazing upon the face of the Buddha will bring you peace.

Ancient priests and tribespeople wore masks to emulate the gods. Masks serve the purpose of distancing the wearer from other people by making the wearer appear strange and mysterious. In magic itself, masks are sometimes worn to aid the invocations of the gods. However, many gods like to change themselves into different things in order to walk among their people. Zeus is one god who changed his identity many times, usually to seduce a new lover, and Odin is known as the god of identity and masks because he often changed his appearance and hid his true identity in order to walk among his subjects.

If you are wearing a mask for whatever reason, whether literally or figuratively, and you feel you are not showing your true self, then perform this spell. Sit in front of a mirror while wearing your mask and say this spell into your reflection:

This mask of mine that I must wear

Shields me from the wear and tear.

Those I love can see the truth of me.

From behind the mask, I am free.

As you sit in front of the mirror, imagine removing that mask so loved ones can see the true you. Keep your guard up when out in public by all means, but always be open and honest with those who truly care for you.

Tudorbeth

 September 29
Friday

2nd ♈

Full Moon 5:58 am

Color of the day: Pink
Incense of the day: Violet

Sukkot begins at sundown

harvest Gratitude Full Moon Spell

Over the centuries, the full moons were given many different names. The September full moon is known in some traditions as the harvest moon. This is the perfect time to harvest your gratitude.

Since this full moon occurs near the autumnal equinox in the Northern Hemisphere, you can reflect on the year, see how far you have come, and count your blessings. Finding reasons to be grateful is a good way to enhance the love in your heart. Place your dominant hand on your heart, think about what you are grateful for, and repeat these words:

On this full moon night, as the moon shines bright, I am grateful for the many blessings I have in my sight.

Harvesting gratitude for your blessings in the present moment will help shift your focus to what you have, instead of what you may think you lack. Harvest your gratitude.

Sapphire Moonbeam

 September 30
Saturday

3rd ♈

☽ v/c 5:50 pm

☽ → ♉ 9:18 pm

Color of the day: Gray
Incense of the day: Pine

Personal Eleusinian Mystery

There are conflicting tales of the content of the Eleusinian mysteries, the initiation rites held every year for the cult of Demeter and Persephone. Dates are also in dispute, although the rituals were generally thought to take place over nine days in late September.

To help you decide where you need renewal, create a personal Eleusinian mystery that begins today. You can extend and deepen it each year. You will need your journal and thirty minutes of uninterrupted time.

Follow your breath into a meditative state, going deep into your own personal cave of experience, emotion, and intuition. Find the light in your soul that burns brightly. Focus on that.

What part of you needs renewal? Think of something you want to keep, not release. What small step can you take now toward that goal?

After your meditation, write in your journal. Track your progress. Next year, take time to build on this year's work.

Cerridwen Iris Shea

October

Days that turn on a breath into rapidly waning light. Wispy, high dark clouds in an orange and turquoise sky. Bright orange pumpkins carved into beautiful art and lit from inside. The eerie music of screeching cats. These fond images of October burn at a Witch's heart, calling to her even across the seasons where she's busy setting up her tent for festival. By the time October finally arrives, Witches and other magic users have already had discussions about costumes and parties, rituals and celebrations, and we look forward with happiness to the whole month of both poignantly somber and brightly playful activities.

In Celtic Europe, our ancestors acknowledged October as the last month of the summer season, with winter officially beginning on Samhain. They carved slits in squashes to keep light in the fields so they could finish their day's work, and when the custom came to America, it eventually evolved into the tradition of carving jack-o'-lanterns. American Witches often use magical symbols to carve their pumpkins, creating beacons for their Beloved Dead. In the spirit of the turn of energies at this time, we give candy to children to ensure that they, our future, will remember the sweetness inside and be good leaders when their turn comes. May we all be so blessed.

Thuri Calafia

October 1
Sunday

3rd ♉

Color of the day: Amber
Incense of the day: Juniper

Senses Awareness

Autumn brings many changes: shortened days and longer nights, cooling temperatures, and magical changes of color and composition. Create time to get out in nature today, even if it's a walk in the park in a cityscape, and fully engage your senses in noticing change.

Today, use your senses to converse and dance with nature. With each breath, let your senses attune and notice something. Breathe.

With your eyes, see the visual changes of color, texture, density, and light patterns. Breathe.

With your ears, hear the changes to birdsong, insect sounds, the flutter of wings, and falling leaves. Breathe.

With your nose, smell the scent of autumn, decay, and endings. Breathe that in.

With your hands, gather one small item to place on your altar, such as a stone, leaf, or seedpod. When you arrive home, make a warm drink, and with your tongue, taste the delight of autumn.

Dallas Jennifer Cobb

 October 2
Monday

3rd ♉

☽ v/c 9:20 pm

Color of the day: Lavender
Incense of the day: Lily

Child Health Day

Be healthy like a child today. Plan your day like a child with nothing to do. In 2021 this date was on a Saturday, the first day of my transition from full-time employment to part-time, with nineteen days to do whatever I wanted before I started working again. I spent most of that time reading. My inner parent kept reminding my inner child of all the chores, projects, and obligations waiting for me, but my inner child ignored such ideas.

Today, indulge in anything that makes your heart as happy as a child. After your joyful day, record all the wonderful things you saw, felt, and experienced. Offer thanks for the child in you:

On this autumn day, allow my inner child to thrive. Whatever comes to mind, I will welcome it with the joy of a child.

Emyme

October 3
Tuesday

3rd ♉

☽ → ♊ 1:03 am

Color of the day: Maroon
Incense of the day: Cinnamon

Weeping Candle Spell

Fire is associated with action, destruction, and transformation. This spell calls upon these qualities of fire to burn away sadness or anger in order to transform it.

When you are feeling extremely stressed or sad, don't hold it in. Instead, find a quiet spot to do this exercise. This spell will help you release your emotions in a healthy way, allowing fire to transform them into new beginnings.

Materials:

• Salt

• 1 black candle

• A candleholder

Make a circle of salt around the candle in the holder for protection. Light the candle. Feel the heat of the fire and notice how it transforms the wick into ash and the wax into liquid and smoke. Allow your feelings to roll through your body. Bawl your eyes out, punch a pillow, even scream (into a pillow if you have neighbors!).

When you feel like you've gotten your emotions out, imagine they've accumulated in front of you in a floating bubble. Hold this invisible bubble in your hands and slowly lower it onto the candle flame. Visualize the flame gobbling up the emotions, turning them into smoke, heat, and ash. Blow out the candle, and keep it ready for next time. Throw the salt away.

Kate Freuler

NOTES:

October 4
Wednesday

3rd ♊

Color of the day: Yellow
Incense of the day: Marjoram

Education Success Spell

Education is so important, and although we may go to school and even university, we never actually stop learning. We may have to retrain for our jobs on a monthly or yearly cycle as new technology brings in new ways of doing things. We also learn at the university of life, as we are constantly learning all manner of things without even realising it. We learn life skills such as cooking and driving a car and how to file a tax return. We basically learn how to survive in the world today. So education isn't just about school or academia; it's a lifelong journey.

If there is something you have to learn and are worried about it, then cast this spell. Write down on a piece of paper in blue ink what it is you have to learn. Roll up the paper like a scroll, hold it in your right hand, and say:

100 percent is what I am aiming for,
Nothing less, nothing more.
I will work both day and night,
Until I get it all right.

Keep the paper in your hand as you meditate on your achievement. Imagine what it will feel like when you've accomplished it. Afterward, keep the paper in a safe place until you have achieved what it is you need to learn, then safely burn the paper and pat yourself on the back for completing the task.

Tudorbeth

NOTES:

October 5
Thursday

3rd ♊

☽ v/c 2:34 am

☽ → ♋ 8:32 am

Color of the day: Crimson
Incense of the day: Nutmeg

Grounding Crystal Spell

It's helpful to ground as we move toward Samhain, with the veil thinning.

For this spell you will need:

• A moss agate (earth, north)

• An amethyst (air, east)

• A sunstone (fire, south)

• A pearl or moonstone (water, west)

• Your birthstone (spirit)

• 15–30 minutes of undisturbed time

Sit facing the north, with the stones lined up so you can easily reach them. Pick up each one in turn, starting with the moss agate. Hold it cupped in your hands until you feel a connection with the stone. Place it in the corresponding direction. Hold your birthstone cupped in your hands over your heart.

Feel each stone tethering you with love to the earth. Remember this loving, stable feeling, so you can recall it when you feel unbalanced.

When you are finished, place your birthstone in front of you and ground any excess energy, placing your palms on the ground. Keep the stones on your bedside table.

Cerridwen Iris Shea

NOTES:

October 6
Friday

3rd ♋

4th Quarter 9:48 am

Color of the day: Rose
Incense of the day: Cypress

Sukkot ends

Taking Stock Meditation

In the fall we harvest and prepare for the cold months ahead. In modern times, even if we're not literally harvesting, we still need to mentally prepare ourselves for a time of rest. Use this meditation to take stock of all you've achieved so far this year. What did you sow and what are you reaping? What goals do you have for the future? Think of this as your personal inventory and write everything down: your hopes, fears, dreams, accomplishments, etc.

Fold your list into a small square and bury it. As you do so, visualize the earth keeping your list safe and secure—a promise to protect your secrets and guard your wishes and goals. See the things you fear being absorbed and no longer a source of worry. Imagine what you want to manifest growing like a seed for the future. Chant these words as you bury the paper:

I plant this list like a seed—

A cycle of reaping and sowing.

I submit to earth these words and deeds,

To aid both ending and growing.

Ember Grant

NOTES:

October 7
Saturday

4th ♋

☽ v/c 3:12 pm

☽ → ♌ 7:24 pm

Color of the day: Blue
Incense of the day: Patchouli

Bathtub Tea

October 7 is known as National Bathtub Day. Immersing yourself in water has many health benefits, in addition to helping you relax. The hot water stimulates blood flow, eases pain in muscles and joints, and helps to increase your oxygen intake.

Pamper yourself by taking a hot, soothing herbal tea bath. Gather dried herbs and place them in a muslin or organza bag. Depending on the desired result, you can add Epsom salts for pain, dried lavender for cleansing properties and skin health, dried rose petals as a stress reducer, and dried chamomile to help with inflammation and healing. Research and discover the herbs that will benefit you the most, and make sure you aren't allergic to any of the ingredients.

Place the herbs/salts in the bag and allow the herbs to release their magical properties into the bathwater. Dim the lights, relax, and drift into a peaceful, healing bathtub vibe.

Sapphire Moonbeam

October 8
Sunday

4th ♌

Color of the day: Orange
Incense of the day: Almond

Spell for the Absolute Truth

Today the Sun, Mercury, and Mars are all in Libra, the sign of the scales of justice. This is an ideal time to see the somewhat harsh but important truths we may not want to look at when it comes to ourselves, other people, situations, or our lives. Put a small white candle, such as a chime candle or a tea light, on a plate. Under the plate place the Justice tarot card and the Ace of Swords. Light the candle, and as you do so, say:

By the powers of this candle,

Reveal truths that I can handle,

That I am able to discern clearly

The illusions I hold on to dearly.

Sit in meditative contemplation and be open to whatever guidance may be revealed during the meditation session. In the next few days, pay attention to your dreams and seemingly random thoughts, conversations, or synchronicities that occur, revealing the truth about yourself, others, or situations and the illusions you may be under regarding them.

Mat Auryn

·October 9
Monday

4th ♌

Color of the day: Silver
Incense of the day: Narcissus

Indigenous Peoples' Day –
Thanksgiving Day (Canada)

Land Back

The only way we can account for history is to try and walk a path of understanding in the present. If you live in the United States and are not yourself genetically Native American, then please take a moment today to learn about whose land you occupy as a colonial settler. Knowing is only half the battle. Give this day a sense of reverence, wear red, and learn earth history. Host a farm-to-table family meal or bonfire in honor of the land and promote awareness.

We can heal our community by speaking to the earth today. Please support Native-led direct actions; discover how you can help the LANDBACK movement. Say a prayer to the spirits that you are already sensing and lift up your voice to honor them. Here is a translation of a Salish prayer to recite:

Hello! Greetings, my relations. Ancestors, I love you. I sense you all around and I hear you. I am listening well and learning to honor

the old ways. Please guide me toward understanding and service to my community. Thank you.

Estha McNevin

NOTES:

October 10
Tuesday

4th ♌

☽ v/c 5:37 am

☽ → ♍ 8:02 am

Color of the day: Black
Incense of the day: Bayberry

Pumpkin Problem Removal

Now is an ideal time to remove problems, obstacles, or annoying health-related issues such as warts. Gather a small pumpkin, a knife and a large spoon, a white tea light candle, a piece of paper, and a black pen.

Hollow out the pumpkin, discarding the seeds. If you wish to remove a blemish or wart, cut a small chunk from the pumpkin, rub it lightly on the blemish, then place it inside the pumpkin. In any case, write what you wish to remove on the paper, mentally pouring your intention into the paper. Place the candle in the pumpkin and light it. Carefully ignite the paper in the flame as you say:

Waning moon and lantern bright,
banish this trouble from my life.

As the paper burns, drop it into the pumpkin, then place the stem "lid" on it to extinguish the candle. Remove the candle and place the pumpkin somewhere hidden outdoors to rot, activating the spell.

Michael Furie

October 11
Wednesday

4th ♍

Color of the day: Brown
Incense of the day: Honeysuckle

Release a Bad Habit Spell

For this spell to banish a bad habit, you'll need a red apple, lemon juice, a rag, and a small knife. First rub the apple with a bit of the lemon juice. Rub it hard with a rag. Think of the habit you wish to get rid of. Now begin to peel the apple with the knife. As you peel, say:

I shed my habit like this peel.

As my habit is removed,

I shall begin to heal.

In your mind, see the habit diminishing as you peel. Let the peeling drop to the floor. End by composting the apple and the peel, or throw them away.

James Kambos

October 12
Thursday

4th ♏

☽ v/c 4:10 pm

☽ → ♎ 8:22 pm

Color of the day: Turquoise
Incense of the day: Apricot

A Blessing upon Farmers

Today is National Farmer's Day (previously known as Old Farmer's Day). This holiday is observed to honor hardworking farmers, their traditional techniques, and their wisdom. Without farmers, we wouldn't have food.

Today, it would be fitting to offer a blessing upon farmers as part of your mealtime blessing. Recite the following blessing before your dinner this evening:

On this day we offer our gratitude:

Gratitude to the deep and fruitful earth,

For the food the fertile earth springs forth.

Gratitude for those who tend the crops,

For their skill, labor, and wisdom.

Gratitude for timeless techniques and necessary innovation.

Gratitude to those farmers who produce our food while minding the health of our earth.

We are grateful for the mindful farmers' discernment, balance, and wisdom,

For farming should be a partnership between humankind and the earth.

To these ends we offer gratitude and blessings. So mote it be.

Blake Octavian Blair

NOTES:

October 13
Friday

4ℏ ♎

Color of the day: White
Incense of the day: Alder

Shell Divination

When you're struggling to make a decision about something because there are too many possible outcomes, try this shell divination to get some guidance. You can use small seashells or halved walnut shells.

Consider your problem, and think of four different outcomes. Choose a word to sum up each outcome, and paint each word on a shell.

Fill a medium-size bowl with water, and put it where it will not be disturbed by people, nature, or animals. State your issue out loud, and place the shells in the water, curved side down, so they float. Let the shells sit in the water. Whichever one sinks first holds the answer to your question.

Keep in mind that this process can take a day or more depending on the shells you're using, so don't forget to check back now and again.

Kate Freuler

 October 14
Saturday

4ℏ ♎
New Moon 1:55 pm

Color of the day: Gray
Incense of the day: Rue

Solar Eclipse

Crossroads New Moon Tarot Reading

Sometimes we feel as if we're at a crossroads in our life. That feeling is even more common on the new moon, when there are so many possibilities in the air. If you want more insight into what the new moon in Libra today means for you, read on.

Draw three cards from your favorite tarot deck, and place them, from left to right, on the table before you. Read the meaning of each card in the manner in which it appears—reversed or upright. These cards represent the three main themes of your life right now.

Draw three more cards and lay them on top of the other three so they cross them. Read these cards upright. These are the "crossroads" you're at. They represent the good things you can create or cause if you work with that energy, or places where you are stuck and you must make a decision. Use this information to create your new moon intentions.

Astrea Taylor

October 15
Sunday

1st ♎

☽ v/c 3:01 am

☽ → ♏ 7:04 am

Color of the day: Gold
Incense of the day: Marigold

Underworld Guide Working

The newly waxing Moon in Scorpio brings with it a lot of excitement and ushers in the first signs of the upcoming Scorpio season. This is an excellent time for magic related to sex and the underworld, and spirits are easily petitioned now for assistance in magic. Perform this working to meet an underworld spirit guide who can help you navigate the present and upcoming Scorpio vibes.

After clearing and grounding your personal energy, stand with the setting sun at your back and say:

As the light fades, I empower the dark.

I call a spirit guide and soon embark;

*Through the underworld
and over the stars,*

Find me, spirit, this task is ours!

Light a candle for the spirit and place it in the west. Allow it to burn out safely on its own. During this time, connect with the spirit and ask for a symbol that you can use later to communicate with it when needed.

Devin Hunter

October 16
Monday

1st ♏

Color of the day: Ivory
Incense of the day: Rosemary

Bast Blessing for Feral Cats

This is a day to celebrate cats of all sorts, no matter where they live. My own experience with feral cats is limited to my college days. Students "adopted" kittens, but when they became more of a burden than just a cute ball of fluff, those growing cats were abandoned, usually at the end of the school year. The dumpsters at my college became the favorite living quarters of these felines, and their numbers increased at an alarming rate.

There are many ways to honor Bast, goddess of cats. You could volunteer at an animal shelter; take clean, old towels, sheets, and other linens to a shelter; or donate money, food, or gift cards. Contact your local shelter if you see feral cats. Call upon Bast for protection:

*Bast, you never meant for any of
your descendants to be abandoned.
Watch over them while they continue
their journey here on earth and
on the rainbow bridge to you.*

Emyme

October 17
Tuesday

1st ♏

☽ v/c 11:44 am

☽ → ♐ 3:36 pm

Color of the day: Scarlet
Incense of the day: Geranium

Tree Magic Practices

Magic is in every part of our world, but at times it is easier to see in nature than in ourselves, especially in autumn or fall. The Green Man is said to exist in the subconscious of those who love nature, plants, animals, and trees. He is nature. He is the forest and he is the trees. He is the animals and he is earth magic at its best.

There is much old lore surrounding tree magic. Here are some magical practices for you to try:

- Planting lilac, honeysuckle, and almond trees in your garden provides financial stability for the family. However, if you plant white lilac, remember that you should never cut it and bring it in the house, as anything white in nature belongs to the Goddess, no matter how tempting its beautiful smell.

- Silver birch, maple, holly, and ash trees are believed to bring luck to the household.

- The monkey puzzle tree is best avoided, as it brings bad luck to the home and family.

- The elder tree is a very sacred tree and is said to protect humans from the spirit world.

- The cherry tree is always said to harbour evil spirits.

- The mighty oak tree is said to be magical. It is believed that if you carry an acorn with you, eternal youth will be yours.

- It is wise to leave an acorn on a windowsill, as it will ward off storms.

- If an oak tree has mistletoe growing round it, this is said to have special powers. The advice is to cut off the mistletoe with a gold knife on the sixth day of a new moon and catch it in a white cloth, not allowing it to touch the ground, as then the mistletoe will lose its power. Place the mistletoe in water and use the liquid as a charm to ward off evil spirits.

Tudorbeth

October 18
Wednesday

1st ♐

Color of the day: Topaz
Incense of the day: Lilac

Visiting a Graveyard

One of the easiest ways to feel the thinning of the veil and honor the dead is to visit a local graveyard. (Only visit a cemetery during posted visiting hours!) Walking the grounds and collecting trash and litter that you might find among the headstones is a great way to show respect and care for the resting place of those who have passed on. You could also leave fresh flowers as offerings on forgotten or neglected graves. These are great ways to gain some powerful spiritual allies.

In the early 1900s, many people used to have picnics at local cemeteries (something that's still seen among those who celebrate the Mexican Day of the Dead), and this is a practice worth reviving. Find a nice grassy spot at the cemetery and prepare a plate for the dead as an offering. You can also close your eyes and extend your senses outward to find out if any of the dead have partaken of your offering or have something to share with you.

Amanda Lynn & Jason Mankey

October 19
Thursday

1st ♐

☽ v/c 3:02 pm
☽ → ♑ 9:55 pm

Color of the day: Purple
Incense of the day: Balsam

Blanket Spell

There's something about a soft, cozy blanket that makes us feel safe and secure. Use this spell to make your favorite blanket extra special by charging it for a specific purpose, such as comfort, healing, or self-love.

First, be sure the blanket is clean and dry. Take it outside and shake it thoroughly, visualizing the air enhancing its freshness. You can even hang it on a clothesline for a few hours if you wish.

The next step is to light some incense and slowly wave the smoke over the blanket, visualizing the blanket being purified and ready for charging. The final step is to roll or fold the blanket so it's small enough to hug tightly against your chest. As you hold it, charge it by visualizing your specific intent. Chant these words to seal the spell:

As I will,

My purpose fulfill.

This blanket will serve

This need I deserve (state your intent).

Each time you use the blanket, it will reinforce its purpose. Recharge it periodically as desired.

Ember Grant

NOTES:

 October 20
Friday

1st ♑

Color of the day: Coral
Incense of the day: Mint

Autumn Leaves Release Spell

Autumn is a magical time of year. Nature teaches us how to navigate phases in our lives. It is wise to work with the transformational energy of the seasons instead of resisting the flow. As the temperatures get cooler, the beautiful autumn leaves dance gracefully as they fall to the earth. This is a visual representation of releasing things in your life with ease and grace.

Find a place where you can sit near the base of a tree. As you ground and connect with the earth energy, take some deep breaths and think about what may be holding you back from achieving your goals and living your best life. Once you feel more grounded, you can say these words:

May the things in my life that no longer serve me fall away effortlessly like the leaves of an autumn tree.

Sapphire Moonbeam

October 21
Saturday

1st ♏

2nd Quarter 11:29 pm

Color of the day: Indigo
Incense of the day: Sandalwood

Autumn Banishing Spell

Trees are pruned in the autumn and winter so that new growth can flourish in the spring. This cutting helps the tree grow bigger and better in the future. The same can be said for things in life that have run their course. Shedding our past is necessary to make room for new opportunities. Perform this spell to cut away the lingering power of experiences that are no longer serving you so you can bloom in the future.

Bring a tree clipping to your sacred space. Hold it in your hands and visualize the experience that you need to let go of. Allow yourself to feel any emotions that arise, even negative ones. Note how the emotions feel within your body, and direct them through the palms of your hands into the wood and leaves. Eventually the sensation will leave your body and sit heavily within the tree clipping.

Go outdoors and place the clipping on the ground. Say:

I return this to the earth,
to wither, fade, and die.

Walk away. As the plant decays into mulch, so will your attachment to the past.

Kate Freuler

Notes:

October 22
Sunday

2nd ♑

☽ v/c 2:00 am

☽ → ♒ 2:06 am

Color of the day: Amber
Incense of the day: Hyacinth

Magical Compote

To fill your home with flavors of the season, create a cauldron of spices that you can cook on low heat to clear negativity from your home and invite ancestral spirits to warm and bless your hearth. The following combination is one we use every year at our temple because it can also bless the air while making a delicious compote. Enjoy!

In a large pot or slow cooker, combine the following:

- 3 oranges, sliced
- 2 apples, seeds removed
- 2 cups mashed pumpkin
- 2 cinnamon sticks
- 1 vanilla bean
- 6 cloves
- 3 allspice seeds
- 2 cups apple juice
- 1 cup honey

Cook for four hours on low heat, then remove the cinnamon sticks and pulverize the mixture in a food processor.

Serve over ice cream or on the side of roasted poultry for a seasonal delight. Store in canning jars for up to one month. This compote tastes wonderful on toast and takes waffles or pancakes to a whole other level with the spices and harvest warmth of the season.

Estha McNevin

NOTES:

October 23
Monday

2nd ♒

☉ → ♏ 12:21 pm

☽ v/c 3:04 pm

Color of the day: Gray
Incense of the day: Hyssop

Manifestation Magic

Today's planetary ruler is the Moon, and the lunar phase is a waxing gibbous. Let's take the opportunity to ride this energy of growth and do a bit of manifestation magic!

Today, place items or images of something you are currently working to manifest in your life on either your existing working altar or one you create for this purpose. For a car, you might choose a picture of the type of a car, a small toy car, or a representation of car keys. If you are trying to manifest a job in a certain field, you might place tools or images of that profession on the altar.

Now make a written list of the real-world actions you will take to help manifest your goal. For a job, you might list the places where you could network with people in the industry. Another action might be to revise your resume. Now let magic and real-world action combine their powers to manifest your goal!

Blake Octavian Blair

 ## October 24
Tuesday

2nd ♒

☽ → ♓ 4:33 am

Color of the day: Red
Incense of the day: Cedar

Spell to Remove a Curse

If someone has employed the spirits of darkness against you, reduce their power with this spell. Upon your altar, spread an old dark cloth. In the center of the cloth, sprinkle some dirt and pepper. Write the name (if you know it) of the person who cast the spell on a piece of paper. Don't try to harm them; just write their name. Now cut the paper into small pieces and throw them onto the cloth with the dirt and pepper, and say:

Your power, like your name, is gone.

The power you had is done.

Earth consumes your power,
pepper stings you.

The curse and your power are through!

Immediately tie up the corners of the cloth to form a bundle. This will contain the curse's power. Throw the bundle into a trash can away from your home. Banish the situation from your mind and move on.

James Kambos

October 25
Wednesday

2nd ♓

Color of the day: White
Incense of the day: Lavender

Tarot Spell for Joy

Today let's call on Euphrosyne, the Greek goddess of happiness, mirth, and hospitality (and one of the Graces) to bless us.

You will need:

• Four of Wands tarot card

• Ten of Pentacles tarot card

• Three of Cups tarot card

• A carnelian stone

Shuffle your tarot deck, thinking of things that give you joy. Pull out the cards listed above and place them in a pyramid, with the Four of Wands and the Ten of Pentacles on the bottom and the Three of Cups at the apex, with all three cards touching at the edges. Place the carnelian where the three cards meet. Say:

Euphrosyne, I ask your blessing.
May my soul be aflame to give
and receive happiness, hospitality,
and laughter. So mote it be!

Keep the spell untouched through the next full moon (on the 28th), then return the cards to the deck and carry the carnelian in your pocket.

Cerridwen Iris Shea

October 26
Thursday

2nd ♓

☽ v/c 2:39 am

☽ → ♈ 6:02 am

Color of the day: Green
Incense of the day: Jasmine

Bewitching Glamor

Many witches and magical practitioners feel their powers peak in late October. Perhaps it's the thinning of the veil that hangs between the worlds, or maybe it's because Samhain is so near. The magical tide could even be attributed to the Halloween practice of dressing up in costumes and celebrating with friends. Whatever the case, it's a great time to practice a glamor spell. This spell can be used with a costume or for bewitching beauty.

Play some mood music. Face a mirror and use some makeup and styling products to make changes to your appearance to be in line with your desired image. Dress in a costume or special clothes. When you're ready to fully enchant your appearance, touch the mirror and say:

I call upon my inner power to
conjure the glamor I desire.

It is so.

Astrea Taylor

October 27
Friday

2nd ♈

Color of the day: Pink
Incense of the day: Thyme

Dark Triple Protection Juice

Both blackberries and raspberries have protective power, and so does the pomegranate. In combination, these three ingredients create a delicious, quick, and seasonally appropriate potion to help keep you safe as the nights lengthen and the shadows loom.

This recipe can be made either with fresh berries and pomegranate seeds in a juicer or by combining the already made juices. Either way, a half cup of each of the juices is a good amount for one serving. Once the juices are mixed, empower them by holding the cup of juice and envisioning an electric purple-black energy streaming from your hands into the liquid, filling it with protective power. When you feel the power has peaked, say:

Bramble berries and Underworld gift,

Let all harm be cast adrift.

Protective power here now held,

With magical potion all harm repelled.

Now drink the potion to absorb the magic.

Michael Furie

October 28
Saturday

2nd ♈

☽ v/c 4:20 am
☽ → ♉ 7:44 am
Full Moon 4:24 pm

Color of the day: Blue
Incense of the day: Ivy

Lunar Eclipse

Illuminating Resources List Making

Late in these days of letting go, I feel my grief so strongly. Gone are spring and summer, and heavily present now is fall. Done with my magical childhood and my robust youth, I turn now to the autumn of my life and feel the vulnerable and delicate nature of my body. I feel the cold more profoundly, the depression brought on by a lack of light, and the need for sleep to restore me.

With the full moon in Taurus shining brightly tonight, use the youthful spring energy of this sign and the bright light of the full moon to illuminate what you need to do to care for yourself now. With pen and paper, write the answers to these questions: *What brings me warmth? What gives me comfort? What sustains me? How do I restore myself when depleted? How do I reset after grief?*

As the autumn days dwindle, let these lists guide you.

Dallas Jennifer Cobb

October 29
Sunday

3rd ♉

Color of the day: Yellow
Incense of the day: Heliotrope

Opening to Mediumship with Our Beloved Dead

As we approach astrological Samhain, when the Sun is at 15 degrees Scorpio, the veil between our world and the spirit world is already greatly thinning, making spirit communication easier. With the Sun and Mercury in Scorpio (as well as Mars, which is Scorpio's ancient ruler), this is a beyond auspicious time to open up the lines of communication with your beloved dead. Create a special place for them and include their photo. You can add offerings of things they enjoyed in life as well as the traditional glass of water and a white candle. Once everything is set up, light the candle and open up the lines of communication by saying:

What is remembered lives within this place.

You are always welcome here in this space.

Though you are gone, I know you are here,

Because in my heart you are always near.

Speak to me in ways I comprehend

If there are messages you wish to send.

Be open to their presence via psychic means, synchronicity, and dreams in the next several days leading up to astrological Samhain. Extinguish the candle.

Mat Auryn

NOTES:

October 30
Monday

3rd ♉

☽ v/c 7:36 am

☽ → ♊ 11:08 am

Color of the day: White
Incense of the day: Neroli

Mediumship Tarot Consecration

It is officially Scorpio season, with the Sun, Mercury, and Mars all stationed now in this sign. This energy is particularly good for those of us who communicate with the deceased, and we can channel the energy into our magical tools to make mediumship easier at any time. This spell is a consecration working that utilizes the potent energy of this moment to bless and empower a tarot or oracle deck to be used as a tool in mediumship. All you need is a deck, a pinch each of mugwort, mint, and rue, and a charcoal to burn the herbs on. Blend the herbs together and burn a bit over the charcoal. Pass the deck through the smoke several times as you chant:

*Death does not silence those
who I seek. Through these cards
their souls shall speak!*

When you intuitively feel that the cards are charged, the working is done. Keep the deck wrapped in black, and use it only for mediumship.

Devin Hunter

 ## October 31
Tuesday

3rd ♊

Color of the day: Maroon
Incense of the day: Ylang-ylang

Samhain – Halloween

Reunite with a Departed Loved One

For many of us, Samhain is about reuniting with loved ones who have crossed over into the realm of the dead. For this spell you will need a picture or an object related to the person you want to connect with, something with a scent that reminds you of the deceased, and a candle. Start by placing the picture on your altar and saying the name of the spirit you wish to reunite with. Next to the picture, place your scented object and breathe in its aroma. Your scented object can be food, something once owned by the deceased, or even an incense or scented oil. Just make sure the scent conjures up memories. Focus on the memories that surface; their energy should bring the deceased close to you. Light the candle and say:

*Though worlds apart, tonight we shall
reunite. (Name of deceased), come to
this place and be with me this Samhain.*

Reach out into the stillness and feel the energy of your deceased loved one around you. Blow out the candle.

Amanda Lynn & Jason Mankey

Page 214

November

The sounds of nature begin to quiet down in November, but this month is far from silent. Yes, the cheery morning birdsong of spring is gone, and crickets are no longer fiddling on warm summer afternoons, but November has its own "voices." On a frosty November morning, you'll hear a faint, faraway gabble. Raise your eyes toward the sky, and coming over the horizon, in a V formation heading south, is a flock of wild geese. The sound makes you pause and wonder: how do they know it's time to migrate? As you rake leaves, the late autumn breeze stirs them, and they softly rustle as they click and swirl up the street. Few sounds say November like the wind. It may be as gentle as a baby's breath or it may roar, carrying the weight of the coming winter as it howls in the night. During the night you can also hear November's most haunting voice: the lone hooting of an owl. Yes, this month has many voices, but every evening I hear the most comforting voice of all. That voice belongs to the crackling of burning logs as my hearth fire wards off the chill of a dark November night.

During this mysterious month, let the voices of November speak to you, igniting your imagination and your magic.

James Kambos

Ŋovember 1
Wednesday

3rd ♊

☽ v/c 8:36 am

☽ → ♋ 5:30 pm

Color of the day: Topaz
Incense of the day: Bay laurel

Ӓll Ꞩaints' Ꝺay

Ꞩpell to honor the Ꝺead

Many people honor the dead at this time of year. Creating a space to acknowledge those who have passed forges a bond between yourself and the dead, allowing a meaningful magical relationship to grow.

Set aside an area on your altar, or create a new altar. Find a photo of those who have passed. Think about what they enjoyed in life, and choose an object to represent this, such as a drink they loved or a tool they often used in their work. Arrange these on your altar and place a few fresh flowers and a glass of water near their photo. Keep the water refilled each day, replace any wilted flowers, and keep the area clean. The act of maintaining the physical altar will sustain your connection to the dead.

When you wish to connect to your dead, light a candle on the altar and enter a relaxed state. Allow them to come to you in whatever form they choose. This could be a flood of fond memories or even a physical sensation. You can simply enjoy their presence, knowing they're still with you. Other times you can ask them for help or guidance in your life. The more frequently you practice this, the more connected you will become.

You can keep this altar space all year round. Honoring the dead isn't just for one season!

Kate Ꝼreuler

NOTES:

November 2
Thursday

3rd ♋

Color of the day: Turquoise
Incense of the day: Myrrh

Feasting Blanket

A blanket is a wonderful way to pass down a tradition. In many cultures, eating outside together while sitting on the earth is a family bonding experience that honors our ancestors. The blankets we choose for family meals are often wool and are rich in colors and traditions because they can reflect the importance of such communal practices. When embroidered to honor family achievements or special events, family blankets become priceless heirlooms that we lovingly pass on.

If you would like to begin a blanket tradition for your family, find ways to honor native artisans and crafters. Support others who are committed to sustainable models of spiritual art to ensure that your family shares in community values that keep our planet verdant and our cultures united in earth-based traditions. Embroider your family name today and share a picnic with your loved ones to tell them of your intention and why you want to share your blanket with them.

Estha McNevin

November 3
Friday

3rd ♋
☽ v/c 11:28 pm

Color of the day: Purple
Incense of the day: Violet

Protection Charm against Spirits

The Sun, Mercury, and Mars are all still hanging out in Scorpio, bringing with them underworld vibes. This can be an exciting time for those of us who enjoy spirits entering our lives, but not all witches like uninvited guests! Cast this spell to protect yourself against unwanted spirits.

All you need are three pinches each of salt, cedar, and rose, plus a small black pouch or piece of cloth with a string to tie the working up with at the end. Put the salt and herbs in the pouch along with a piece of your hair. Tie the pouch up using three knots. Each time you tie a knot, say:

Hidden from spirits I do not know,
protected by allies, both high and low.

After you tie the final knot, say:

So must it be!

Carry the charm with you until the threat passes.

Devin Hunter

November 4
Saturday

3rd ♋

☽ → ♌ 3:21 am

Color of the day: Gray
Incense of the day: Sage

Scream Water

This is a slightly unusual method of magical cleansing. Water is naturally magically "magnetic" and has the ability to absorb and carry energy. This quality makes it an ideal medium of cleansing. If you feel as though you need an inner cleansing—if you feel run down or agitated or are worried that someone has sent bad vibes your way—get a cup of cold water and take a swig of it, holding it in your mouth. Visualize any incorrect, harmful energy in your body being drawn to and absorbed by the water. Swish it around in your mouth to complete this energy collection, then gargle it as you would mouthwash, making an audible sound with the intention of pushing all the bad energy out into the water. Finally, quickly spit the water into a sink and rinse the sink clean. It is done.

Michael Furie

November 5
Sunday

3rd ♌

4th Quarter 3:37 am

Color of the day: Gold
Incense of the day: Almond

Daylight Saving Time
ends at 2:00 a.m.

Extra hour of Power

Daylight saving time ends in most areas of the United States today. At 2:00 a.m. the clocks roll back and we "gain" an extra hour. Let's seize that hour and make it into an Hour of Power!

Set aside an hour today for spiritual study, spellcraft, ritualizing, meditation, or any other activity that will benefit your spiritual practice. Do something you feel will build your spiritual power and benefit you as we move into the future. It could be a shamanic journey, taking time to perform self-Reiki, or perhaps reading a few chapters in a spirituality-related book. In recent years, thankfully, modern popular culture has brought to light the need for self-care. It is well-known wisdom that if we take care of ourselves, then we can be a source of support for others. Enjoy your Hour of Power!

Blake Octavian Blair

November 6
Monday

4th ♌

☽ v/c 2:25 am

☽ → ♍ 2:39 pm

Color of the day: Silver
Incense of the day: Clary sage

Spell to Forgive Rudeness

If we allow it, aging brings maturity and wisdom. It allows our minds to open. One of my tried-and-true and heartfelt mantras is "Humor is no excuse for rudeness." Another hard-learned fact is that one does not have to put voice to every thought.

Here is a spell to help us be less rude and to forgive the rudeness of others:

The words pierce our hearts,
the laughter hurts our soul;

Laughter does not forgive rudeness,
spoken thoughts must be ignored;

Do not take into your heart and soul
such carelessness; to forgive is to bless.

Emyme

November 7
Tuesday

4th ♏

Color of the day: Black
Incense of the day: Cinnamon

Election Day

Election Day Fate Spell

Elections can bring out the worst in people, especially if we don't vote for those who eventually win. During this time, it can feel like our hands are tied and our fate is up to the universe. We can feel like a ship bobbing along on an ocean current, not knowing where we belong.

If you feel that you need to reestablish your fate, then cast this spell. It doesn't need to be cast on this particular day. It can be cast anytime you feel like your life is in the hands of the goddesses of fate.

In Greek mythology, the goddesses of fate were three sisters who determined the fate not only of every mortal but also of the gods.

Safely light a white candle and imagine the Fates listening. Talk to them about what is it that you actually want in life. Do you have a problem or decision that you want them to sort out for you? Imagine what the goddesses of fate would look like and begin to talk to them. Tell them your desire and then finish by saying:

Goddesses of fate,

Your decision I await.

Grant me one wish, I implore.

Grant me success, no less, no more.

Be gentle with my life, be tender with my fate.

Goddesses of my life, ensure that now all will be great.

Keep the candle burning for at least three hours after the spell and then extinguish it safely. Never leave a candle burning unattended.

Tudorbeth

NOTES:

November 8
Wednesday

4th ♍

☽ v/c 11:55 pm

Color of the day: White
Incense of the day: Honeysuckle

Close the Veil

For many of us, late October to early November is a time to remember our beloved dead, and we may choose to commemorate those we've lost by giving them a place on our altars. When resetting our altars after Samhain, we think it's a good idea to give our lost loved ones a heartfelt and memorable goodbye.

Start by picking up each individual item celebrating your beloved dead from your altar and saying the name of the person the item is matched to aloud. Jason usually does this by saying something like this:

> Marie Mankey, beloved grandmother, mother, and wife.

After you pick up each of the items, reverently pack them away securely. Then say:

> The veil thickens, and once more I must say goodbye to those I have loved and lost in this world. But what is remembered always lives, and as we move away from Samhain, I know that the spirits of those I have honored here will forever be close to me. Until next we meet when the veil thins, blessed be!

Amanda Lynn & Jason Mankey

NOTES:

November 9
Thursday

4th ♏

☽ → ♎ 3:08 am

Color of the day: Purple
Incense of the day: Mulberry

hot Chocolate Spell for Self-Love

Hot chocolate is nearly universally loved. There's something about it that warms the heart and the soul. It can even make us feel as if we're drinking love itself. You can use this spell with a homemade drink or a beverage from a coffeehouse. For an extra boost of magic, add a pinch of cinnamon or instant coffee.

Gather these materials:

- 1 cup hot milk
- 2 tablespoons chocolate powder
- 2 tablespoons sugar
- Pinch of sea salt
- ¼ teaspoon vanilla
- Saucepan
- Whisk
- Mug
- Spoon

In the saucepan, combine all of the ingredients except the vanilla. Whisk them together until the sugar dissolves. Pour the hot cocoa into a mug, then add the vanilla. Stir it clockwise with a spoon and say:

Rich cocoa, sweet sugar, creamy milk, and luscious vanilla. As I imbibe this lovely drink, I find these aspects within me.

Take a sip. Make any adjustments to your liking. Enjoy!

Astrea Taylor

Notes:

November 10
Friday

4♄ ♎

Color of the day: Rose
Incense of the day: Vanilla

Shuffling Psychic Clarity into Your Tarot Deck

The Sun in mystical and psychic Scorpio today makes it an auspicious time to charge your tarot deck. Divide your deck into five piles: the four suits of the minor arcana and a pile of the major arcana. Pick up the suit of swords and shuffle the cards, declaring:

Reveal to me by suit of air

The words, thoughts, and truths laid bare.

Next, pick up the suit of wands and shuffle the cards, saying:

Reveal to me by suit of fire

Career, ambitions, and desire.

Shuffle the suit of cups, saying:

Reveal to me by suit of water's flow

All relationships and the emotional.

Shuffle the suit of pentacles and say:

Reveal to me by suit of pentacle

Finances, home, and the practical.

Shuffle the major arcana cards and say:

By the arcana of World to Fool,

I charge you as a psychic tool.

Combine the five piles of cards and shuffle them all together, declaring:

To see the future, present, and the past,

On whatever subject that might be asked.

Mat Auryn

NOTES:

November 11
Saturday

4th ♎

☽ v/c 10:05 am

☽ → ♏ 1:39 pm

Color of the day: Blue

Incense of the day: Magnolia

Veterans Day –
Remembrance Day (Canada)

Veterans Day Remembrance Meditation

Today, as we honor veterans, perform this meditation in remembrance. Decorate your altar with red and white roses. You can use silk flowers if you can't find real ones. If you have veterans in your life to honor, put photos of them on your altar or write their names on pieces of paper instead. Light a white candle for each of them. If you don't know any veterans personally, simply direct your honor in a general manner. As the candles burn, meditate on the dedication and service of veterans. Here's a prayer you can use during your meditation:

For all those who serve,
in the past and today, we honor
and value the price that they pay.

Please let their service not be in vain.
Let them find comfort to heal their pain.

Allow the candles to burn out safely. If possible, make a donation to a veterans' organization.

Ember Grant

November 12
Sunday

4th ♏

Color of the day: Yellow

Incense of the day: Frankincense

Biome Bowl

Today, cast clarity into the air you breathe and explore all of the types of mold, yeast, and bacteria floating around. Once you know who you live with, it can be life-enriching. Good yeast can flavor your bread and bloom sourdough in your home, while harmful protozoa can cause disease if not discouraged by burning herbs or antibacterial spices that clear the air.

Into a clean glass pie plate, mix one packet of agar gel or fruit pectin with one pinch of salt and one pinch of sugar. Chant the following intention:

Everything living, draw near this glass

And make your imprint as you pass;

Reveal the spark of all life in bloom

And help me to know the
biome of this room.

Photograph the spores that bloom in the pie plate this week. Explore microbiology and fun botany games as you adventure in the worlds within our world, for we actually live among some amazing bacterial civilizations.

Estha McNevin

4th ♏

November 13
Monday

New Moon 4:27 am

)) v/c 6:03 pm

)) → ♐ 9:23 pm

Color of the day: Ivory
Incense of the day: Hyssop

Lucky Seeds Spell Manifestation

A new moon is a powerful time for manifestation magic. The great luminaries (lights) in our lives, the Sun and the Moon, are conjunct today, sitting together in space. This makes the moon invisible to us, and concentrates huge amounts of energy from the two planets.

Initiation, planting, and manifestation spells are common at the new moon. It is a time of beginnings. This new moon occurs in Scorpio, which rules transformation, opportunity, change, and regeneration, among other things.

Close your eyes and ask yourself:

What do I choose to transform?

Now envision your hand planting small seeds of intention in the fertile soil of the earth.

Say:

*I am a magical being, this
I have always known.*

*Water flows in my blood,
earth makes up my bones.*

I tend the fires of my heart and

breathe the air of inspiration,

And plant these seeds of transformation.

Blessed be.

Dallas Jennifer Cobb

Notes:

November 14
Tuesday

1st ♐

Color of the day: Maroon
Incense of the day: Geranium

Clean Kitchen Spell

Thanksgiving is early this year, so let's clean the kitchen (even if you're not cooking in it).

Call on Hygeia, the Greek goddess of cleanliness, or Hestia, the Greek goddess of the hearth, to bless your mop and filled bucket. Burn some cleansing incense (such as rosemary) and put on your favorite upbeat music. Open the windows.

Mop the floors, wipe down the counters, scrub the sink, clean the stove, clean out the refrigerator, and do any dishes lying around. Take out the garbage.

Dance around the kitchen, singing along with the music, if you want! That will get the energy moving.

When you're finished and everything is put away, turn off the music. Stand in the middle of the room. Open your arms, palms up, and feel the clean, fresh energy.

Say:

Thank you, (name of goddess), for today's blessing. May the energy of health, prosperity, and abundance fill this space. So mote it be.

Cerridwen Iris Shea

November 15
Wednesday

1st ♐

☽ v/c 5:57 pm

Color of the day: Brown
Incense of the day: Lilac

Bury Your Sorrow Spell

Read the following verse, and follow the instructions. May it help you if you're dealing with sorrow or grief.

When the geese fly beyond the southern horizon's bounds,

And silver frost kisses the frozen ground,

Find a rock and hold it to your aching heart.

Tell it your sorrow so your healing may start.

Then go to a lonely place where leaves lie sere and dead.

Think of the sad words you have just said.

Now dig a small earthly grave to contain your grief.

Bury the rock, cover it with earth and decaying leaves.

Walk away and allow the grave to consume your sorrow.

May your heart be filled with hope come tomorrow.

James Kambos

November 16
Thursday

1st ♐

☽ → ♑ 2:41 am

Color of the day: Green
Incense of the day: Jasmine

Drum Balance Spell

November is known as International Drum Month. Ancient people knew the benefit of using drum beats to connect with the energy of their souls, the universe, and the rhythm of the earth. Using drums to create rhythms is an activity that can help restore balance.

Drumming helps to synchronize and ground your personal energy. When you use a hand drum made from natural materials and hit it with a drum stick in your dominant hand, the energy of that motion will help the rhythmic vibration of the drum travel up through your arm, resonate through your heart space, and then travel back down to the hand holding the drum beater. Repeating this movement will foster the balance within. This type of drumming can be done with or without music. Once you practice this technique more, you can utilize it anytime.

Sapphire Moonbeam

November 17
Friday

1st ♑

Color of the day: Coral
Incense of the day: Alder

homemade Bread Day

The pandemic that began in March 2020 forced many of us to stay at home and gave rise to many "old-fashioned" crafts and hobbies. Bread has been a staple of life for thousands of years. Suddenly, there was time and reason to create our own bread.

The internet is full of recipes and instructions for making bread with a machine or by hand. Be it plain white or artisanal bread, the possibilities are endless.

As your bread is created and baked, you and your family will be looking forward to the tasting—and the house will smell wonderful. Perhaps make it a Friday night ritual and have fresh bread all weekend. Incant:

*Bread is life! Welcome life
into our home with the
ancient blessing of bread.*

Emyme

November 18
Saturday

1st ♑

☽ v/c 3:27 am

☽ → ♒ 6:28 am

Color of the day: Black
Incense of the day: Pine

Moon in Aquarius
Inspiration Spell

For a few hours this morning, the Moon will be void-of-course, but then the energy eases and we feel the full promise of the Aquarius Moon! During this time we can harness the inwardly directed power of Aquarius to find inspiration in all areas of life. For creative types, this is a great time to break through blocks and finish projects. If you are struggling with creativity, you can cast this spell to harness the power of the Aquarius Moon and blast open your creative flow.

Around an orange candle, place three pennies head-side up in the shape of an upward-pointing triangle. Light the candle and say:

Aquarian muse and creative sprite,
deep thoughts flowing just in sight.

Inspired and lifted all in one, three
times over let this be done!

Let the candle burn out safely on its own. Keep one penny and give the other two away.

Devin Hunter

 November 19
Sunday

1st ♒

Color of the day: Amber
Incense of the day: Juniper

Essential Petition Magic

This is one of those classic techniques that everyone should have in their magical repertoire. A petition spell is, in essence, a magical method of requesting assistance or intervention from an otherworldly (usually divine) power. The basic ingredients for this spell are a pen, a clean, new piece of paper, a candle, and a fireproof vessel such as a cauldron.

Before attempting a petition spell, think deeply about what you are seeking and whom you are asking for help. Craft a carefully worded intention on the paper, asking for exactly what you want (adding "without harm" or "for the highest good" for safety) and addressing it to your chosen being (a deity, ancestor, spirit guide, etc.). Light the candle while calling upon the being, then read your petition aloud. Follow this by carefully lighting the paper in the candle flame and dropping it into the cauldron to burn out.

Michael Furie

November 20
Monday

1st ♒

☽ v/c 5:50 am

2nd Quarter 5:50 am

☽ → ♓ 9:29 am

Color of the day: Lavender
Incense of the day: Lily

Jar of Potential

Even though this season often brings to mind death and endings, it's important to remember that darkness is also a place of creation and potential. All that is born comes from darkness, and in knowing this, we can look at the darkness in a positive light. This spell is designed to help you welcome and understand what the darkness has to offer while providing a sense of hope and excitement for what is to come.

Materials:

• A jar with a large opening

• Black paint and a brush

• A container for mixing paint

• Biodegradable glitter

Pour a small amount of paint into the container. Stir in the biodegradable glitter, creating what looks like a sparkling night sky. Paint the inside of the jar thoroughly with the black paint, being sure not to leave any cracks where light can get in.

When it's dry, find a quiet moment to gaze into the dark you've created within the jar, and imagine the glitter pieces are all tiny seeds of potential germinating.

Throughout the dark months, any time you have a hope or wish, gaze into the jar and visualize your desire, planting seeds in the fertile darkness so that they might sprout and grow.

Kate Freuler

NOTES:

November 21
Tuesday

2nd ♓

Color of the day: Gray
Incense of the day: Basil

Window Fluff Your World

Window fluff was a popular Yuletide fad in the 1950s because it mimicked a snowy scene and allowed the kids to paint the winter onto any window in the house. Easy to make, it smells amazing and deters spiders and other pests like ticks. Kids especially will delight in hours of creative fun. To make it more sustainable, the fluff can be collected from the windows and recycled for use in the laundry or mopping water when all that spring cleaning begins in earnest.

Gather these ingredients:

- 6 drops peppermint oil
- 2 drops pine oil
- 1 drop eucalyptus oil
- ¼ cup warm lemon juice, freshly squeezed
- 1 egg white
- 1 cup potato starch
- 1 cup borax
- Warm water as needed

Start by adding the three oils to the lemon juice. Then, in a standing mixer, whip the egg white into hard peaks, then slowly add the starch and borax, alternating with the lemon juice mixture. Keep mixing on medium low until light and fluffy. If dry, add warm water as needed to achieve a light and fluffy consistency. Wear gloves and hand-paint snowy scenes on windows or dip, press, and peel lace to create patterns.

Estha McNevin

NOTES:

November 22
Wednesday

2nd ♓

☉ → ♐ 9:03 am

☽ v/c 10:10 am

☽ → ♈ 12:19 pm

Color of the day: Yellow
Incense of the day: Marjoram

Soup Spell

Try a little kitchen witchery while preparing a soup or stew. No matter what type you're making, use this spell to enhance its nourishing qualities. You can do this as you prepare it and just before eating.

During preparation, as you stir, visualize the ingredients blending together, creating a healthy harmony of nutrients. Stir clockwise and chant:

As witches made brew in
cauldrons of old,

This tradition today I gladly uphold.

Let magic infuse this meal I create,

To nourish and heal all
those who partake.

When you're ready to eat, gently stir (again clockwise) the contents of your bowl and repeat the chant. Eat and be well.

Ember Grant

November 23
Thursday

2nd ♈

Color of the day: Crimson
Incense of the day: Clove

Thanksgiving Day

Thanksgiving Reflection

Magick isn't just about getting the things we want; it's also about personal growth, and Thanksgiving is a powerful time to do a little personal development work. Take a moment to think about the various injustices currently taking place and what you can do to help those whose rights and opportunities are being trampled on. Write these things down on a small piece of paper or an index card.

Place a pillar candle (and its holder) on top of your piece of paper, then light your candle while saying:

May the words written here remind
me to be aware of the suffering of
others and my commitment to help
right those wrongs. So mote it be!

Keep your candle in sight during the day, and take some time between bites of turkey and cranberry sauce to reflect on how we can and should do better as a society. Keep your card or piece of paper once the candle burns down (or you blow it out) to serve as a reminder to help others.

Amanda Lynn & Jason Mankey

November 24
Friday

2nd ♈

☽ v/c 12:40 pm

☽ → ♉ 3:29 pm

Color of the day: Pink
Incense of the day: Orchid

Candle Vision Spell

Gazing at a candle flame for divination is known as fire scrying. It can be useful for determining what's ahead and preparing for the future. Nutmeg is used in this spell for its ability to enhance psychic abilities. You will need a white chime candle, a few drops of oil, nutmeg powder, and a lighter.

Dress the candle with the oil from bottom to top. Say:

This will help me see the future.

Sprinkle the candle with nutmeg from the bottom to the top and repeat the phrase.

Turn off the lights and safely light the candle. Say:

Flaming fire, speak to me.
Show me a vision of what may be.

Gaze through the flame. Let your mind become soft. Allow yourself to become one with the flame, in a way. If any shapes appear, follow them and watch their stories. You can ask questions if you wish. When you're done, thank the candle and blow it out.

Astrea Taylor

 November 25
Saturday

2nd ♉

Color of the day: Indigo
Incense of the day: Ivy

Put Up Your Feet Spell

We are deep in the holiday season, and the pace will only get more frenetic. So take some time to do a spell for your feet.

Soak in a footbath with Epsom salts and some of your favorite oils. Give yourself a pedicure if you wish. Peppermint lotion soothes and is also good for prosperity and protection.

Once your feet are completely dry, put on a favorite pair of fluffy, comfy socks.

Lie on the bed or the couch with your feet above the rest of you, propped on something comfortable. Say:

I bless my feet, which keep me
rooted to the earth and allow
me to reach for the sky.

I am grateful for all they
do all day, every day.

Today I celebrate them,
and I let them rest.

Spend the rest of the day relaxing with your feet up!

Cerridwen Iris Shea

November 26
Sunday

2nd ♉

☽ v/c 4:52 pm

☽ → ♊ 7:40 pm

Color of the day: Orange
Incense of the day: Hyacinth

Baking with Intention

Today is National Cake Day. We don't need an excuse to celebrate the wonders of cake, but it is nice to have one! Today would be a great day to indulge in a little kitchen magic. Pick an intention you've wanted to work on, then find a cake whose ingredients align with your goals and whip it up in the kitchen. Create an incantation to go along with it. Since today's planetary ruler is the Sun, let's look at an incantation you might use while baking an orange cake, which would incorporate the solar energy of the oranges and help lift the health, happiness, and prosperity of the home. As you bake and whisk together the batter, recite:

Cake of happiness and prosperity,

Golden oranges bright and sunny,

As I whisk and bake thee, bring to me

The sweetness of these qualities.

By solar power, so mote it be!

Now enjoy serving up this delicious spell to your housemates!

Blake Octavian Blair

November 27
Monday

2nd ♊

Full Moon 4:16 am

Color of the day: Gray
Incense of the day: Rosemary

Consecration of a Magic Cupboard

Practical magic is what I like, and I want to be able to get all my magical resources in an instant when I feel the inspiration or need to cast a spell of a particular type. As witches, we seem to amass over time a large supply of magical resources and equipment, from pots and pans to oils, incense, herbs, salts, and all manner of things.

Therefore, I created a magic cupboard, a place in my kitchen where all things used for magic and magic only are given special pride of place. I do not have these items mixing with everyday things. For example, I do not allow a pan that was used for a spell to be used for everyday cooking. There are a couple of reasons for this: one, it diminishes the spell and magic, and two, I want to avoid cross-contamination between the spell ingredients and the food, especially if I'm cooking for other people. Plus, it goes against what I was taught regarding magic: to grow your knowledge of magic and always respect your magical resources.

In your kitchen or wherever you have room, clean out the cupboard you will be using and then waft some sage around it to cleanse it or place a bowl of salt in it for twenty-four hours. Then remove the salt and place your magical items in the cupboard. As you do so, say this spell over the items:

In this cupboard, safe you shall be

From all manner of negativity.

When you are called, I ask of thee,

To perform in perfection in my witchery.

The space doesn't have to be a cupboard and can even be just a box or a bag. It just needs to be something special to keep your magical resources separate from your everyday items.

Tudorbeth

Notes:

November 28
Tuesday

3rd ♊

☽ v/c 8:03 pm

Color of the day: Red
Incense of the day: Ginger

Prayer to Understand Magickal Knowledge

The Jupiter-ruled sign of Sagittarius governs study, philosophy, and spiritual pursuits. Today the Sun, Mercury, and Mars are all in Sagittarius. This is a great time to focus on your study of the magickal arts and to ensure you understand the concepts and practices that are ideal for your soul's journey along the path of witchery.

This simple prayer is meant to be performed before you engage in any sort of learning activity related to magick or spirituality, whether that's picking up a book to read, listening to a teacher, or attending a workshop. This prayer can be recited out loud or mentally. I like to take a deep breath, relax, and recite it as an intimate whisper to my higher self.

As I study the arts of the mysteries

Of the path of ancient witcheries,

I understand the wisdom of philosophy

*And theories and practices
that are meant for me,*

*That nourish my mind
and nourish my soul,*

*That enhance my magick
to meet my goals.*

Mat Auryn

NOTES:

November 29
Wednesday

3rd ♊

☽ → ♋ 1:54 am

Color of the day: Topaz
Incense of the day: Lavender

Night Magic

Having had and raised a child, I spent many years indoors in the evening, observing early bedtimes. Recently I realized I was afraid of the night, and wanted to reclaim it. I started the practice of walking in the village at night with my dog.

Initially I was aware of my racing heart. I told myself, "There is nothing here in the dark that isn't here in the light." Dispelling negative notions, I searched for positivity.

I trained my eyes to see the night magic—how the middle of the street beckons when empty of cars, what the church steeple looks like when the moon is behind it, and the way the light falls, creating new awareness of structures.

Tonight, take a short walk in the dark. Let your heart slow and your eyes grow accustomed to the dark. See the night magic.

Dallas Jennifer Cobb

November 30
Thursday

3rd ♋

Color of the day: White
Incense of the day: Nutmeg

Feast for a Household Spirit

Many homes have a household spirit. Follow this verse to let your resident spirit know they're welcome. Household spirits have been around for thousands of years. The ancients treated their house spirits in a similar manner, with small gifts or some food, like I've done here.

When the clock strikes midnight,

Upon a plate of pure white,

Serve a slice of crusty bread

And an apple shiny and red.

And pour a glass of ruby red wine,

Now invite your spirit to sit and dine.

When the visit ends, I truly believe,

To bid your guest well, let them take their leave.

Occasionally a house spirit will move on, but not always, especially when they feel welcome. The next day, compost the food and pour the wine respectfully upon the earth.

James Kambos

December

December features a palette of cool colors: white snow, silver icicles, evergreen, and, of course, blue—the bright cerulean sky on a clear, cold winter's day, or the deep navy velvet of the darkening nights, culminating on the longest night of the year, the winter solstice. This hue is reflected in December's birthstones: turquoise, zircon, tanzanite, and lapis. The notion of a stone representing each month has been linked to ayurvedic beliefs that suggest correspondences between the planets and crystals. It wasn't until the eighteenth century that associating stones with a birth month became a popular practice in the Western world.

Even if you weren't born in December, you can still tap into the power of this month's special stones. Zircon increases bone stability, which is good for moving over icy terrain. Use turquoise, a rain-making stone, to summon snow. Turquoise also heals and brings peace. Engage tanzanite's powers for psychic visions for the impending new year. Lapis—the mirror of the winter night sky, and a stone that can be found in the breastplate of the high priest—brings wisdom and awareness.

Natalie Zaman

December 1
Friday

3rd ♋

☽ v/c 8:07 am

☽ → ♌ 11:00 am

Color of the day: Coral
Incense of the day: Mint

Magical Bracelets

Our hands pick up lots of things. Some of the unintentional things we pick up are germs, but we can also pick up random energy. To help dissolve the influence of these unwanted energies, we can use magically charged bracelets, almost like a dryer sheet neutralizes static electricity in clothing. The bracelets can be made of any material, from silver to natural cord.

On a plate, carefully pour a large ring of salt. In the middle of the salt, stack two bracelets and set a gray candle in the middle. Light the candle and visualize the bracelets glowing with a strong gray aura that will dissipate any harmful or disharmonious energy. When you're ready, say:

Circles of power worn on the wrist, dissolve the harm while leaving the blessed; charged with power for protecting me; as I will, so mote it be.

Extinguish the candle and put one bracelet on each wrist.

Michael Furie

December 2
Saturday

3rd ♌

Color of the day: Blue
Incense of the day: Sandalwood

Remedy for Being Constipapered

Years ago, many businesses decided to go paperless. The goal was to become paper-free. It never happened. A degree of success was achieved as computer technology advanced. In our private lives, many of us also decided to go paperless. Some achieved it and some did not. I, and many others, became nearly paperless by paying almost all household bills online. Still, I found myself too often "constipapered," bogged down with catalogues, sale flyers, and bills that could not be paid online. Several times a year, a pile of junk paper had to be jettisoned into the recycling bin.

This is a good day to go through all your paperwork before the winter. As you organize, sort, and toss, incant:

Soon the Wheel of the Year will turn and life will become dormant.

Bring organization to our home for this time of Yule to Imbolc.

Emyme

December 3
Sunday

3rd ♌

☽ v/c 9:11 pm

☽ → ♍ 10:50 pm

Color of the day: Yellow
Incense of the day: Eucalyptus

Affirmation to Dispel the Dark

It's easy to feel melancholy during the cold months of the year as the days get shorter and there's less sunlight. Use this affirmation to lift your spirits and bring some cheer when you're feeling down.

In a clear glass candleholder, light a white candle (any type) and set it on top of a mirror. Then place enough clear quartz crystals around the candle to make a circle. This is your circle of light, and it's powerful enough to chase away any darkness. Meditate on the light. See how it reflects off the mirror and crystals, and visualize it filling you with pure joy and gratitude. Chant these words:

When despair is in my heart,

Let this light dispel the dark.

Whisper things you're thankful for. Allow the candle to burn out safely.

Ember Grant

December 4
Monday

3rd ♍

Color of the day: Ivory
Incense of the day: Neroli

Liquid Love Spell

Venus enters Scorpio today, bringing focus to our relationships, especially those that are romantic or sexual in nature. Specifically, we will likely find ourselves wanting to be around those we are attracted to and seeking—nay, requiring—their attention more than usual. Cast this spell to get the attention you deserve right now from your partner(s), and use the energy to set the stage for a sensual evening of connection.

Cleanse a piece of red jasper or black tourmaline and place it in a bowl of water. Holding the bowl with both hands, present it to the east and say:

Crystal virtue, sexy and true, into this water your power imbue.

Bring on connection and make it deep, give us something worthy to keep.

Heart to heart, through body and soul, make us two pieces of the same whole!

Sprinkle the water around your home, especially in the bedroom.

Devin Hunter

December 5
Tuesday

3rd ♍

4th Quarter 12:49 am

Color of the day: Scarlet
Incense of the day: Bayberry

Banishing What Doesn't Serve You

While we're still in the early part of December and entering the last phase of the calendar year, it's the perfect time to begin thinking about what you don't want to bring into the next year with you, especially with the Sun still in Jupiter-ruled Sagittarius, governing cleansing and purification.

Throughout the month, as ideas come to you, write something you don't want to take into your life moving forward. It could be a less-than-ideal personal quality or trait, a bad habit, or a situation that stresses you out or makes you unhappy. Write each idea on an individual slip of paper and place them in a small jar. Throughout the month, as you drop a slip of paper into the jar, say:

Burden and vice that I place in this jar,

Soon the distance between us will be far.

On New Year's Eve, empty out the jar and read each slip of paper silently to yourself. Ritually burn the papers in a bonfire, your fireplace, or a fire-safe dish such as a cauldron.

Mat Auryn

Notes:

December 6
Wednesday

4th ♏

☽ v/c 8:50 am

☽ → ♎ 11:35 am

Color of the day: Brown
Incense of the day: Lilac

Peace on Earth Spell

With the holiday season in full swing, you might be feeling stressed. How do you keep your center at this time of year? Start each day with Words of Power and a visualization that you can carry with you all day. Charge yourself each morning with these or similar words:

There is one Power,

The Power is perfect protection.

*I am a perfect manifestation
of this Power,*

I am perfect calm, I am perfect peace.

Now raise your power (dominant) hand and turn clockwise in a circle. As you turn, "see" a stream of white light radiating from your hand. See this light sealing you in a shield of protective energy. As you go through your day, if you must deal with a difficult situation, remember your Words of Power, the white light, and the fact that you are calm and peaceful. Shield yourself with this meditation and you'll find peace on Earth this holiday season.

James Kambos

December 7
Thursday

4th ♎

Color of the day: Green
Incense of the day: Carnation

hanukkah begins at sundown

The Light Within

The candle and the lamp are two illuminating technologies that drove human language and culture. We harbor them in the window to inspire light, even in the darkest of places. The flame is an emblem of the Fool's willingness to achieve true authenticity. To be gifted with fire-building knowledge is a birthright of humans, second only to language.

At dusk, light a candle or lamp and offer your prayers to the celestial beings as they shine upon true will and human potential. Moonrise marks an annual commemoration of the light of creation. Fire, in a single flame, was a spark of ingenuity that evolved human civilization. With this in mind, ignite and pass the flame, envisioning your true purpose this evening. As you celebrate love and light, visualize the journey of your soul and celebrate your adaptive intelligence.

Estha McNevin

December 8
Friday

4ħ ♎

☽ v/c 8:05 pm

☽ → ♏ 10:35 pm

Color of the day: Pink
Incense of the day: Rose

Steady Income Spell

Sometimes prosperity spells bring a temporary increase of finances, but what many people really need is an ongoing stream of dependable income. Cast this spell when you're searching for a long-term job or other means of ongoing financial support.

Materials:

- A dollar bill (Fake money is okay.)
- A green or gold chime candle, anointed with peppermint oil
- A candleholder
- A nail
- A hammer
- A piece of wood that the nail can be hammered into, or a spot on your wall that you can put a nail in

Place the bill on your altar. Put the candle in a holder, and set it on top of the money. Light the candle and visualize a stream of income coming into your life. You can envision an actual river flowing toward you, filled with bills and coins. Extinguish the candle or let it burn down while supervised.

Take the bill and hammer the nail through it, securing it to the wall or your block of wood. Hammering the bill ensures that money will come to you and stay for as long as it is nailed down.

Kate Freuler

NOTES:

December 9
Saturday

4th ♏

Color of the day: Black
Incense of the day: Rue

Fire Divination Spell

During the dark months of the year, you can practice divination with fire. Pyromancy is the art of scrying and seeing divinatory signs in fire and flames. If you have a fireplace, you can practice gazing at a fire. You can also use a candle.

Take at least three deep breaths. While you breathe, work on clearing your mind and being fully present in the moment. Once you feel more relaxed, allow your gaze to soften and begin watching the flame(s) without trying to force an outcome. Stay in this relaxed state and be open to the shapes/signs/symbols that you may see. Fire divination takes practice. To get in a receptive, magical frame of mind, you can say:

In this fire, on this night, help me gaze with perfect sight.

Show me a sign and reveal to me the message that I need to see.

Blessed be!

Extinguish the fire safely when you are done.

Sapphire Moonbeam

December 10
Sunday

4th ♏

Color of the day: Orange
Incense of the day: Marigold

Human Rights Day

Today is Human Rights Day, in honor of the adoption of the Universal Declaration of Human Rights in 1948.

Call on Aequitas, the Roman goddess of equality and fairness, and Themis, one of the Greek goddesses of justice.

Read the Universal Declaration of Human Rights. Then place a small scale on your altar. Light a white candle and say:

I, (your name), believe in equality and justice for all. I call upon Aequitas and Themis to help me walk in fairness, compassion, and justice every day, no matter the obstacles. Help me embody these qualities in the world.

Let your candle burn out safely, or relight it and repeat the spell for nine nights.

Research human rights organizations and choose one to work with for the coming year, giving either money or time, in the quest for human rights for all.

Cerridwen Iris Shea

December 11
Monday

4th ♏

☽ v/c 3:57 am

☽ → ♐ 6:11 am

Color of the day: Silver
Incense of the day: Narcissus

Mystic Charity Spell

'Tis the season to give to the charities that are closest to our hearts. You can make your donation even more special by dedicating it to your favorite deity, a helpful spirit, or a special person you love (or one you've lost). Including them in the charity can increase the positive feelings you get from it, and it can also build your working relationship with them.

First, choose a charity. If you're using cash or a check, write the name of the deity, spirit, or person on it. If it's an e-payment, start to process the payment and write their name in one of the fields. Silently say:

With deepest love and trust,
I make this donation in the
name of _____.
In your name, may it do good.

Take a moment to envision the money helping the charity. Make the donation with no expectations, only happiness in your heart.

Astrea Taylor

 December 12
Tuesday

4th ♐

New Moon 6:32 pm

Color of the day: Red
Incense of the day: Basil

Moon Journal Spell

The moon in all her splendour grants gifts every night when she looks down upon us. However, there are certain times during her 29.5-day cycle when she is stronger for certain intentions in our spellwork. One of those days is the new moon, that beautiful silver crescent we see in the indigo night sky. This is the perfect time to start a moon journal, which is similar to a regular journal with one exception: it is devoted entirely to the moon cycles and your affirmations.

Buy or create a small book of no more than thirty pages. Safely light a white candle, and on the first page write down your intentions for the month. Write what you want to accomplish this month. It can be anything from being successful in an exam to being a good friend, getting organised in your magic work, chasing your ambitions, or accomplishing absolutely anything you desire. You can have as many goals as you want, but remember you only have about thirty days to accomplish them, so limit yourself to about five to ten intentions for the month.

On the front cover of your moon journal, write:

I am full of opportunity and potential.

Then cast the following spell over the intentions you have written. Place your right hand on the first page, covering your written intentions, and say:

From now until thirty days have passed,

Until my intentions are amassed,

Blessed moon, please grant me

All these dreams aplenty.

Meditate on your intentions for a while by the candle and then blow it out. Watch the rising smoke drift up toward the new moon, and imagine it telling the moon your intentions.

Every day for the next thirty days, record in your journal what phase the moon is in, such as waxing, waning, crescent, gibbous, first quarter, third quarter, etc. In addition, explain in a few sentences where your intentions are: have they begun, are they halfway through, or have you accomplished one or all of them? Enjoy your moon journal.

Tudorbeth

December 13
Wednesday

1st ♐

☽ v/c 1:48 am

☽ → ♑ 10:31 am

Color of the day: White
Incense of the day: Bay laurel

Stirring the Cocoa Cauldron

Today is National Cocoa Day, a day devoted to celebrating the richness of cocoa. If you're in a location with a colder climate in December, chances are you'll love celebrating this holiday with a mug of hot cocoa. Plus, due to cocoa's associations with comfort food, luxury, and abundance, drinking it is great sympathetic magic to attract those qualities into your life. A mug is just another form of magical cauldron, so let's get the magic brewing! As you stir your mug-cauldron of hot cocoa, recite an incantation such as the following:

Magical cocoa, bean and brew,

Abundance, prosperity, and comfort through and through.

As I stir thee, rich dark brew,

May I embody these qualities my whole life through!

Enjoy your tasty treat. Cheers!

Blake Octavian Blair

December 14
Thursday

1st ♑

Color of the day: Purple
Incense of the day: Apricot

Mercury Retrograde Precautions

Mercury stationed to turn retrograde yesterday. It may also be a hectic time before Yule and other winter holidays.

Before and after a planet moves retrograde, it goes through a period called a "station," where it is barely moving and is adjusting to the U-turn. During the two-week shadow phase before Mercury goes retrograde, take the necessary Mercury retrograde precautions. Move ahead at a gentle pace and do not sign anything binding. Back up all data to password-protected (or firewall-protected) cloud storage, change overused log-in codes, and make sure important bills are paid in a timely fashion. Research the god Mercury and all his powers. Chant:

Mercury, the winged messenger, give us the blessings of all you protect.

Emyme

 December 15
Friday

1st ♑

☽ v/c 11:04 am
☽ → ♒ 12:56 pm

Color of the day: Rose
Incense of the day: Cypress

hanukkah ends

Your Inner Light

As the Winter Solstice approaches, this is when most witches welcome back the light of the sun and prepare for the freshness of the new year. As we continue through the dark half of the year, this is a great time for us to find our own inner light and focus on our personal strength that has held us up as this year comes to a close.

Sit in a comfortable position in a dark room, or use a blindfold if necessary. Take a few deep breaths and allow your mind and body to calm down and relax. Imagine yourself in a pitch black space where nothing is visible. As you think of how amazing and strong you are, feel yourself getting brighter and emitting a light that illuminates the space you are in. Remember that you are loved, worthy, and magical. Continue to find those elements that make your inner light shine so brightly that you shine like the sun, and feel the warmth of your light throughout your body.

As you finish your meditation, keep the thoughts of your inner light within you for the remainder of the day.

Amanda Lynn & Jason Mankey

NOTES:

 December 16
Saturday

1st ♒︎

Color of the day: Indigo
Incense of the day: Ivy

The Great Mother's Embrace

Not every child has what they need. Perhaps, like me, you lacked the safety and security of compassionate, protective parents. Today, take the time to feel the Great Mother's embrace, creating a connection to the sacred feminine, so that you, too, can experience the nurture of a good mother.

Without that early life modeling, it took me a long time to learn how to mother myself. I focused on what a good mother would do, and began to provide those acts and sentiments for myself.

Close your eyes and ask the child inside:

What do you need?

Listen for the answers. Say:

I am here for you.

Then become the Great Mother: make up a cozy, comfy bed; drink warm milk with honey; tuck yourself in; stroke your hair. Whisper:

I love you, sweetie. Be blessed in sleep.

Wrap your arms around yourself and sleep in the Great Mother's embrace.

Dallas Jennifer Cobb

♥ December 17
Sunday

1st ≈

☽ v/c 7:04 am

☽ → ♓ 2:58 pm

Color of the day: Gold
Incense of the day: Heliotrope

Self-Love Potion

We all deserve self-love. Generate true self-appreciation with this magical potion. You will need:

- 7 drops rose essential oil
- 7 drops geranium essential oil
- 7 drops amber oil
- 1 cup rose water
- 7 small rose quartz stones
- An 8-ounce spray bottle

Combine all of the ingredients into the spray bottle and decorate it with your name and the symbol for Venus (♀). Activate the potion by shaking the bottle and seeking to love yourself. Spray the air, and anoint the mirrors and windows of your home with the symbol for Venus. Envision the many ways that you are free to love and celebrate yourself. If you follow your intuition, this potion will revive your ability to see the best in yourself and others, drawing self-compassion into your life.

Estha McNevin

December 18
Monday

1st ♓

Color of the day: White
Incense of the day: Lily

Spell for Prophetic Dreams

Try this spell to encourage prophetic dreams. You'll need a cotton ball and any combination of the following essential oils: jasmine, rose, mugwort, and calendula. Put three drops of any or all of these oils on the cotton ball. Add an additional three drops of clary sage essential oil to increase vividness, if desired.

Place the cotton ball in your pillowcase. As you drift off to sleep, whisper the following words and know that you will not only remember your dreams but also gain insight and understanding that you can use:

I compel dreams that foretell;

Insightful and clear—nothing to fear.

Ember Grant

December 19

Tuesday

1st ♈ ♓

2nd Quarter 1:39 pm

☽ v/c 4:03 pm

☽ → ♈ 5:47 pm

Color of the day: Maroon
Incense of the day: Cinnamon

Blessings of holly

B y this time of year, the berries on holly—a traditional symbol of winter celebrations—will have turned red. Having been raised in Millville, New Jersey, (one of) the holly capital(s) of the US, I chose holly as one of the two plants on my personal totem. Two majestic holly trees flanked the entrance to the driveway of the home in which I grew up. Holly has a rather slow growth rate; those two trees had been there for approximately fifty years. In Celtic mythology, holly is revered and rules over half of the year, as a companion to the oak.

Should you be lucky enough to have a holly tree or bush on your property, this is the perfect time to prune it and use the trimmings as winter holiday decorations. Remember to thank the holly and cleanse it with burning herbs or a saltwater mixture before bringing it in your home.

Chant:

Holly, whether a bush, tree, or wand,

Protect this home from unwanted entities, poisons, and lightning.

As you make room for the oak,

We rejoice in your arrival again soon.

Emyme

NOTES:

December 20
Wednesday

2nd ♈

Color of the day: Yellow
Incense of the day: Honeysuckle

Relish the Dark Spell

Tomorrow is the Winter Solstice, when we celebrate the longest night and the return of the light. So tonight, let's take some time to relish the darkness.

You will need three small candles and just over an hour of undisturbed time in your bedroom, after dark.

Lie on your bed without any lights on in the room. Let natural light or outdoor artificial lights come through the window. For forty-five minutes, lie quietly in the dark, listening. Try not to fall asleep. Let your thoughts wander. Be aware of any sounds, scents, and emotions.

After forty-five minutes, sit up and light the first candle. Feel the way the dark embraces the light. Five minutes later, light the second candle. Feel the way the light and the dark are more in balance. Five minutes later, light the third candle. Feel the way the light now embraces the dark. After five more minutes, either extinguish the candles to use in your Winter Solstice ritual or let them burn down safely.

Cerridwen Iris Shea

December 21
Thursday

2nd ♈

☽ v/c 9:47 pm
☽ → ♉ 9:50 pm
☉ → ♑ 10:27 pm

Color of the day: Turquoise
Incense of the day: Balsam

Yule – Winter Solstice

Solstice Secret Reveal

Happy Winter Solstice, witches! Tonight is the longest night of the year, and people all over the world are celebrating the metaphorical rebirth of the Sun. In addition to the traditional festivities, this is an excellent time to harness the energy of the Sun's unique transition and direct it to reveal hidden information that until now has been difficult to find. Mythologically, the Sun begins its journey back from the underworld now, and we can ask the Sun to bring with it lost information and forgotten secrets.

Write a question you need answered on a piece of paper and safely burn it in a heatproof container. Collect the ashes and scatter them to the wind at dawn and say:

Ashes to ashes, dust in the wind.

As the Sun rises, this message I send!

You should have your answer by Midsummer.

Devin Hunter

December 22
Friday

2nd ♉

Color of the day: Coral
Incense of the day: Alder

Mental Magick Protection

With the Sun and Mercury in Saturn-ruled Capricorn today and Saturn in visionary Pisces, this is a very auspicious time to enhance your personal boundaries and protection through the use of your mind's eye. Get in a relaxed meditative state. Close your eyes and visualize the glyph of Saturn (♄) glowing on your chest, to get in sync with this planetary power.

Now visualize yourself standing firmly in the middle of a temple of protection. The temple surges with protective energy. As this energy surrounds you, visualize it turning into a shining suit of impenetrable armor. Envision yourself holding a shield in one hand and a powerful sword in the other. Focus on the feeling of security and protection on all levels. Then declare:

By sword and shield

And armor bright,

I am safe from

Attack and blight.

When you're ready, open your eyes, knowing that the protection provided by this suit of armor, sword, and shield is around you. You don't need to hold the visualization; just know it's there.

Mat Auryn

NOTES:

December 23
Saturday

2nd ♉

Color of the day: Gray
Incense of the day: Pine

Saturnalia Altar Spell

The winter is a time of rest and sleep. Animals all over the world hibernate at this time. The cold winter nights creep quickly toward the day, and frozen nights keep all huddled tightly in their beds. And yet at this time of year was one of the greatest ancient festivals: Saturnalia, which lasted from December 17 to the 23rd.

Saturnalia was a celebration of the god Saturn, and with it came parties, gifts, and carnivals. In modern times, this has become our holiday season, with Christmas and Yule. However, we can still join in the activities of Saturnalia and rejoice in the gifts of this god of plenty, wealth, and agriculture, amongst many other things.

Create a Saturnalia altar in your home to bring in the wealth and abundance of the season. It doesn't have to be a huge, elaborate altar; it can be anything from a particular corner of a room to a shelf with just a few symbolic items on it.

On your Saturnalia altar, place a red candle, some gold coins, a packet of seeds, and some olive oil. If you can find a small statue or image of the god Saturn, that would be great, but it's fine without. The very fact that you are acknowledging his festival will suffice. In front of your altar, stand or kneel and hold out your hands in a receiving pose, with palms up, and say:

Here in my room, now upon the shelf,

Saturnalia gifts, I grant myself.

Lord of plenty and of wealth,

Send me lots of money and health.

If you like, you can light the candle while you say your spell, but never leave a candle unattended and always remember to extinguish it. If you perform this spell every year and every night of Saturnalia, it will become a tradition.

Tudorbeth

NOTES:

December 24
Sunday

2nd ♉

☽ v/c 1:40 am

☽ → ♊ 3:15 am

Color of the day: Amber
Incense of the day: Frankincense

Christmas Eve

Celebrate the Book Flood

Today is Jolabokaflod, a celebration that originated in Iceland but has spread to become a global sensation! In the World War II era, when many things were rationed and scarce, there was still access to paper in Iceland. Thus, for holiday gift giving, Icelanders turned to books. It is now a cultural tradition to gift books to loved ones on Christmas Eve and spend a cozy evening at home, reading with hot drinks, chocolate, and perhaps a fire.

Now that the rest of the globe has caught wind of this delightful holiday, consider celebrating it with your family or a close friend or two. Even if you don't exchange books, grab a book from your own queue. With your hearth fire (or a few candles) well supervised, the airy knowledge from books, the watery treat of hot drinks, and the earthy nourishment from your snacks, you'll have an elementally balanced celebration!

Blake Octavian Blair

December 25
Monday

2nd ♊

Color of the day: Ivory
Incense of the day: Rosemary

Christmas Day

"I Am Enough" Chant

When my mother remarried during my teenage years, Christmas became a painful time. She and her new partner lavished each other with gifts and gave me little. When I began to observe Pagan sabbats, I was relieved to leave behind the painful memories of Christmas. Whether you celebrate Yule, Hanukkah, Kwanzaa, or Christmas, use this chant to affirm your intrinsic worth. Look at yourself in the mirror, chanting:

> *I have enough, I do enough,*
> *I give enough, I am enough.*
> *Enough is enough. So be it.*

Gather with friends and family, chanting:

> *I have enough, I do enough,*
> *I give enough, I am enough.*
> *Enough is enough. So be it.*

Go out into the world, chanting:

> *I have enough, I do enough,*
> *I give enough, I am enough.*
> *Enough is enough. So be it.*

Self, friends, and family, out there in the world, we are enough. So be it.

Dallas Jennifer Cobb

December 26
Tuesday

2nd ♊

☽ v/c 2:55 am

☽ → ♋ 10:15 am

☽ Full Moon 7:33 pm

Color of the day: Gray
Incense of the day: Cedar

Kwanzaa begins –
Boxing Day (Canada & UK)

Comforting Warmth Tea Spell

During the hubbub of the holiday season, it's comforting to take a moment for rest and reflection. This tea spell promotes centeredness and cleansing. Throughout this spell, use slow, mindful breaths and movements to enhance the comfort qualities.

Gather these materials:

• Kettle

• 8 ounces water

• 1 teaspoon lemon balm

• ½ teaspoon sage

• Teapot

• Strainer

• Teacup

Take a deep breath, pour the water into the kettle, and boil it. Measure the herbs and place them in the teapot. As you wait for the water to boil, stretch or give yourself a light massage.

When the water boils, turn the stove off. Take another deep breath before pouring the water over the herbs.

Let the tea brew for five minutes, then strain it into your cup. Inhale the aromas and say:

May blessings rain upon me
as I take time for myself.

Take a sip when the tea is cool enough to drink. Enjoy the peaceful moment.

Astrea Taylor

NOTES:

December 27
Wednesday

3rd ♋

Color of the day: Topaz
Incense of the day: Lavender

Spiderweb Spell to Release a Creative Block

Spiders and their webs are ancient symbols of creativity. The spider weaves the web autonomously, from its own body, much like our ability to manifest is self-generated. This spell calls upon the magic of the spiderweb to release a creative block, whether it's in your art, your writing, or your magic.

Materials:

• A picture of a spiderweb

• Enough sand to just cover the picture of the web

• A tool pertaining to your creative project (a paintbrush for an artist, a pen for a writer, etc.) or a selenite wand

Put the picture on a flat surface and gently cover it with enough sand to just slightly obscure the image.

Beginning at the center of the web, use your utensil to trace it through the sand, pushing the sand aside to reveal the pattern of the spiderweb, while chanting:

I weave the web, my mind is free, unleashing creativity.

When you're done, take the picture outside and blow the sand away from you. Hang the picture somewhere near your creative space for inspiration.

Kate Freuler

NOTES:

December 28
Thursday

3rd ♋

☽ v/c 5:57 pm

☽ → ♌ 7:23 pm

Color of the day: Crimson
Incense of the day: Mulberry

Purification and Protection, to Taste

Salt and pepper are staple kitchen items, which only adds to their magical usefulness. Both salt and black pepper are magically related to cleansing, banishing, purification, and protection. These two seasonings can be charged with power and then used on food to energize it with magic. To begin, gather a container of salt and a container of pepper along with a black or white candle. Place the candle in the center of a flat surface, then the pepper to the left of the candle and the salt to the right. Light the candle, grasp the salt in your right hand and the pepper in your left, and envision pure white light pouring from your hands into the seasonings as you say:

Pepper and salt, charged and cleansed, all hindrances now cast away; whenever consumed, your power will lend protection from harm, keeping evil at bay.

Extinguish the candle and use the salt and pepper as usual.

Michael Furie

 December 29
Friday

3rd ♌

Color of the day: White
Incense of the day: Orchid

Repairing Relationships

Relationships can fray, and we may find ourselves moving away emotionally from people we truly care about. Luckily, with a little bit of magick, we can fix the relationships that are important to us. For this spell you will need two pieces of string (or rope) long enough that they can be tied together.

Place the two pieces of string in front of you and designate one as yourself and the other as the person you are having trouble with. Hold the "you" piece of string and visualize yourself happy with your friend, perhaps savoring old memories. Repeat this with the other string. Once both pieces of string have been charged, tie them together while saying:

May what was broken be mended. May the bonds that brought us together be renewed. So mote it be!

Place the tied-together pieces of string in a small bag and store in a secure place. Soon your relationship will be mended.

Amanda Lynn & Jason Mankey

 December 30
Saturday

3rd ♌

Color of the day: Blue
Incense of the day: Magnolia

Find a Lost Item Spell

While some people are tidy and organized, if you are anything like me, you may have a tendency to misplace things. If you've lost something in your house that you are desperate to find, you can use this spell.

Instead of imagining where the item is not located, visualize where it actually could be, or the last place you think you saw it. Stand in the middle of your house or the room where you think the item might be. Close your eyes. Take a few deep breaths in order to ease any anxiety you may have about the urgency to find the missing item. Open your eyes slowly and say these words:

Show me the item.

Return it to me.

Reveal where it is hiding.

Allow me to see.

Once you are more calm and confident, the item should be easier to find.

Sapphire Moonbeam

December 31
Sunday

3rd ♌

☽ v/c 12:18 am

☽ → ♍ 6:53 am

Color of the day: Orange
Incense of the day: Juniper

New Year's Eve

A Holly Spell for New Year's Eve

Tonight we tie another knot on the endless cord of time. It's time for hope and resolutions. Holly is an excellent spell ingredient to use when you wish to clear away any negative vibrations, because it catches and holds anything you wish to banish. You'll need four holly leaves and a small ritual fire in a cauldron or other heatproof container. Ground and center. As you speak the following words, cast the holly leaves into the fire, one at a time.

On this night I release all anger,

I release all doubt.

I release all negativity,

I release all fear.

I will walk in peace

Throughout the coming year.

Let the fire safely burn out. See your issues from this year fading with the dying embers. In the next day or two, when the ashes are cool, scatter them upon the earth.

James Kambos

Daily Magical Influences

Each day is ruled by a planet that possesses specific magical influences:

Monday (Moon): peace, healing, caring, psychic awareness, purification

Tuesday (Mars): passion, sex, courage, aggression, protection

Wednesday (Mercury): conscious mind, study, travel, divination, wisdom

Thursday (Jupiter): expansion, money, prosperity, generosity

Friday (Venus): love, friendship, reconciliation, beauty

Saturday (Saturn): longevity, exorcism, endings, homes, houses

Sunday (Sun): healing, spirituality, success, strength, protection

Lunar Phases

The lunar phase is important in determining best times for magic.

The new moon is when the moon and sun are conjunct each other. It corresponds to all new beginnings and is the best time to start a project.

The waxing moon (from the new moon to the full moon) is the ideal time for magic to draw things to you.

The full moon is when the sun and moon are opposite each other. It is the time of greatest power.

The waning moon (from the full moon to the new moon) is a time for study, meditation, and little magical work (except magic designed to banish harmful energies).

Astrological Symbols

The Sun	☉	Aries	♈
The Moon	☽	Taurus	♉
Mercury	☿	Gemini	♊
Venus	♀	Cancer	♋
Mars	♂	Leo	♌
Jupiter	♃	Virgo	♍
Saturn	♄	Libra	♎
Uranus	♅	Scorpio	♏
Neptune	♆	Sagittarius	♐
Pluto	♇	Capricorn	♑
		Aquarius	♒
		Pisces	♓

The Moon's Sign

The moon's sign is a traditional consideration for astrologers. The moon continuously moves through each sign in the zodiac, from Aries to Pisces. The moon influences the sign it inhabits, creating different energies that affect our daily lives.

Aries: Good for starting things but lacks staying power. Things occur rapidly but quickly pass. People tend to be argumentative and assertive.

Taurus: Things begun now do last, tend to increase in value, and become hard to alter. Brings out an appreciation for beauty and sensory experience.

Gemini: Things begun now are easily changed by outside influence. Time for shortcuts, communications, games, and fun.

Cancer: Stimulates emotional rapport between people. Pinpoints need, supports growth and nurturance. Tend to domestic concerns.

Leo: Draws emphasis to the self, to central ideas or institutions, away from connections with others and emotional needs. People tend to be melodramatic.

Virgo: Favors accomplishment of details and commands from higher up. Focus on health, hygiene, and daily schedules.

Libra: Favors cooperation, compromise, social activities, beautification of surroundings, balance, and partnership.

Scorpio: Increases awareness of psychic power. Favors activities requiring intensity and focus. People tend to brood and become secretive under this moon sign.

Sagittarius: Encourages flights of imagination and confidence. This moon sign is adventurous, philosophical, and athletic. Favors expansion and growth.

Capricorn: Develops strong structure. Focus on traditions, responsibilities, and obligations. A good time to set boundaries and rules.

Aquarius: Rebellious energy. Time to break habits and make abrupt change. Personal freedom and individuality are the focus.

Pisces: The focus is on dreaming, nostalgia, intuition, and psychic impressions. A good time for spiritual or philanthropic activities.

Glossary of Magical Terms

Altar: A table that holds magical tools as a focus for spell workings.

Athame: A ritual knife used to direct personal power during workings or to symbolically draw diagrams in a spell. It is rarely, if ever, used for actual physical cutting.

Aura: An invisible energy field surrounding a person. The aura can change color depending on the state of the individual.

Balefire: A fire lit for magical purposes, usually outdoors.

Casting a circle: The process of drawing a circle around oneself to seal out unfriendly influences and raise magical power. It is the first step in a spell.

Censer: An incense burner. Traditionally a censer is a metal container, filled with incense, that is swung on the end of a chain.

Censing: The process of burning incense to spiritually cleanse an object.

Centering yourself: To prepare for a magical rite by calming and centering all of your personal energy.

Chakra: One of the seven centers of spiritual energy in the human body, according to the philosophy of yoga.

Charging: To infuse an object with magical power.

Circle of protection: A circle cast to protect oneself from unfriendly influences.

Crystals: Quartz or other stones that store cleansing or protective energies.

Deosil: Clockwise movement, symbolic of life and positive energies.

Deva: A divine being according to Hindu beliefs; a devil or evil spirit according to Zoroastrianism.

Direct/retrograde: Refers to the motion of a planet when seen from the earth. A planet is "direct" when it appears to be moving forward from the point of view of a person on the earth. It is "retrograde" when it appears to be moving backward.

Dowsing: To use a divining rod to search for a thing, usually water or minerals.

Dowsing pendulum: A long cord with a coin or gem at one end. The pattern of its swing is used to answer questions.

Dryad: A tree spirit or forest guardian.

Fey: An archaic term for a magical spirit or a fairylike being.

Gris-gris: A small bag containing charms, herbs, stones, and other items to draw energy, luck, love, or prosperity to the wearer.

Mantra: A sacred chant used in Hindu tradition to embody the divinity invoked; it is said to possess deep magical power.

Needfire: A ceremonial fire kindled at dawn on major Wiccan holidays. It was traditionally used to light all other household fires.

Pentagram: A symbolically protective five-pointed star with one point upward.

Power hand: The dominant hand; the hand used most often.

Scry: To predict the future by gazing at or into an object such as a crystal ball or pool of water.

Second sight: The psychic power or ability to foresee the future.

Sigil: A personal seal or symbol.

Smudge/smudge stick: To spiritually cleanse an object by waving smoke over and around it. A smudge stick is a bundle of several incense sticks.

Wand: A stick or rod used for casting circles and as a focus for magical power.

Widdershins: Counterclockwise movement, symbolic of negative magical purposes, sometimes used to disperse negative energies.

About the Authors

Mat Auryn is a witch, professional psychic, and occult teacher. He is the multi-award-winning author of the international bestselling book *Psychic Witch: A Metaphysical Guide to Meditation, Magick & Manifestation*. He is a High Priest in the Sacred Fires Tradition of Witchcraft. As a psychic witch, Mat has had the honor and privilege of studying under some of the most prominent witchcraft teachers and elders. He has been featured on Oprah Daily and Cosmopolitan and in many other magazines, radio shows, podcasts, books, anthologies, and periodicals. You can follow him on Twitter or Instagram @MatAuryn or visit his website at www.MatAuryn.com.

Blake Octavian Blair is a shamanic and druidic practitioner, ordained minister, writer, Usui Reiki Master-Teacher, and musical artist. Blake incorporates mystical traditions from both the East and West with a reverence for the natural world into his own brand of spirituality. He is an avid reader, knitter, nature lover, and member of the Order of Bards, Ovates & Druids. He lives with his loving husband in the New England region of the USA. Visit him on the web at www.blakeoctavianblair.com.

Dallas Jennifer Cobb lives an embodied life. Studying somatics, trauma therapy, astrology, and magic, she spends time in nature, where all of these converge. A Pagan, mother, feminist, writer, and animal lover, she has conjured a sustainable lifestyle with an abundance of time, energy, wisdom, and money. Widely published, she writes about what she knows: trauma and neurological recovery, magic, herbs, astrology, deep ecology, and vibrant sustainability. She is eager to connect with like-minded beings. Contact her at jennifer.cobb@live.com.

Emyme is an eclectic, enjoying retirement from the forty-hour workweek. Expanding on the wealth of knowledge surrounding all things Wiccan and Pagan, she is busy creating a grimoire and writing alternative fairy tales. Contact Emyme at catsmeow24@verizon.net.

Kate Freuler lives in Ontario Canada, and is the author of *Of Blood and Bones: Working with Shadow Magick & the Dark Moon*. She owns and operates White Moon Witchcraft, an online witchcraft boutique. When she isn't crafting spells and amulets for clients or herself, she loves to write, paint, read, draw, and create. Visit her at www.katefreuler.com.

Michael Furie (Northern California) is the author of *The Witch's Book of Potions, Supermarket Sabbats, Spellcasting for Beginners, Supermarket Magic, Spellcasting: Beyond the Basics*, and more, all from Llewellyn. A practicing Witch for more than twenty-five years, he is a priest of the Cailleach. He can be found online at www.michaelfurie.com.

Ember Grant has been writing for the Llewellyn annuals for twenty years and is the author of four books, her most recent being *Mythology for a Magical Life*. In addition, she is an avid photographer and poet. She shares a home in the woods with her husband and two feline companions. You can find her on Instagram @poetofthewoods.

Devin Hunter (San Francisco, CA) is the bestselling author of *The Witch's Book of Power, The Witch's Book of Spirits*, and *The Witch's Book of Mysteries*, as well as the critically acclaimed pictorial formulary *Modern Witch: Spells, Recipes & Workings*, all from Llewellyn. Initiated into multiple occult orders, Devin is the founder of the Sacred Fires Tradition of Witchcraft and the cofounder of the Black Rose Tradition of Witchcraft. He hosts an A.V. Club and Glamour Magazine–favorited podcast called *Modern Witch*. His fifth book from Llewellyn, *Crystal Magic for the Modern Witch*, was released in summer 2022.

James Kambos celebrates his 25th year writing for Llewellyn Publications. He writes articles and essays on folk magic, magical living, and herbs. He holds a degree in history and geography from Ohio University. He lives in the beautiful hill country of southern Ohio.

Amanda Lynn has been dedicated to Witchcraft since childhood. For thirteen years she was a priestess in her local community, where she developed a penchant for ritual creation and spellcraft. These days, when she's not taking long walks in cemeteries or circling with one of her covens, she studies aromatherapy, esoterica, and intuitive magic. You can often find her checking out new music and wearing lots of glitter.

Jason Mankey is a third-degree Gardnerian High Priest and helps run two Witchcraft covens in the San Francisco Bay Area with his wife, Ari. He is a popular speaker at Pagan and Witchcraft events across North America and Great Britain and has been recognized by his peers as an authority on the Horned God, Wiccan history, and occult influences in rock and roll. He is the author of *The Horned God of the Witches* and *The Witch's Book of Spellcraft*, both from Llewellyn. You can follow him on Instagram and Twitter @panmankey.

Estha McNevin (Missoula, MT) is a Priestess and Eastern Hellenistic oracle of Opus Aima Obscuræ, a nonprofit matriarchal Pagan temple. Trained in the Lake District, UK, in Gardnerian Wicca, she has served as a Priestess, academic lecturer, freelance author, and artist since 2001. Along with cohosting public sabbats, Estha organizes annual philanthropic volunteer projects, teaches classes, advocates for vulnerable clients, and employs permaculture techniques to manage the temple orchard where the community conducts its ceremonies each dark and full moon. Please explore www.opusaimaobscurae.org and www.instagram/esthamarelda.

Sapphire Moonbeam is a rainbow energy artist, metaphysical jewelry maker, card reader, nature photographer, and nature lover. She is the artist and author of the Moonbeam Magick oracle card deck. Sapphire sells her artwork, jewelry, and oracle deck worldwide and also teaches intuitive abstract art classes at locations around the world. She has a worldwide following at her Sapphire's Moonbeams page on Facebook. Visit her website at SapphireMoonbeam.com.

Cerridwen Iris Shea has worked in the Craft since 1994 and is now, chronologically, a Crone. She is a full-time writer, publishing under multiple names in fiction and nonfiction. She started as an urban witch, spent a decade as an ocean witch, and is now a mountain witch, but always a kitchen witch. Her website is www.cerridwenscottage.com.

Astrea Taylor is an eclectic/intuitive pagan witch, writer, and speaker whose life goals include empowering other witches and encouraging them to use intuition in their witchcraft. She's the author of *Intuitive Witchcraft*, *Air Magic*, and *Modern Witchcraft with the Greek Gods*. She blogs as *Starlight Witch* on Patheos. When she's not coleading the Aurora Fire dance group, she presents workshops and rituals at festivals across the country. Learn more at www.AstreaTaylor.com.

Tudorbeth is a hereditary practitioner of witchcraft. Her knowledge of magic and the Craft stems from her Celtic ancestry. She has written many books, including *A Spellbook for All Seasons: Welcome Natural Change with Magical Blessings*, published by Eddison. She also wrote a trilogy of spell books on Hedgewitchery for Llewellyn, starting with *The Hedgewitch's Little Book of Spells, Charms & Brews*, published in 2021, and *The Hedgewitch's Little Book of Seasonal Magic*, published in 2022. Her latest book by Llewellyn is *The Hedgewitch's Little Book of Flower Magic*. She can be found on her social media pages as Tudorbeth.

Notes

Notes

Notes

Notes

Notes

Notes

2022

SEPTEMBER

S	M	T	W	T	F	S
				1	2	3
4	5	6	7	8	9	10
11	12	13	14	15	16	17
18	19	20	21	22	23	24
25	26	27	28	29	30	

OCTOBER

S	M	T	W	T	F	S
						1
2	3	4	5	6	7	8
9	10	11	12	13	14	15
16	17	18	19	20	21	22
23	24	25	26	27	28	29
30	31					

NOVEMBER

S	M	T	W	T	F	S
		1	2	3	4	5
6	7	8	9	10	11	12
13	14	15	16	17	18	19
20	21	22	23	24	25	26
27	28	29	30			

DECEMBER

S	M	T	W	T	F	S
				1	2	3
4	5	6	7	8	9	10
11	12	13	14	15	16	17
18	19	20	21	22	23	24
25	26	27	28	29	30	31

2023

JANUARY

S	M	T	W	T	F	S
1	2	3	4	5	6	7
8	9	10	11	12	13	14
15	16	17	18	19	20	21
22	23	24	25	26	27	28
29	30	31				

FEBRUARY

S	M	T	W	T	F	S
			1	2	3	4
5	6	7	8	9	10	11
12	13	14	15	16	17	18
19	20	21	22	23	24	25
26	27	28				

MARCH

S	M	T	W	T	F	S
			1	2	3	4
5	6	7	8	9	10	11
12	13	14	15	16	17	18
19	20	21	22	23	24	25
26	27	28	29	30	31	

APRIL

S	M	T	W	T	F	S
						1
2	3	4	5	6	7	8
9	10	11	12	13	14	15
16	17	18	19	20	21	22
23	24	25	26	27	28	29
30						

MAY

S	M	T	W	T	F	S
	1	2	3	4	5	6
7	8	9	10	11	12	13
14	15	16	17	18	19	20
21	22	23	24	25	26	27
28	29	30	31			

JUNE

S	M	T	W	T	F	S
				1	2	3
4	5	6	7	8	9	10
11	12	13	14	15	16	17
18	19	20	21	22	23	24
25	26	27	28	29	30	

JULY

S	M	T	W	T	F	S
						1
2	3	4	5	6	7	8
9	10	11	12	13	14	15
16	17	18	19	20	21	22
23	24	25	26	27	28	29
30	31					

AUGUST

S	M	T	W	T	F	S
		1	2	3	4	5
6	7	8	9	10	11	12
13	14	15	16	17	18	19
20	21	22	23	24	25	26
27	28	29	30	31		

SEPTEMBER

S	M	T	W	T	F	S
					1	2
3	4	5	6	7	8	9
10	11	12	13	14	15	16
17	18	19	20	21	22	23
24	25	26	27	28	29	30

OCTOBER

S	M	T	W	T	F	S
1	2	3	4	5	6	7
8	9	10	11	12	13	14
15	16	17	18	19	20	21
22	23	24	25	26	27	28
29	30	31				

NOVEMBER

S	M	T	W	T	F	S
			1	2	3	4
5	6	7	8	9	10	11
12	13	14	15	16	17	18
19	20	21	22	23	24	25
26	27	28	29	30		

DECEMBER

S	M	T	W	T	F	S
					1	2
3	4	5	6	7	8	9
10	11	12	13	14	15	16
17	18	19	20	21	22	23
24	25	26	27	28	29	30
31						

2024

JANUARY

S	M	T	W	T	F	S
	1	2	3	4	5	6
7	8	9	10	11	12	13
14	15	16	17	18	19	20
21	22	23	24	25	26	27
28	29	30	31			

FEBRUARY

S	M	T	W	T	F	S
				1	2	3
4	5	6	7	8	9	10
11	12	13	14	15	16	17
18	19	20	21	22	23	24
25	26	27	28	29		

MARCH

S	M	T	W	T	F	S
					1	2
3	4	5	6	7	8	9
10	11	12	13	14	15	16
17	18	19	20	21	22	23
24	25	26	27	28	29	30
31						

APRIL

S	M	T	W	T	F	S
	1	2	3	4	5	6
7	8	9	10	11	12	13
14	15	16	17	18	19	20
21	22	23	24	25	26	27
28	29	30				